Culture, Mind, and Society

Series Editor
Peter G. Stromberg
Anthropology Department
Henry Kendall College of Arts and Sciences
University of Tulsa
Tulsa, OK, USA

The Society for Psychological Anthropology—a section of the American Anthropology Association—and Palgrave Macmillan are dedicated to publishing innovative research that illuminates the workings of the human mind within the social, cultural, and political contexts that shape thought, emotion, and experience. As anthropologists seek to bridge gaps between ideation and emotion or agency and structure and as psychologists, psychiatrists, and medical anthropologists search for ways to engage with cultural meaning and difference, this interdisciplinary terrain is more active than ever.

More information about this series at
http://www.palgrave.com/gp/series/14947

Elizabeth Fein · Clarice Rios
Editors

Autism in Translation

An Intercultural Conversation on Autism Spectrum Conditions

palgrave
macmillan

Editors
Elizabeth Fein
Duquesne University
Pittsburgh, PA, USA

Clarice Rios
Department of Social Psychology
Federal University of Rio de Janeiro
Rio de Janeiro, Brazil

Culture, Mind, and Society
ISBN 978-3-030-06632-1 ISBN 978-3-319-93293-4 (eBook)
https://doi.org/10.1007/978-3-319-93293-4

This Palgrave Macmillan imprint is published by the registered company Springer Nature Switzerland AG
The registered company address is: Gewerbestrasse 11, 6330 Cham, Switzerland

Series Preface

Psychological Anthropologists study a wide spectrum of human activity: child development, illness and healing, ritual and religion, personality, political and economic systems, just to name a few. In fact, as a discipline that seeks to understand the interconnections between persons and culture, it would be difficult to come up with examples of human behavior that are outside the purview of psychological anthropology. Yet, beneath this substantive diversity lies a common commitment. The practitioners of psychological anthropology seek to understand social activity in ways that are fitted to the mental and physical dimensions of human beings. Psychological anthropologists may focus on emotions or human biology, on language or art or dreams, but they rarely stray far from the attempt to understand the possibilities and the limitations of on-the-ground human persons.

In this collection of papers, psychological anthropology is brought to bear on the complex challenge of autism. The book is unique in a number of ways. First, the standpoint of the "Global North" is most often taken for granted in academic work, this in spite of the fact that other perspectives may considerably enrich our understanding of the phenomena we study. This volume exemplifies something that ought to happen more often, a collaborative dialogue between the academic perspectives of the north and a robust conceptual system developed elsewhere, in this case, the South American "Collective Health" tradition. Second, rather than considering autism as a fixed diagnostic category inscribed into the structure of the universe, papers in this collection place autism in social and political contexts in order to illustrate variations in the conceptualization of autism and of the treatment and experience of men and women on the autism spectrum. The result is a volume that is valuable for both theory and practice, a broadening of our thinking not only about autism but also about human experience more broadly.

Tulsa, USA

Peter G. Stromberg

Acknowledgements

The editors of this book first met at a meeting of the Society for Psychological Anthropology. Ever since then, SPA has been a fertile intellectual home for this project. We are therefore honored to be publishing this book within the SPA series, *Culture, Mind and Society*. We'd like to thank Peter Stromberg, Yehuda Goodman, Rachel Daniel, and Kyra Saniewski for their welcome of this book and their invaluable help preparing it for publication. We'd also like to thank Derek Hook, Daniela Manica, and an anonymous reviewer for their helpful comments on various parts of this manuscript, Benjamin M. Gaddes for editorial assistance, and Lisa Rivero for a meticulous and conceptually sound index.

The workshop that produced this book was supported by the Lemelson/Society for Psychological Anthropology Conference Fund, made possible by a generous donation from the Robert Lemelson Foundation. For the past decade, the Foundation has funded meetings organized around innovative topics in psychological anthropology, ranging from cross-cultural critiques of attachment theory to the power of comic books to enhance understandings of medical care. These workshops have advanced both the theory and practice of psychological anthropology, in the kind of new directions that can emerge only from protected time and space for good conversations and sustained thought. In supporting an international collaboration that took place in a country going through significant political and financial upheaval, the Foundation took on a new set of logistical challenges. We appreciate their willingness to take a chance on this workshop, and we hope this publication will continue the tradition of excellent work emerging from this program.

A number of people also helped to make the workshop possible. Denize Barros contributed the striking design for our workshop materials. Christine Pollock and the Duquesne University Office of Research assisted with the handling and disbursement of funds, as did CEPESC (*Centro de Estudos, Pesquisa e Desenvolvimento Tecnológico em Saúde Coletiva*) at Rio de Janeiro State University (UERJ). After the event was over, Ted Gideonse made the videos of our conference talks available on the SPA Vimeo channel. They can be viewed at https://vimeo.com/album/3897481. Also included there are opening remarks by Kenneth Camargo Jr., whose introduction to the tradition of Collective Health helped to place our work in context.

We would also like to thank and acknowledge the diverse audience that showed up to a public meeting held at UERJ, Rio de Janeiro as part of our workshop. Among the audience, composed of health and education professionals, as well as parents of children with autism, we would like to particularly thank Iranice Nascimento and Monica Accioly. Iranice and Monica have been involved with autism activism in Rio de Janeiro for almost 20 years now. Their hard work and persistence, working with very limited resources and under very adverse conditions, have been a great inspiration for us throughout the whole process of organizing the different events that composed the workshop in Rio.

Finally, our deepest respect and admiration go to all the administrative staff and professors at UERJ, who supported in various ways the events that took place at the university. They have been working under continuously deteriorating conditions, for the past year with late salaries, and yet have kept the university open as place for intellectually and politically engaging forums. As they often say, these days: *UERJ resiste!*

Contents

Notes on Contributors

Michael B. Bakan, Ph.D. is Professor of Ethnomusicology at Florida State University. Dr. Bakan's research explores the musical lives of autistic individuals as composers, performers, and engaged listeners. He has published widely on Indonesian *gamelan* music and has performed as a percussionist with renowned musical artists including George Clinton, John Cage, and Tito Puente.

Benilton Bezerra Jr., M.D., Ph.D. is Associate Professor at the Institute for Social Medicine, State University of Rio de Janeiro. Dr. Bezerra is a psychoanalytic psychiatrist who played a key role in Brazilian psychiatric reform. His current research focuses on contemporary reconfigurations of psychiatric diagnosis and their impact on subjectivity and identity.

Pamela Block, Ph.D. is Professor and Director of the Concentration in Disability Studies for the Ph.D. Program in Health and Rehabilitation Sciences at Stony Brook University and the Graduate Certificate in Disability Studies. She is also a former President of the Society for Disability Studies (2009–2010), and a Fellow of the Society for Applied Anthropology. Dr. Block studies multiple marginalization and the intersections of gender, race, poverty, and disability in Brazil and the United States.

M. Ariel Cascio, Ph.D. is a cultural anthropologist who studies science and medicine, and especially the social study of autism. Their work has been funded by the US–Italy Fulbright Commission and the Social Sciences and Humanities Research Council of Canada's Banting Fellowship Program. They are currently a postdoctoral fellow at the Neuroethics Research Unit of the Institut de recherches cliniques de Montréal (Québec, Canada), and the data referenced in this book come from their doctoral work at Case Western Reserve University (Cleveland, OH, USA).

Jurandir Freire Costa, M.D. is a psychiatrist, psychoanalyst, and Full Professor at the Institute for Social Medicine of the State University of Rio de Janeiro. He has written on historical and contemporary topics related to the connections between subjectivity and society and psychoanalysis and culture.

Bárbara Costa Andrada, Ph.D. is a researcher at the Center for Research in Mental Health Public Policies at the Institute of Psychiatry, Federal University of Rio de Janeiro. She is a psychotherapist and Ph.D. in Collective Health, and researches the intersections between mental health public policies, disability rights, and autism.

Cassandra Evans, Ph.D. is an Adjunct Lecturer in Health and Rehabilitation Science, Stony Brook University and Adjunct Philosophy Instructor, Molloy and St. Jospeh's and Suffolk Community colleges. Cassandra is a disability studies scholar with backgrounds in philosophy and rehabilitation counseling who analyzes mental health systems and interventions for individuals with persistent mental disabilities in the United States.

Elizabeth Fein, Ph.D. is Assistant Professor, Department of Psychology, Duquesne University. Dr. Fein is a psychological anthropologist and licensed clinical psychologist who uses clinical ethnography to explore the intersections of culture and neurodevelopmental difference.

Clara Feldman is a Ph.D. student, Institute for Social Medicine, State University of Rio de Janeiro. She is a psychotherapist whose research looks at autism in the Brazilian public mental health care system.

Roy Richard Grinker, Ph.D. is Professor of Anthropology, George Washington University. Dr. Grinker has published extensively on the manifestation and treatment of autism across diverse cultures.

Rossano Cabral Lima, M.D., Ph.D. is Associate Professor at the Institute for Social Medicine, State University of Rio de Janeiro. A child and adolescent psychiatrist, Lima is a co-author of the national guidelines for autism treatment in the mental health system of Brazil.

Francisco Ortega, Ph.D. is Full Professor at the Institute for Social Medicine of the State University of Rio de Janeiro and Research Director of the Rio Center for Global Health. He has published, among other books, *Corporeality, Medical Technologies and Contemporary Culture* (London: Rutledge, 2014) and with *Fernando Vidal, Being Brains: Making the Cerebral Subject* (New York, Fordham University Press, 2017).

Dawn Prince-Hughes, Ph.D. is the author of seven books including the national best-seller *Songs of the Gorilla Nation: My Journey Through Autism* and has been nominated for a MacArthur Fellowship. Her accounts of her life on the autism spectrum explore issues of commonality and difference both within and across primate species.

Clarice Rios, Ph.D. is Lecturer at the Social Psychology Department of the Federal University of Rio de Janeiro (UFRJ). She is a psychological anthropologist whose current research explores the biopolitics of autism treatment within the Brazilian Unified Health System. She is also interested in embodied and tacit knowledge in the context of lay autism expertise.

Laura Sterponi, Ph.D. is Associate Professor of Language, Literacy and Culture, University of California Berkeley, Graduate School of Education. Dr. Sterponi brings together developmental psychology and applied linguistics to study the sociocultural underpinnings of learning through ethnographic and discourse analytic methods. Her current work focuses on the interactional affordances of language practices such as formulaic language and reported speech in autism spectrum conditions.

Enrico Valtellina, Ph.D. collaborates with the University of Bergamo, Italy. The author of multiple works on Disability Studies, History of Psychiatry, and other philosophical and literary topics, he has increasingly focused his work on relational disability since realizing that he is lost somewhere on the autism spectrum.

Thomas S. Weisner, Ph.D. is Professor of Anthropology, Emeritus, Departments of Psychiatry and Anthropology at UCLA. Dr. Weisner's research and teaching interests are in culture and human development; ecocultural theory and methods; medical, psychological and cultural studies of families and children at risk (including children and adults with developmental disabilities, ADHD, and autism); mixed methods; and evidence-informed policy. His publications and further information are available at www.tweisner.com.

CHAPTER 1

Introduction

Elizabeth Fein and Clarice Rios

1.1 Where Did This Book Come From?

All knowledge emerges from a network of somewheres. Its production is bound up in particular histories of particular people, who bring distinctive sets of pragmatic arts to the balance of their resources and vulnerabilities. This book is no exception. The editors of this volume, who are also the instigators of the workshop from which it emerged, first met at the Society for Psychological Anthropology biannual conference in San Diego in 2013. Both of us were working on autism in cultural context, and both of us were at transition points in our own professional lives, facing uncertain futures. Clarice, who had trained as an anthropologist at the University of Chicago and UCLA, was completing a postdoctoral fellowship at the Research Program in Subjectivity, Health and Medicine at the State University of Rio de Janeiro, amidst psychoanalysts and philosophers studying the impact of psychiatric knowledge and discourse on the formation of subjectivities. Elizabeth had just completed training in clinical psychology and anthropology at the University of Chicago's

E. Fein (✉)
Department of Psychology, Duquesne University, Pittsburgh, PA, USA

C. Rios
Department of Social Psychology, Federal University of Rio de Janeiro, Rio de Janeiro, Brazil

E. Fein and C. Rios (eds.), *Autism in Translation*, Culture, Mind, and Society, https://doi.org/10.1007/978-3-319-93293-4_1

interdisciplinary Department of Comparative Human Development; a year later, she would take a position in Psychology at Duquesne University, a department advocating for a culturally and historically situated, meaning-centered psychology grounded in traditions of phenomenological philosophy. We felt a synergy, not only between our own interests but also between the communities we inhabited and the intellectual currents and eddies swirling within their flows and obstructions. In response to both the opportunities and uncertainties before us, we decided we needed to make something. Over the following year, we met via video-conferencing each week to discuss what its parameters might be. Out of those conversations, the plan for the conference that would produce this volume was born.

As our ideas coalesced, our aim became to create an event that would place into dialogue two intellectual traditions: psychological anthropology and the South American tradition of Collective Health. These fields have multiple points of commonality with manifold implications for autism. Both take as their subject the complex interplay of individuals and their sociocultural contexts; both have developed theoretical and methodological tools to connect the levels of analysis that are frequently divided in debates about autism and issues of global health more broadly. However, due to differences and distances in language and geography, these two fields had not experienced much cross-pollination. Our hope was to start a conversation between them.

Encompassing the fields of social science, epidemiology, and health policy, Collective Health takes a social and political approach to the study of health and disease, working to articulate and propagate a model of health that is "socially established through intersubjective pacts within economic, social and cultural contexts" (ABRASCO 2004, in Ivo de Carvalho et al. 2007, 10). Collective Health possesses a distinct epistemological ethos characterized by a careful attention to the relationships between the individual and the state, especially around contested politics of health, and a deep grounding in the lived realities of service provision (Langdon and Follér 2012). Similarly, psychological anthropology has a long history of examining the interaction between psyche and sociocultural life, in all the particularities of each. As Tom Weisner explores in his contribution to this volume, psychological anthropology engages with the daily life experience of individuals, families, and communities, developing conceptual tools for both identifying and working across levels of analysis. We were particularly aware of "the position of psychological anthropology to engage in bridging research, practice, and policy," especially when put into conversation with other disciplines and domains of practice (Korbin and Anderson-Fye 2011, 415).

As a phenomenon with irreducibly individual and interpersonal instantiations, possessing both robust similarities and intriguing differences across contexts, autism serves as a powerful point of departure from which to consider questions at the intersection of these two fields. How do individual differences that exceed or transcend local norms get conceptualized, diagnosed, and treated within different societies with different medical infrastructures and expectations for social relations? How do diverse processes of socialization affect the cross-cultural manifestation of individual differences? How do relationships between the individual, the community, and the state shape political claims about disability, biosocial identity, and public health? How do individuals living under such descriptions understand their condition and themselves? Dis/ability is inextricably linked to the relationship between self and society (Ingstad and Whyte 1995); the power of autism to destabilize and reinscribe assumptions about sociality, intersubjectivity, and communication refracts these issues in disruptive and potentially generative ways.

In order for anthropological theory to effectively address these questions, we felt, its development needs to be driven by the inclusion of paradigms from outside the global North. However, the dominance of English as a scholarly language, the scarcity of resources within academic environments in low- and middle-income countries, and the challenges of speaking across deep-seated and long-standing ontological and epistemological differences all contribute to the marginalization of South American intellectual traditions within supposedly globalized discourses. In particular, as we observed the increasing influence of work in the field of Global Mental Health (GMH), we were becoming increasingly concerned about the dominance of Northern perspectives and priorities within this growing field and its interventions. One aim of this event was to begin, in some small way, to destabilize this dominance.

A core premise of this event has always been that the contexts of knowledge production matter. Physical spaces and arrangements, institutional infrastructures, status hierarchies, and their impact on spatial position, the sheer distance that a voice can carry, when amplified (or not) through one technology or another—all of these things constitute a matrix through which ideas are born and through which they rise and fall. It felt important to us to come together in a physical way, to be in each other's presence in an intentionally chosen location. We opted to locate the conference at the State University of Rio de Janeiro, taking advantage of the rich theoretical and philosophical approaches thriving within the Research Program in Subjectivity, Health, and Medicine while addressing an identified need within the program for training in ethnographic research methods. Countering the trend for South American intellectuals to train abroad and study literatures that may not be attuned to the needs and questions most relevant to the South American context, we hoped instead to introduce methodological tools that could be effectively adapted to address issues related to the organization of health and of governance unique to the Brazilian context.

We hoped, especially, to counter tendencies within Global Mental Health to depict the Global South as a place of lack, in need of rescue through Northern intervention. As Khan et al. (2012) observe, "[i]t is critical to note that the landscape of supportive interventions in LIMCs [low-to-middle-income countries] has not been void of alternative approaches to those developed in high-income countries, and that these approaches provide equally viable targets for research" (157); however, these approaches are often overlooked within discourses that focus on the absence of appropriate services. We sought to explore the wide range of understandings and practices already in place for addressing autism spectrum conditions and other developmental differences. In doing so, we follow Whitley's (2014, 501) call to offer "no opposition without proposition": a call to counter-balance critique of mental health interventions with an exploration of possible solutions to the problematics thus posed.

In planning the event, we made a conscious decision to prioritize depth of representation over maximizing geographic diversity. We could have opted to hold a "cross-cultural" conference in which we sought scholars from as many different countries as possible. (One agency denied our application for funding on the grounds that we had not done so). Instead, rather than attempting to seek "thin" representation from the widest variety of places and perspectives, we focused instead on establishing a "thick" and in-depth dialogue between two scholarly traditions that were each located within particular geopolitical and historical contexts.

In selecting our participants, however, psychological anthropology and Collective Health provided guiding principles rather than constraints upon acceptable disciplinary identities. We approached people whose work explored autism situated in particular contexts, whether those contexts be geographic, aesthetic, or linguistic. We sought scholars who were themselves positioned with regard to autism in a variety of ways: scholars who are themselves on the autism spectrum; scholars who have family members, partners, and friends on the autism spectrum; scholars who have worked with people on the spectrum in clinical contexts, and those who have worked with people on the spectrum in artistic and academic collaborations. All participants, in their work, address autism across levels of analysis, from individual development to global discourses, with a focus on the particular cultural and material contexts in which each of these phenomena manifests.

We were very fortunate to receive funding from the Lemelson/Society for Psychological Anthropology Conference Fund. Since 2008, this program has funded a number of small conferences and workshops that allow in-depth work on innovative and significant topics in psychological anthropology. Through the generosity of this program, we were able to fly eleven conference participants to Rio de Janeiro, hold the conference, and present our work to the public on the final day of the conference, via a complex assemblage of translators and audiovisual equipment.

1.2 The Event

Once our funding had been confirmed, we sent official invitations to the community of scholars with whom we had been planning the event.[1] Each participant was asked to prepare a twenty-minute presentation, and invited to consider the following questions:

Conceptual framework: What do you understand yourself to be looking at, or looking for, or looking through, in your work? How do you define terms like "autism" and "culture" in your own work? What models of person, society, and the relationship between them inform your work?

Method: How do you go about finding out what you find out, and how does that affect what you find? What research paradigms do you use in your investigations? What challenges have you run into and how did you address those challenges?

Findings: What have you found out about autism, its social, cultural, and political contexts, and the relationship between the two?

Each presenter was also assigned a discussant, and some time for discussion of their work, adding up to about an hour in total. The end of each day was capped with a summative discussion, the goal of which was to identify and track emergent themes. The entirety of the conference was filmed, and the videos are available to view at the Society for Psychological Anthropology Vimeo channel. These recordings became an important part of the workshop methodology, as it allowed us both to make the event available to a wider audience and also to revisit particularly thought-provoking moments as we were preparing this volume.

Over four days of paper presentations, lively discussions, and an outreach event to the broader scholarly and clinical community of Rio de Janeiro, we grappled with our own differences in position and perspective, struggling over language barriers, unfamiliar sets of assumptions, jet lag, and the human tendency to cling to the familiar when disoriented. We were all, on some level, differently abled at this event than we were accustomed to being, whether this was because we were working in a foreign location, as was the case for the visiting North American scholars, or working in a non-native language, as was the case for the hosting scholars. In working through our own understandings and misunderstandings of each other, we generated new understandings: of the relationship between political systems, cultural models of self and social life, and individual lived experience. We did more than talk, and listen, trying desperately to fit everything we wanted to say into the number of hours we had allotted; we guided each other through explorations of the Rio streets at night, we danced to samba music together and shared meals and long walks through gardens heavy with branches. We took a trip to the Museum of Images of the Unconscious, founded by the pioneering Jungian psychiatrist Nise da Silveira and honoring her rejection of primitive electroshock and lobotomy in favor of expressive art therapies. We climbed the winding stairs of the *Hotel e Spa da Loucura* (Hotel and Spa of Madness), adorned with elaborate graffiti murals, where clients experiment with art, music, and theater as means of symbolic healing.

The final day of the conference ended with a meeting to discuss the form this publication would take. From the beginning, we agreed that we wanted to produce a publication that would capture some elements of the experience we had just shared. Particularly, we wanted to preserve both its dialogic character and its element of surprise. As we talked, we threw words and phrases up on a white board, trying to characterize where we'd been and where we hoped to go: Community. Decentering. Representation of togetherness. Collision. Conflict. Psychic connection.

Synergy. Dequotative. Voices. Ways of caring, knowing, speaking, seeing, being, being uncomfortable. Close to nature. Committed Fair Witness. Institutionalization. Price. Access. Things that really bother people (some but not all of which are labels). Holding hands. Effort of defining terms. Territories. Knowledges. Experiences. And some memorable phrases from the event: *I'd like to sleep on a bed of your voice and your ideas. There's a saying: keep one eye on the cat and one eye on the fish. Who owns autism? Maybe autism owns us.*

On that last day, we also held a meeting open to the public, attended by about 150 mental health practitioners, scholars, educators, and advocates from Rio de Janeiro and beyond. We presented, we took questions. But the most memorable moments came when we moved outside of our prepared words piped through translation headphones. Clarice offered an impassioned, extemporaneous call for Brazilian scholars and practitioners to embrace their/our own expertise even while enthusiastically embracing approaches from abroad. Michael B. Bakan shared his gift of rhythm with us in a collective drumming exercise. Dawn Prince-Hughes got us up out of our chairs—the whole hall full of us—swinging our arms, opening up our mouths and faces, and experimenting with how it felt to move and communicate like gorillas.

It is impossible to relate to your colleagues in quite the same way after sharing such an experience. In a sense, this workshop instantiated what Callard and Fitzgerald have memorably described as "a delicate, difficult, transgressive, risky, playful, and genuinely experimental interdisciplinarity" (2015, 4), in which "experimental theatre and experimental poetry promise as much—in terms of methods, knowledges, modes of construing, and intervening in the world—as the rich legacy of experimentation in the natural sciences" (ibid., 9). Our intent in bringing these participants together into a shared physical space shares something with their call to create a "temporary, local assemblage of motivation, interest, people and machinery—in which we, and our collaborators, are able momentarily to think something exterior to both the conventions of experimental practice, and the taken-for-granted dynamics of epistemic power that underwrite its conduct" (Fitzgerald and Callard 2015, 18). We built good bones for the event—a schedule, guiding questions, a strong mission; but at heart, our goal was to bring some people together in a place and see what happened. This book is our attempt to show you what emerged.

1.3 The Volume

The volume aims to capture the unique nature of this inter-cultural conversation, as well as to carry it forward. We invited participants to form international teams and work together on collaborative pieces, and did our best to set up groups of chapters and commentators that spanned across both geographic and disciplinary territories. The volume itself is structured as a continuing conversation: it contains individual stand-alone pieces that can be read in isolation; however, each section also contains a response piece from a discussant, synthesizing the themes of that section, and the volume also contains two commentaries by participants on the event as a whole.

The first section of the volume, "Political Histories of Autism" consists of two comparative, collaborative essays examining autism and neurodiversity in the context of psychiatric reform movements in the US, Italy, and Brazil. Rossano Cabral Lima, Clara Feldman, Cassandra Evans, and Pamela Block draw on their many years of studying autism and disability in the United States and Brazil to chronicle post-deinstitutionalization efforts to advocate for the recognition of the full humanity and personhood of autistic people. In both countries, schisms have formed between groups that share this common goal. This chapter compares how these tensions have taken form within the United States and Brazil, in the context of each country's particular and "radically different political and economic histories, health systems, conceptions of health, and ideals about the relationship between individuals and the state" (Lima et al., this volume). M. Ariel Cascio, Bárbara Costa Andrada, and Benilton Bezerra Jr. also take up the question of psychiatric reform—this time in Italy and Brazil—looking at how the biologically based and diagnosis-specific approaches once rejected by psychiatric reformers are now embraced by a new wave of critics to post-reform policies. In his discussant remarks, Francisco Ortega examines the presence of polarizing conflicts throughout these two comparative case studies, observing how families within these systems model pragmatic practices of integration.

The second section of the volume focuses on issues of "Voice, Narrative and Representation." The section begins with Michael B. Bakan exploration of the question: what does it mean to be an ethnomusicologist of autism? The piece calls for, and exemplifies, a form of appreciative listening, surrounding and foregrounding an essay written by a musician diagnosed with

Syndrome. Elizabeth Fein tells a series of stories—about three young men diagnosed with autism spectrum conditions, about her experience getting trained on the Autism Diagnostic Observation Schedule, and about conferences where autism is attributed to environmental contamination—to explore the possibility of understanding autism as a mode of engagement with the world, characterized by a deep involvement with external systems of organization. Jurandir Freire Costa and Roy Richard Grinker collaborate on an essay that brings phenomenology and philosophy of mind to an analysis of first-person accounts of autism, approaching the issue of cognition and rationality from the perspectives offered in these accounts as a way of challenging claims about the nature of autistic cognitive impairment. Laura Sterponi's discussion identifies two strategies she sees in these essays, which she calls *denotational layering* and *non-referential signification*, as ways to "engage with the silence and interrogate the unspeakable" (Sterponi, this volume).

The third and final section focuses on the concept of autism and how it organizes both individual lives and social and economic systems. Clarice Rios provides an ethnographic account of the Brazilian parent association she calls *Círculo da Esperança* (Circle of Hope). Participants in the program develop a form of autism expertise that bridges specialized knowledge of autism that comes from abroad with their locally developed and situated ability to translate the tacit knowledge of their own social worlds to their autistic children. Philosopher and historian of science Enrico Valtellina provides a witty and incisive analysis of the diagnosis of Asperger's Syndrome as both a classification and an event, drawing on Althusser's notion of interpellation to narrate his own changing relationship with the diagnosis. Roy Richard Grinker argues that the economic power of autism can be understood through the figure of the fetish—a sacred object set apart. In the discussant remarks that conclude the section, M. Ariel Cascio links the many meanings of autism to classic anthropological questions, exploring implications of "the autism concept" for debates on normality and abnormality, mind and body, socialization and enculturation, political economy, and social organization.

The volume closes with two sets of reflections by participants. Thomas Weisner shares insights from a long career at the intersection of psychological anthropology and the study of disability, tracing connections between autism and the core concerns of psychological anthropology: difference as both biological and social, the centralities of lived experience, the intersection of vulnerabilities, the complexities of social and linguistic competence, the importance of daily routines for organizing family and community life, and the historical and institutional forces that structure all these things. Dawn Prince-Hughes closes out the volume with her lyrical and gently humorous meditations on the immediacy and messy power of connection between living beings.

1.4 Broader Themes

The goal of this volume is to contextualize autism within a range of socio-political contexts, by illuminating the historical, cultural and economic circumstances that lead to particular conceptualizations of autism and exploring the impact of these conceptualizations on the daily lives of those affected. The papers in this volume thus move beyond what Solomon and Bagatell (2010) have criticized as a tendency toward "less and less attention in autism research to phenomena that cannot be studied at the neurobiological or molecular level, such as human experience, social interaction, and cross-cultural variation," (2) instead examining autism in the context of politics, economics, aesthetics, and citizenship. Pieces in this volume critically interrogate the construction of autism as both a subjective and objective category, while seeking to remain grounded in the lived experience of people for whom this category organizes access to much-needed services, and/or provides a deeply meaningful way to make sense of life experiences. We attend to the historical, economic, and socio-political conditions that hinder or foster such experiences. In doing so, we seek to elucidate some of the complex and contingent ties between arenas too often oversimplified as "the global" and "the local" (Bemme and D'souza 2014). Authors in this volume engage with the ways in which autism spectrum conditions—of all sorts, including the conditions under which autism can emerge as a coherent category—travel through different borders and contexts. They grapple with education and public health structures, self-advocacy and parent activism, the entanglement between experience and psychiatric knowledge/expertise, and the various forms of re-presentation and authorship afforded by these conditions.

At the heart of all of these processes is the ongoing work of meaning-making, and the works in this volume all engage with the question of meaning and its negotiations across a wide variety of contexts. The chapters by Cascio et al. and Lima et al. compare culturally and historically situated approaches to autism to show how meaning is not determined by a single type of rationality and logic, but is contextually and historically dependent. As pieces by Michael B. Bakan, Enrico Valtelina, and Freire Costa and Grinker explore, meaning is affected by who is speaking and experiencing, and who is the audience. Meaning is not solely determined by available cultural content, but is created where that content is taken up through widely diverse modes of engagement with culture, as Fein's chapter argues. Rios's ethnographic study of *Círculo da Esperança* demonstrates how meaning-making activities around autism draw from sociocultural local worlds as well as from specialized knowledge. Meaning-making activities are also materially based, shaped by economic and geopolitical dynamics and flows that have a life of their own, and that do not always map onto the concerns of academic researchers or autism advocates, as Grinker incisively argues in his essay on the economics of autism. Amidst these flows, in a world of connectedness, it is hard to distinguish purely "local cultural beliefs," as powerful discourses and practices around autism spread all over the world. Instead, we heed Marcus' (1998) call for multi-sited ethnographies, of which this book as a whole could be considered an example. He criticizes the "conventional single-site mise-en-scene of ethnographic research" and argues that "for ethnography [...] there is no global in the local-global contrast [...] The global is an emergent dimension of arguing about the connection among sites in a multi-sited ethnography" (83).

The quality of this connectedness has changed with time. Technological devices that have allowed for information to flow at a fast pace have also changed our sensibilities and traditional meaning-making processes. At the same time, there is still a unique generative power to sharing a bit of place and time—as we saw at the workshop itself. These pieces thus seek to explore the ways in which meaning-making is both fluid and situated.

As the volume slowly came together, we confronted a number of questions about how to translate a situated, polyvocal conversation into a series of traveling texts. We grappled particularly with questions of attribution[2]: how should we credit "Gordon Peterson" and the many other autistic creators whose words have been folded into texts by neurotypical (or at least neurologically unmarked) authors who aim to amplify and re-present their expressions? How to include each other's words in our own pieces, making space for the impact our discussants had on the shape, form, and contents of our papers? Like many other forms of echolalia, these scholarly dequotatives evoke the complex ethics of repetition. We have made a series of choices here that balance the conventions of academic writing with a desire to honor the forms of expression that are silenced by such conventions; we acknowledge that a wide variety of other choices would also have been possible.

Time and place matter to the production and dissemination of knowledge, and time keeps moving on. The chapters in this book have been written and the book edited and assembled between 2015 and 2018: a time when massive historical changes have continued in Brazil and in the United States. In both cases, the politics of health, and the role of states and societies in the maintenance of health of individuals and societies, has played a major role in the eruption of simmering political conflicts. In Brazil, the long historical process that led to Psychiatric Reform has been under intensifying pressures since democratically elected president Dilma Rousseff was removed from the presidency in 2016. This event initiated a long political crisis, aggravated by a deepening economic crisis, that not only affected public policies around autism in Brazil but the very academic structure in which Brazilian scholars in this volume have been developing their research. In the United States, Donald Trump was elected president, ushering in a whirlwind of dismantled state programs, shifting geopolitical allegiances, and rising far-right nationalist violence. Our weekly phone meetings have continued, and our small talk has turned now to more urgent check-ins: How are you doing? How are you dealing? Are you safe? What have you come to understand differently, this week, about governance? And the reverberations of the workshop continue to extend outward in new ways: the video of our public meeting continues to be shared across social media in Brazil, catalyzing conversations we could not have predicted. We hope this volume will also provide a venue for carrying these conversations forward into whatever the future holds.

Notes

1. While most of the scholars with whom we had planned the event were able to attend, a few were in the end unable to join us. We'd like to particularly acknowledge Elizabeth "Ibby" Grace, Elinor Ochs, and Michael Orsini, who, while not able to be there in person, felt very much present in spirit.
2. Thanks to Benjamin M. Gaddes, whose work editing these chapters put him into frequent contact with such choice-points, for emphasizing the significance of this issue.

References

Bemme, Doerte, and Nicole A. D'souza. 2014. "Global Mental Health and Its Discontents: An Inquiry into the Making of Global and Local Scale." *Transcultural Psychiatry* 51 (6): 850–874.

Callard, Felicity, and Des Fitzgerald. 2015. *Rethinking Interdisciplinarity Across the Social Sciences and Neurosciences*. New York: Palgrave Pivot.

Fitzgerald, Des, and Felicity Callard. 2015. "Social Science and Neuroscience Beyond Interdisciplinarity: Experimental Entanglements." *Theory, Culture and Society* 32 (1): 3–32.

Ingstad, Benedicte, and Susan Whyte, eds. 1995. *Disability and Culture*. Berkeley: University of California Press.

Ivo de Carvalho, Antonio, Marica Falia Westphal, and Vera Lucia Góes Pereira Lima. 2007. "Health Promotion in Brazil." *Global Health Promotion* 14 (1): 7–12.

Khan, Naila Z., Lilia Albores Gallo, Aurora Arghir, Bogdan Budisteanu, Magdalena Budisteanu, Iuliana Dobrescu, Kirsty Donald, Samia El-Tabari, Michelle Hoogenhout, Fidelie Kalambayi, Rafal Kawa, Isaac Lemus Espinoza, Rosane Lowenthal, Susan Malcolm-Smith, Cecila Montiel-Nava, Jumana Odeh, Cristiane S. de Paula, Florina Rad, Adelaide Katerine Tarpan, Kevin G.F. Thomas, Chongying Wang, Vikram Patel, Simon Baron-Cohen, and Mayada Elsabbagh. 2012. "Autism and the Grand Challenges in Global Mental Health." *Autism Research* 5: 156–159.

Korbin, Jill, and Eileen Anderson-Fye. 2011. "Adolescence Matters: Practice- and Policy-Relevant Research and Engagement in Psychological Anthropology." *Ethos* 39 (4): 415–425.

Langdon, Esther Jean, and Maj-Lis Follér. 2012. "Anthropology of Health in Brazil: A Border Discourse." *Medical Anthropology* 31: 4–28.

Marcus, George E. 1998. *Ethnography Through Thick and Thin*. Princeton, NJ: Princeton University Press.

Solomon, Olga, and Nancy Bagatell. 2010. "Autism: Rethinking the Possibilities." *Ethos* 38 (1): 1–7.

Whitley, Rob. 2014. "Beyond Critique: Rethinking Roles for the Anthropology of Mental Health." *Culture, Medicine and Psychiatry* 38: 499–511.

PART I

Political Histories of Autism

CHAPTER 2

Autism Policy and Advocacy in Brazil and the USA

Rossano Cabral Lima, Clara Feldman, Cassandra Evans and Pamela Block

2.1 Introduction

Brazil and the United States have some commonalities concerning social policies and advocacy for people with autism during the twentieth century as well as in the beginning of the twenty first century. Within both countries, medical rationales were once used to segregate people who would now get a diagnosis of autism into inhumane institutional settings. In these two countries, powerful alliances of mental health professionals, family members of people on the autism spectrum, and (in some cases) autistic people themselves have fought to obtain full inclusion in society for autistic people. In both cases, a scarcity of resources available to vulnerable populations, and disagreements about how to allocate these resources, have led to schisms between groups that ideally would

R. C. Lima (✉) · C. Feldman
Institute for Social Medicine, State University of Rio de Janeiro (UERJ), Rio de Janeiro, Brazil

C. Evans · P. Block
Health and Rehabilitation Science, Stony Brook University, Stony Brook, NY, USA

E. Fein and C. Rios (eds.), *Autism in Translation*, Culture, Mind, and Society, https://doi.org/10.1007/978-3-319-93293-4_2

work collaboratively with each other. Finally, in both Brazil and USA, there are struggles over who gets to define what autism is, and thus to shape policy, delineate, and control services and grant (or deny) access to resources for treatment and research. However, these two countries have radically different political and economic histories, health systems, conceptions of health, and ideals about the relationship between individuals and the state. Consequentially, as far as mental health and autism advocacy is concerned, activist movements have taken very different forms and led to very different sets of contentions and controversies.

Psychiatric Reform and deinstitutionalization in Brazil took place within the formation of the *Sistema Único de Saúde* (Brazilian Unified Health System—SUS). The SUS arose within a larger reform in the health system, also known as the Sanitary Reform, which began to take shape in the mid-1970s, but was only fully consolidated by the end of the 1980s. This reform grew out of a widespread social movement, involving different sections of society that were brought together during the struggle to restore democracy after a long period of military dictatorship. Politically and ideologically, the health reform adopted the viewpoint that health is not "an exclusively biological issue to be resolved by medical services, but a social and political issue to be addressed in public" (Paim et al. 2011, 1784). This widespread debate and political mobilization around health led to the incorporation of the right to health in the 1988 constitution. The notion of health as a citizen's right laid out the foundations of the SUS, which translated into three basic principles—universality, integrality, and equity. Together, these principles aim at amplifying access to health care to all Brazilian citizens (universality), while taking into account the different needs and life conditions of the populations served (equity) and the wide range of possible actions for health promotion (integrality). As a result of this history, psychosocial, communitarian, and political projects are fundamentally and explicitly intertwined with health service provision in Brazil.

The assumption that mental health professionals are involved in social, political, and activist projects as an intrinsic part of their professional practice is less prevalent within the United States. In the U.S. case, the federal arm of mental health care is organized around a form of bioscience primarily geared toward removing diseases through intervention on the body; the Vision Statement of the National Institute of Mental Health, for example, reads simply "NIMH envisions a world in which mental illnesses are prevented and cured" (National Institute of

Mental Health, n.d.). Public and private funding tends to prioritize research into the presumed neurogenetic causes of autism, with a focus on prevention and cure, often at the expense of funding social, vocational, and community supports for people living with autism (Singh 2015). Activist and advocacy programs thus find themselves in conflict with clinical agendas in their attempts to build community and raise awareness of the psychosocial needs of people on the autism spectrum. Meanwhile, however, these activist movements also tend to ideologically foreground issues of personal rights and autonomy, even as they also advocate for health as a collective good.

In both cases, arguments about fundamental human rights have been central to political advocacy around mental health reform movements. In the United States, mainstream mental health reform has taken place within a broader framework of political and civil rights; in Brazil, the political activism that accompanied the redemocratization period in the last decades has more explicitly connected political and civil rights with social and economic rights, such as the "right to health." In other words, while in the US the most significant political movements have concentrated on safeguarding individual liberties from external coercion, in Brazil, social movements came together during that period to fight both for individual liberties and for the public services that are essential to freedom and agency, such as the right to health care, education, food, and employment, among other things. However, in both settings, scarcity of funding and limitations on resources have led to difficulties in honoring these rights in practice; many of the controversies around autism treatment arise out of these gaps between assumed human rights and the social resources necessary to honor them.

In what follows, we will show how these different conceptions of health, personhood, and citizenship have promoted different sets of allegiances and conflicts between different sectors of autism communities, by comparing the history and "lay of the land" of autism advocacy in the US and Brazil. To achieve its objectives, this chapter initially presents the processes of institutionalization and deinstitutionalization of disabled and mentally ill people in USA, as it is a major step in the task of understanding the construction of the current status of autism. After that, we introduce the middle-twentieth century figure of the "exceptional child" (with mental deficiency) in Brazil as well as Brazilian Psychiatric Reform and its twenty-first century impact on people with autism. Finally, we point out the tensions among different mental health, educational and disability studies approaches to autism in both countries. By providing a comparative history and the current state of affairs, we aim to show what the two countries have to teach and learn from each other.

2.2 Twentieth Century Institutionalization in the USA

From the early to late twentieth century in the United States, approaches to psychiatric and mental disabilities were largely characterized by exclusion, warehousing, experimental surgeries, tentative treatments, and physical restraints.[1] The congested urban asylums that contained people then considered mad and feebleminded created social problems in larger metropolitan areas like Chicago, Philadelphia, Boston, and New York and provided the impetus for mental hygiene planners to consider non-urban alternatives. For this reason, the overcrowding in city asylum populations gave way to the creation of farm colonies for the feebleminded, insane, and nervous (Rembis 2011).

It is likely that these institutions contained many people who today would be on the autism spectrum. What would now be considered autism was then conflated with feeblemindedness and/or mental retardation (MR) (Eyal 2013), thus placing Autistic people under the same constraining approaches that were used for those conditions at the time. As late as 1942, Kanner labeled people who would today be on the spectrum as feebleminded and idiotic, even though he championed for their rights and advocated against eugenics and euthanasia (Kliewer and Drake 2013). Furthermore, though many asylum residents were committed for less grave afflictions, the majority of these populations were identified with schizophrenia, and what was then considered as childhood schizophrenia would most likely be considered autism nowadays, as Bleuler named and identified schizophrenia in 1911 and Kanner would not introduce autism as a psychiatric category until 32 years later. This diagnosis sealed the fates of individuals, consigning them to endure the most experimental of treatments and harshest of restraints. "Once a child diagnosed with autism or childhood schizophrenia was placed in a state hospital, he or she was no longer treated as a child" (Silberman 2015, 208). The same experimental drugs, ECT, and insulin therapy used for psychosis were also used on autistic children. In 1950, the first discovery of neuroleptics—anti-psychotic medicines—was recorded.

Subsequent research trials and experiments with these drugs persisted in mental hospitals throughout the United States in the 1950s (Silberman 2015).

By the mid-1940s, US mental hospitals recorded the highest number of patients both in its own history, and in the world overall. However, at the same time, legislature and federal funding were moving toward finding alternatives to institutions and to the dangerous interventions in use there. In 1946, President Truman passed the National Mental Health Act. Originally a response to advocacy on behalf of veterans with mental health needs, the Act paved the way for establishing the nation's National Institutes of Mental Health (NIMH). Three years later, in 1949, NIMH became a formal institute aimed at furthering a commitment to mental health research (NIMH 2017). Following that, United States Public Law 84–182 created the Mental Health Study Act of 1955 (NIMH 2017). This mandated reevaluating causes and effects of mental illness, requiring that investigators consider economic and social variables as aggravating factors during their research as well (Hinshaw 2007; NIMH 2017).

In 1959, the U.S. Mental Health Act was passed. The Act outlined involuntary commitment procedures and established psychiatrists' authority to declare individuals as insane and be held for initial observation in 72- and 24-hour time frames. Shortly afterward, in the 1960s and 1970s, once the successes of Thorazine in hospitals were fully acknowledged, widespread use of the first-generation neuroleptics/anti-psychotics to treat psychosis, schizophrenia, and autism became common (Silberman 2015), and hospitals experienced quieter patients and fewer admittances.

2.3 The Cultural Context of Deinstitutionalization in the USA

President Kennedy passed the Community Mental Health Centers Construction Act in 1963, shifting funding priorities from building more hospitals to community care (Hinshaw 2007). At the height of institutionalization, before pharmacological therapy became prevalent, the country estimated institutionalizing 560,000 individuals. The United States' effort to deinstitutionalize reduced the number of psychiatric beds in state mental institutions from 560,000 to 45,000 or more than half a million beds—a 95% release rate in the short decades spanning the mid 1950s to early 1970s (Hinshaw 2007; Johnson 2014).

Rights of the mentally ill and other groups were bolstered by pharmaceutical advances, public advocacy, and the broader cultural shifts that characterized the USA in the 1960s. At the same time that this movement gained momentum, civil rights protests fought for humane treatment of women, racial minorities, and people with disabilities. Social commentators like Szasz,[2] Foucault, and Goffman focused attention on the ways in which insanity could be understood as deviation from social norms. The publication (1962) and then the film (1975) of Ken Kesey's book *One Flew Over the Cuckoo's Nest* depicted diagnosis and hospitalization as the violent imposition of repressive constraints upon nonconformists whose creative energies challenged the status quo. Deinstitutionalization therefore took place within a broader political and cultural ethos that emphasized the liberation of the autonomous individual from oppressive social organizations. Additional indirect forms of action were at play as well.[3] For example, William Gronfein (1985) stresses that at the same time the American government was beginning to look at mental health differently because variables like Medicaid and Medicare were paying for community-based treatments.

Sadly, thousands of patients or "residents" were still found experiencing squalid conditions in modern-day America. As late as the 1970s, when a popular American talk show host Geraldo Rivera exposed Willowbrook State School in Staten Island for savage, sub-human conditions, the United States was forced to look at its institutionalization procedures again. Opened in 1951, Willowbrook was a public hospital for children with developmental disabilities. While anti-psychotics and psychosurgeries designated for the mentally ill would typically not be protocol for this population, reports uncovered abusive medical experiments injecting the children with hepatitis, terrible overcrowding, restraints, and disease rampant in this institution (Carlson 2010; Johnson 2014). Rivera likened the scenes and inhumanity to "America's Nazi concentration camps" (Carlson 2010, 131). Public response to the discovery was so severe that the hospital endured a class action lawsuit and was forced to close shortly thereafter. This tragedy spurred the National Research Act in 1974 and gave impetus for the Belmont Report, which influenced university review boards to require strict ethical standards for projects with human subjects (Johnson 2014). It also furthered what had by then become a national movement to deinstitutionalize individuals living with intellectual, developmental, and psychiatric disability.

The ideological commitment to freeing people from institutions in the United States has not been accompanied by a similar commitment to providing the resources and support necessary for community and family care. Though the time was culturally ripe for a shift toward liberation from institutions, the national ambivalence toward providing funding manifested in ongoing shifts in funding levels between presidential administrations. While Presidents Kennedy and Johnson established a network of Community Mental Health Centers to provide community care, President Nixon's presidency eliminated much of the funding for these centers. The Carter administration worked to undo the funding reductions only to be reversed by the next round of cuts in services and supports by President Reagan. Because of funding lapses in the 1980s, many of the half million individuals were left without social supports, like job search assistance, medication and, for some, housing. "By the end of the twentieth century, community facilities in New York City evidenced the squalor and neglect formerly associated with large state hospitals" (Hinshaw 2007, 80). The 1980s then saw an unprecedented increase in jail and prison populations. (Hinshaw 2007; Ben-Moshe 2013; Luhrmann 2007).[4]

Escaping the grips of unregulated and unseen abuses in American institutions thus came with its benefits and its pitfalls. The social and political movements that urged for better treatment of confined and committed individuals also resulted in additional pressure and unanswered questions for caregivers. Along with the desirability for deinstitutionalization and normalization came enormous pressures on parents who were now in charge of community care:

> The absence or deterioration of both community and institutional supports leaves families as exclusive providers of ongoing care for disabled relatives. This structural failure to recognize the uncompensated labor of familial caregivers contributes to untold hardships on an individual level. The families of disabled children, like those who care for the chronically ill, the elderly, or people with severe mental illnesses, have few options for their continuing care. (Silverman 2012, 123)

The shift in policy toward an emphasis on decentralized community-based alternatives was justified not only by the belief that it was more humane, but also by the belief that it would save money. The push to get people out of institutions was not matched by resources needed to support them well in the community, where they were not always welcome.

Essentially, the release of disabled individuals—whether psychiatrically, developmentally, or cognitively disabled—resulted in an abundance of unsupported people into the community.

2.4 Deinstitutionalization and the Emergence of the Autism "Crisis" in the USA

Eyal (2013) notes that it was the combination of deinstitutionalization with parental involvement that produced the epidemic of autism. Deinstitutionalization meant that old categories from the custodial era were replaced with new ones. The categorization of moron, feeble-minded, idiot, imbecile, became mentally deficient, educable, trainable, or untrainable, which then in the community became mildly, severely, or profoundly mentally retarded. This happened "while creating instead a new institutional matrix—community treatment, special education, and early intervention programs—wherein autism could be identified, differentiated, and multiplied" (Eyal 2013, 868). Parents working in the community and advocating for community treatment, interventions, and new curriculum also became contributors to knowledge production about their own children. They no longer relied solely upon the "experts" to collect data from within the institutions. They were able to contribute their "expertise" to developing new knowledge systems. Eyal concludes that this was not previously possible "within the institutional matrix of custody" (879). Children who present as autistic would not be recognizable in the confines of an institution—"mental deficiency" was a homogeneous category that ignored nuances of a spectrum. Now, given the parents' recognition as part of a team of authorities—including teachers, therapists and psychologists—and the non-custodial nature of treatments, efforts to habilitate, rather than restrain or cure, offer the potential for discovering effective means of communication and acceptance for people with autism.[5]

However, parents did more than become partners with professionals in identifying and diagnosing children—they also fought passionately to identify supports and resources for their children, often under conditions of significant scarcity. In order to achieve this, the autistic child (or, in what became a more widely accepted phrasing, the *child with autism*) emerged as a significant figure of concern in the United States. Special education and medical service systems proliferated as more and more children received the autism diagnosis, and through it became eligible for these services. The majority of funding and resources devoted to autism spectrum conditions, in the United States, focused on detection, diagnosis, and early intervention and treatment for autistic children, much of it taking place within public education system. Far fewer resources were available for these children once they became adults and aged out of the school system (Gerhardt and Lainer 2011). The consequence was a dramatic rise in diagnosed cases of autism, accompanied by a shortage of social roles and acceptable life paths for autistic people. Suddenly there was an autism crisis, an epidemic. What had previously been invisible was suddenly an all-too-visible threat.

Public education and supports were guaranteed to disabled children in the US through the passing of Education for all Handicapped Children Act (EHA) and the Developmental Disabilities Assistance and Bill of Rights Act (DD Act) in 1975 (Weigerink and Pelosi 1979). The DD act focused on supporting three disability populations: autism, cerebral palsy and MR. At first, the services and educational supports provided were more beneficial to those with intellectual disability, as there were established treatments for this population. Elaborated services specifically for autistic children and adults were not developed until the 1980s. In fact, it was not unusual for autistic children to be as MR, as this was seen as a more hopeful diagnosis, with more treatment options available. Autism was also a diagnosis with some stigma attached to it due to assumptions, then in vogue via popularized forms of psychoanalysis, that the disorder developed as a result of cold and rejecting parenting. If mothers did not seem to fit the model of "refrigerator mother" associated with this theory, the children were more likely to be classified as MR.

Many parents understandably rejected the "refrigerator mother" (and father) theory of autism, and looked for alternative explanations that foregrounded biological over psychosocial causes. One highly influential parent researcher (Rimland 1964) directly opposed this thesis by developing his own theories about autism's cause, first identifying that autism had neurogenetic origins and later proposing exposure to environmental toxicity as a significant factor. Rimland's (1964) approach had a huge impact on the way autism was perceived and treated in the United States, in ways still very apparent today. Outgrowths of Rimland's approach include the anti-vaccination movement, which is still very alive and well, though the supposed scientific basis for this was proved fraudulent

(Wakefield 1998). Nevertheless, these remaining constituents continue subjecting children and their environments to interventions aimed at limiting or extract the toxins, such as lead, mercury, and gluten from the child's body. Some of these interventions are benevolent or neutral, but others are quite dangerous, such as bleach purges or chemical castration reminiscing days of experimental treatments tested upon the insane (Food and Drug Administration 2015; Rivera and McDaniel 2013; Tsouderos 2009). Organizations such as Autism Speaks and Defeat Autism Now (now renamed the Autism Research Institute, in response to concerns raised by the autistic community) grew out of the intervention approach.

In the context of significant cultural ambivalence around dependency and the welfare state, the locus of the identified problem became the autistic body rather than the psychosocial context of the autistic person. As Broderick (2010) has analyzed, the rhetoric of many parent advocacy groups increasingly linked the urgency of the challenges facing autistic people and their families to ideas of autism as a biomedical disease best treated through medical practice (rather than, for example, education), a conceptualization which itself became connected with metaphors of autism as an abductor and autism as "the enemy." Intervening biologically to prevent or cure autism became a major focus of both public and private initiatives, while funding for social and community supports continued to lag behind (Singh 2015).

The major controversies around autism in the United States today were born out of this historical set of circumstances, shaping the form they take. These controversies are characterized by contentious battles—among researchers, clinicians, parents, and increasingly, autistic people themselves—over the causes of autism and solutions to it. Is autism as we know it today a new condition, a crisis brought about by modern environmental toxicities, or has autism always been a part of humanity? Is autism necessarily a life-destroying tragedy, or can it be considered a form of human diversity that brings challenges and benefits? Should money be spent on prevention research or on helping autistic people better live their lives? What is the best way to help autistic people develop their independence and sense of autonomy? These issues arise out of a sociocultural context in which liberation of the individual from constraint and oppression is focal, and the psychosocial needs that persons might have from the community around them are less clearly foregrounded and less fully elaborated.

Brazil's debate on autism and the constitution of a service system have developed along very different historical and ideological lines that have greatly influenced the educational and treatment trajectories for autistic children—and led to a different set of disputes, focused instead on the responsibilities of the Brazilian state toward its citizens and their right to health.

2.5 "Exceptional Children" and the First Autistic Associations in Brazil

In order to better understand the historical background for autism services in Brazil, it is necessary to go back to the first half of the twentieth century. While Leo Kanner and Hans Asperger were formulating theories about autism in the United States and Austria in the 1930s and 1940s, the first initiatives in Brazil to provide assistance to "exceptional children" were being developed by *Associação Pestalozzi. Sociedade Pestalozzi* was incorporated in 1932, in Belo Horizonte—State of Minas Gerais—by a group of physicians, educators, and religious people, under the leadership of a European *émigré*, psychologist and educator Helena Antipoff (1892–1974). In the mid-1940s, Antipoff moved to Rio de Janeiro and created a national headquarters, the *Sociedade Pestalozzi do Brasil* (Block 2007; Block and Cavalcante 2014; Campos 2003).

Among the many children who were educated by the association, there were children that would, nowadays, be diagnosed as autistic, despite not being described as such at the time. The organization promoted a combination of educational and therapeutic strategies from the fields of Education and Health, and also stressed the specialized training of professionals and parents (Block 2007; Block and Cavalcante 2014; Campos 2003). Similar to the term "special" in the US, the term "exceptional" is currently under critique in Brazil as a term of patronizing and pejorative difference. However, the term was brought into use by Antipoff in the 1930s to provide a better alternative than other commonly used terms of this era, such as "abnormal," "subnormal," "retarded" and "deficient" (Block and Cavalcante 2014).

In the 1950s, with Antipoff's encouragement and support, a number of parents with intellectually disabled children, first in São Paulo and Rio de Janeiro, and quickly in other parts of the country, formed mutual support groups. In 1954, Beatrice Bemis, an American mother of a child with Down Syndrome, visited Brazil to speak about the US organization

ARC (then known as the Association for Retarded Children), a model for organizing groups of parents of intellectually disabled children. Modeled on the ARC movement in the United States, these Brazilian support groups eventually became the *Associação de Pais e Amigos de Pessoas Excepcionais* (Association of Parents and Friends of Exceptional People—APAE). APAE had the goal of providing assistance, mainly educational, to "mentally disabled individuals" (Block 2007).

Lack of state support for these vulnerable groups led to the mobilization of such parent advocacy groups and resulted in the proliferation of private associations, organized along APAE's model, and whose main purpose was to provide education, social and therapeutic assistance to children and adults with disabilities (Block and Cavalcante 2014). Throughout the twentieth century, APAEs and Pestalozzis continued growing in number. By the end of the twentieth century, there were a few hundred Pestolozzi societies, but there were well over one thousand APAES (Block 2007; Cavalcante 2003). However, as in the United States, the concept of autism was still not a central organizing force in this movement, being generally combined with MR and other disability conditions.

Autism gained visibility in Brazil when the first *Associação de Amigos do Autista* (Association of Friends of Autistic Individuals—AMA) emerged, in the early 1980s in the state of São Paulo, composed of a group of parents who had the goal of providing assistance, developing expertise, and helping autistic individuals (Mello et al. 2013). This association has developed awareness campaigns aired on television, and promoted workshops, congresses, and international interchange programs. These programs recruited foreign professionals to contribute to the training of parents and professionals, and inspired the establishment of a network of services and other associations. In 1988, the *Associação Brasileira de Autismo* (Brazilian Association of Autism—ABRA) was created from 5 Brazilian states' AMAs (São Paulo, Rio de Janeiro, Minas Gerais, Sergipe and Distrito Federal). The AMA became a pioneer in supporting the cause of autism, by building a kind of expertise adapted to the demands experienced by many families, and by aligning practical and politic actions that contributed to new paths for autism in Brazil.

At the same time that these autism associations grew and gained political strength in different parts of Brazil, another social movement, Psychiatric Reform, was taking its first steps, demanding changes in the provision of psychiatric care on regional and national levels.

For many years, both movements developed parallel to each other, with little or no interlocution between them. Only from the beginning of the twenty first century would their agendas intersect.

2.6 The Brazilian Psychiatric Reform Movement

These developments occurred in the context of major political shifts in Brazil. In the 1980s, Brazil went through a period of re-democratization, marked by the redefinition of State's responsibilities to citizens and a new set of commitments to equality and to the welfare state, culminating in the enactment of the 1988 Federal Constitution (Couto and Delgado 2015). These changes extended to the relationship between psychiatric patients and treatment systems. During the same period, the Brazilian Psychiatric Reform movement was growing, causing a change in cultural, technical, and therapeutic paradigms concerning insanity and its treatment.[6] The Mental Health Professionals Movement, which started at the end of the 1970s, expanded in the following decade, encompassing psychiatric patients and their relatives and resulting in changes in public psychiatric assistance. Large-scale hospitals, which used to be the symbol and the core of psychiatric treatment, were being challenged and the era of deinstitutionalization began.

During the Brazilian civilian-military dictatorship (1964–1985), there had been a significant growth of private, government-funded, psychiatric hospitals. These hospitals coexisted with the huge Brazilian state-owned urban asylums or farm colonies, most of them built at the beginning of twentieth century (Resende 1987). In the late 1970s and early 1980s, as government censorship became less of a problem, reports of precarious living conditions in hospitals, such as in Barbacena, Minas Gerais and in Jacarepaguá, Rio de Janeiro, were made public by newspapers and TV news stations (Firmino 1982; Hidalgo 2011; Arbex 2013). Thus, mental health workers, relatives of mental patients, and the general public learned about these Brazilian "concentration camps"—so called by the Italian psychiatrist Basaglia in 1979—and this public knowledge gave political momentum to the *Movimento da Luta Antimanicomial* (Psychiatric Deinstitutionalization Movement) and the Psychiatric Reform process. From the 1990s, this process became the new official Brazilian mental health policy (Bezerra 1994; Tenório 2001), and since then the government mental health budget has been gradually shifted from psychiatric hospitals to a network of communitary services.

As Amarante (2007) highlights, the psychiatric reform process questioned not only the institutions that dealt with madness, but also the whole knowledge and practice framework within which they were embedded. To better understand the influences that constituted the Brazilian Psychiatric Reform, it is worth clarifying that ideally the transformation should go beyond the restructuring of services. One major epistemological influence on Brazilian Psychiatric Reform was the above-quoted Franco Basaglia—head of the Italian Democratic Psychiatric Movement. Basaglia critiqued the way that psychiatry equated mental disease with a natural object, thus relegating the person experiencing the condition and his or her social environment to the background. While classic psychiatry disregarded the person in order to deal with disease, Basaglia's proposal was to place the "disease in brackets," (Amarante 2007, 66) so that one could focus on the person living the experience, something that may be interpreted as an epistemic attitude. (For more information about Basaglia and the Italian Democratic Psychiatry, we refer readers to Cascio, Andrada, and Bezerra Jr., in this volume.)

In line with Basaglia's theoretical principles and practical experiences of deinstitutionalization in Italy, many local examples of alternatives to psychiatric hospitalization confirmed the possibility of building novel approaches for dealing with insanity. For example, in 1989, in the city of Santos, State of São Paulo, the municipal government intervened in the local asylum, *Casa de Saúde Anchieta*, and served as a model for encouraging the expansion of communitarian daily care of people with severe mental disorders in Brazil (Amarante 1998; Tenório 2001). However, despite the existence of several reform movements for over 20 years, the official acknowledgment of the Brazilian Psychiatric Reform process only took place, from a legal standpoint, in 2001, by means of Law 10.216. This law provides for the protection and rights of people affected by mental disorders, and reorients their mental health care, prioritizing treatment carried out through community-based services.

Brazilian Psychiatric Reform enabled extremely significant changes by means of the gradual closure of psychiatric hospitals and the building of substitute services. An important piece of this process was the development of *Centros de Atenção Psicossocial* (Centers for Psychosocial Attention—CAPS), Day-Hospitals, Community Centers, working cooperatives and Therapeutic Residences (collective housings for patients coming out of extended psychiatric hospitalizations), as elements composing the gradual substitution of total institutions. Among these, the

Centers for Psychosocial Attention are especially significant. CAPS are non-mandated open day services, located in the communities where the patients live, and are responsible for providing assistance to people with severe and persistent mental disorders, while looking to maintain, strengthen, and preserve users' social ties.[7] Initially, the CAPS prioritized adult patients, especially those coming from extended psychiatric hospitalizations or those who manifested their first crisis, so as to avoid their admittance in psychiatric hospitals. Autism did not fit into any of these criteria since it is almost always diagnosed in childhood and it is often misrecognized as schizophrenia or MR in undiagnosed adults. As a result, it was not included in the Psychiatric Reform's agenda until the end of the twentieth century.

2.7 The Rise of CAPSi and Its Impact on Autism Care

Between the first and second decades of the twenty-first century, autism became more prominent in the mental health field, due to a greater emphasis on child mental health in public policies. During the III National Conference of Mental Health that took place in 2001, attended by professionals, managers, users, and their relatives from all over Brazil, childhood and youth mental health was for the first time discussed as a specific topic (Brasil 2002). The result was a proposal to create a service network to focus attention on the issue. The *Centros de Atenção Psicossocial Infanto-juvenis* (Centers for Psychosocial Attention for Children and Youth—CAPSi) were developed as the central system through which services for youth would be coordinated, working together closely with other sectors, such as education, social welfare, legal and advocacy (Brasil 2004). After the enactment of Ministry of Health's resolution 336, in 2002, which regulated several modalities of CAPS, among them, CAPSi, a slow, but progressive expansion in the number of these service centers has taken place. There were 76 in 2006, 101 in 2008, 128 in 2010, and 201 in 2014 (Brasil 2015). Such centers tend to be located in medium-sized and large cities and, at least in some regions of the country, provide services for a significant number of autistic individuals. A survey carried out in 2011 in 14 CAPSi of Rio de Janeiro's metropolitan area showed that 35% of the patients using these services were diagnosed with autism (Lima et al. 2017). Surveys evaluating CAPSi from other regions of Brazil indicated a presence of Developmental Disorders (according to ICD 10), which include autism, ranging from 14.2% (Hoffman et al. 2008) and 16.2% (Delfini et al. 2009) to 27.5% (Ronchi and Avelar 2010). The majority of Rio de Janeiro's CAPSi offer individual and collective spaces of treatment to children and adolescents, including those with autism and other kinds of disorders (a minority offer exclusive spaces or schedules for autistics), make home visits and provide individual or collective family care.

While CAPSi seeks to provide integrated psychosocial attention, recent studies have indicated some significant limitations to the services provided. Little emphasis is placed within these services on systematic inter-sector partnership for shared care strategies, as a way of expanding the social inclusion for people with autism (Lima et al. 2017). Visani and Rabelo (2012), based on research with medical records from several CAPSi, reported that the treatment of autistic children begins late due to lack of early detection programs and delayed diagnosis by other health professionals, resulting in delay in referrals to CAPSi.

Lima et al. (2014), in a focus group-based research, found that families affected by autism had both praise and criticism for CAPSi. The families praised the speed with which they were able to obtain treatment through CAPSi after a "pilgrimage" through others services, and they point out their children's improvement, valuing CAPSi as space of socialization. But some criticized a lack of "focus" of the clinical services, and demanded more specific treatments for autism. Families complained about the high turnover in staff and highlighted the difficulties in continuing treatment for autistics once they become adults. Moreover, most parents considered the frequency and duration of therapies to be insufficient, and highlighted the structural precariousness of some CAPSi (regarding the upkeep of the facilities, size and number of attendance rooms, lack of telephone, transport, and medicines, etc.). At the same time, family members emphasized the support they receive by the service's team, but many of them complained about the lack of information on the children's disorder, leading them to seek and share knowledge on the web. According to Lima et al. (2017), the vast majority of CAPSi of Rio de Janeiro's metropolitan area reported that they do not maintain relations with autistic family associations. Despite not being present in all geographic areas covered by CAPSi, these associations play a key role in Brazil nowadays; the gap between them and CAPSi suggests that the ideal of collaboration and dialogue articulated within the philosophy of Psychiatric Reform has not been fully realized.

Many of the controversies currently brewing over autism care in Brazil arise out of such difficulties of implementing comprehensive, integrated, psychosocial care under conditions of significant economic scarcity. Within psychiatric reform, the "right to health" was adopted in part as a mechanism for bringing about more widespread social transformation. However, these political transformations were taking place in the context of global neoliberal reforms and increasing income inequality. Biehl (2005) observes that "these prominent discourses on human rights and the practices of citizenship as related to health coincided with [...]the reduction of public health funding as a result of the country's economic and political transformations" (130). While the ideals of psychiatric reform emphasize inter-sectoral collaboration and full access to services sufficient to produce universal health, in practice, these ideals are difficult to comprehensively attain. Parents who have become frustrated with the services available through CAPSi have begun to pursue the right to health through alternative channels. Recently, this has involved fighting to redefine autism from a problem of "social suffering" to a disability, adopting an increasingly global discourse of disability rights to marshal new resources for care.

2.8 Tensions and Misunderstandings Involving Parent Activists, Mental Health and Rehabilitation Professionals in Brazil

In the beginning of the twenty first century, the health status of disabled people was brought into the spotlight in Brazil. The ratification by the Brazilian Government, in 2009, of the Convention on the Rights of Persons with Disabilities, enacted by the UN in 2007, inspired the development of the *Plano Viver sem Limites* (Living Without Limits Plan). This plan encompassed 15 federal agencies and coordinated actions focused on persons with disabilities in the areas of health, education, accessibility, and social inclusion. As part of this Plan, the Health Care of People with Disabilities Network was created within SUS, Brazil's Unified Health System (Brasil 2012a).

Parents of autistic children, who had been advocating for the rights of their children for a long time, also benefited from the growing attention to the rights of persons with disabilities. In 2012, as a direct result of parent activism, the Law 12764 of 2012, also known as the "Autism Act" or "Berenice Piana Act" (in honor of a family member who first worked to submit the bill), officially brought autism to the scope of the Living Without Limits plan. This act instituted the Protection Policy of the Rights of Persons with Autism Spectrum Disorder. For legal purposes, persons with ASD were officially designated as persons with disabilities, being extended the same rights given to the latter by other pre-existing Brazilian laws. The guidelines of the new law include an emphasis on collaboration between service sectors, the participation of the community, focused attention to health services provision (including early diagnosis, multi-professional services, and access to medicine and nutrition services), access to employment, the dissemination of public information about the condition, and incentives for the training of professionals and for scientific research. With respect to the education sector, the law ensures the right to schooling in a regular classroom and, whenever necessary, to specialized paraprofessional support (Brasil 2012b).

Meanwhile, the Brazilian Autism Association (ABRA) pressured the Ministry of Health into developing a protocol to regulate assistance to persons with autism in Brazil. At the end of 2011, a working group dedicated to this subject was formed. The group included the Ministry's Office of Mental Health and Office of Health Care of People with Disabilities, professionals and managers of the public health system, professors and university researchers and representatives of family associations. After a few meetings, however, internal disagreements in the Ministry caused a division into two groups, one coordinated by the Office of Mental Health (Brasil 2013b) and another coordinated by the Office of Health Care of People with Disabilities (Brasil 2013a). The Ministry ended up publishing two separate documents simultaneously, with health policies designed for the same audience—persons with autism.

In spite of several similarities and the participation of ABRA representatives in the drafting of both, there are some differences between them. The document produced by the disability network is closer to ABRA's initial charge, which leaned toward a specialized approach to service provision for autism within the public sector. It prioritizes indicators and screening instruments for the identification of developmental delays, in addition to suggesting habilitation and rehabilitation strategies in the health network for people with disabilities. The document written by the mental health network, although also presenting criteria for the early identification of risks for developing Autism Spectrum

Disorders, emphasizes the organization of the Psychosocial Support Network for the assistance of people with autism, in addition to including a chapter about interprofessional practice within education, social support, and policies for people with disabilities (Oliveira et al. 2017). Overall, the mental health document emphasizes an inclusive approach to service provision, following the philosophy of the *Sistema Único de Saúde* (Unified Health System—SUS), which adopts a more holistic conception of health. In fact, integrality, one of the key principles of SUS, represents, among other things, criticism of a growing tendency toward overspecialization within the health sector.

The existence of two official documents targeted to the same audience not only evidenced alliances and antagonisms between parent activists and different sectors of public health system, but has also caused practical problems, including an overlapping of policies and resources destined to the same target audience. After discussions within the Ministry of Health, specifically within the field of mental health, a committee was instituted with the purpose of coordinating actions of both the mental health and the disability network. Between 2013 and 2016, this committee met once or twice a year, and was composed of members of the Ministry of Health and the authors of both documents, in addition to invited participants connected with key associations and social movements, such as the *Movimento Psicanálise, Autismo e Saúde Pública* (Psychoanalysis, Autism and Public Health Movement—MPASP), and the *Associação Brasileira para Ação por Direitos da Pessoa com Autismo* (Brazilian Association for Rights of People with Autism—ABRAÇA). The establishment of this committee was an attempt to overcome the different conceptions and strategies existing in the fields of disability and psychosocial attention.

The participation of MPASP in the Ministry of Health's committee must be understood in the context of the significant role played by psychoanalysis in the Psychiatric Reform. Representing one of the pillars of the psychosocial attention, along with the Italian Democratic Psychiatry, the psychoanalytic tradition is even stronger in relation to child/youth mental health. English-speaking authors such as Melanie Klein and Donald Winnicott were initially among the most influential scholars for Brazilian psychoanalysts and mental health professionals. However, they were gradually replaced by those who spoke French, following the line established by partners or followers of psychoanalyst Jacques Lacan, such as Rosine and Robert Lefort, Maud Manonni, Éric Laurent, Virginio Baio,

Alfredo Zenoni, Antonio Di Ciaccia and Jean Claude Maleval. Such influence is especially felt in some of the CAPSIs, mainly those located in cities which contain university psychology programs strongly influenced by psychoanalysis. The focus group-based research published by Lima et al. (2014), quoted above, showed that most professionals within Rio de Janeiro's CAPSi argued that no single theoretical or clinical approach should be favored within CAPSi. At the same time, this research also found that psychoanalysis was the theoretical framework most frequently endorsed by practitioners—even though many of them praised the diversification of approaches, criticized theoretical rigidity, and claimed to base their practice on their own experiences and "insights" rather than on any particular theory.

Professionals of the mental health sector are highly critical about the conceptualization of autism as a disability. The concept of disability in Brazil is historically tainted by negative connotations: it is associated with a history of excluding children considered *retardadas* (a term similar in meaning and stigma to the English word *retarded*), who were predominantly poor and black, in public or philanthropic shelters, or even psychiatric hospitals, throughout the twentieth century (Couto 2004; Lobo 2008).[8]

Parent activists, on the other hand, found in the notion of autism-as-a-disability the possibility to make demands for "specialized treatment," through the Health Care to the Person with Disability Network. For many parents, especially those involved with the approval of the Autism Act, the mental health network is simply not qualified to assist autistic children. Thus, for them, insisting on assisting people with autism through the mental health network means denying them proper care. They argue that having access to specialized treatment for autism is, on the one hand, part of their right to health guaranteed by the Constitution of 1988,[9] and on the other hand, the only way into giving their children the opportunity to eventually become full members of Brazilian society.

As we can see, the Brazilian autistic landscape is complex and dynamic, incorporating new elements and approaches while re-interpreting old ones. It is worth noting some of them. First, the Basaglian prescription of "placing the disease in brackets" (Amarante 2007, 66), coupled with the strong presence of psychoanalysis, leads Brazilian public mental health professionals to have a critical stance regarding psychiatric diagnoses as presented in the DSM and ICD (Elia et al. 2010; Amarante e Freitas 2015), including the very diagnosis of autism spectrum disorders. The CAPS, for example, are places for treatment of people presenting "severe mental suffering" (Brasil 2004, 15), regardless of the nosological category. This position is not so evident in the Brazilian policies for autistic people that are an outgrowth of disability rights legislation, but is somewhat aligned with a critical approach to the medical model of disability. Second, despite the strong influence of psychoanalysis in the public mental health network, Brazil has also witnessed the expansion of behavioral treatment strategies. Such procedures are imported and adapted from the United States, being available mainly in private practice, psychiatric and parents' associations, and university psychiatric services. Inside the psychiatric associations, for instance, this approach is generally associated with an emphasis on the biology of autism, including genetics and neuroscience. Last, but not least, the growing emphasis on the inclusion of persons with disabilities also led to the enactment of laws that mandate school inclusion at all levels and modalities, compelling schools to reorganize themselves to include autistic children in regular classrooms.[10] This met with resistance from many schools and families, who demand segregated educational services whenever it is not possible to include the students in regular classrooms (based on where they stand on the autism spectrum).

Finally, it is important to notice that the tensions and misunderstandings between parent activists, rehabilitation, and mental health professionals in Brazil cannot be reduced to divergences around therapeutic approaches, but must be understood within a larger discussion about the social rights guaranteed by the Brazilian Constitution of 1988, such as universal access to health care and education, and disagreements over how inclusion is best achieved. This scenario also evidences the intricate relationship between the articulated ideals shaping health policies and the Brazilian health system, and the actual landscape of health and educational services available for autistic people and their families. While professionals from both networks, as well as parent activists, mobilize their experiences and theoretical biases to formulate their understanding of what is at stake in the aforementioned antagonisms, the inevitable gap between political and therapeutic ideologies and the reality of daily practices and challenges faced by parents, professionals and autistic people alike keep pushing these antagonisms forward.

2.9 Treatment, Education, and Rights of Autistic Children in the USA

In the United States, basic services and supports for autistic children and some adults have been firmly established since the 1970s. However, there is little consensus about the appropriate treatment for autism. Points of contention focus around a few key questions: Should autism be treated as an adversary to be fought, or a valued form of human diversity to be accepted and accommodated? How should resources be allocated between biomedical science with a goal of cure and/or prevention of autism, and social services and education that can improve quality of life for autistic people? Should treatments for autism seek to erase prototypically autistic behaviors such as "stimming" (repetitive self-stimulatory behaviors, which can be pleasurable and self-regulating for people on the spectrum) or should these behaviors be celebrated as cultural expressions, as do the autistic activists and scholars who published in the book Loud Hands: Autistic People Speaking (Bascom 2012)? Is autism a new and dangerous threat, or is it part of the spectrum of human variation that brings not just deficits, but also benefits to the human whole? As in Brazil, these deep and divisive disagreements over how autistic people can best become full members of their social worlds are grounded in locally specific understandings of the relationship between a person and their society. In the United States, these disagreements tend to revolve around interventions upon the body, especially those that foreground issues of personal autonomy, the relationship between individuality and conformity, and the kinds of social supports required for independent living. Unlike in Brazil, where a significant number of psychiatrists in the public system are closely associated with a tradition of political activism and resistance to oppression, in the United States, the medical mainstream and its form of bioscientific expertise and intervention is often positioned as inimical to activist movements whose goal is social inclusion for people on the autism spectrum. However, medical intervention is also often depicted as a necessary condition of social inclusion within a society that is deeply ambivalent about state support for individual well-being.

The controversy over Applied Behavioral Analysis (ABA) illuminates these tensions. First popularized by Lovaas (1987), who introduced it in part as a means of changing effeminate behavior in boys, ABA became far more widespread as a behavioral intervention for autistic children.

It is an integral part of the treatment protocols advocated by many major parent-founded autism advocacy organizations, particularly those whose goal is or has been to cure or otherwise eliminate autism (i.e., Autism Speaks, n.d.). The technique is meant to train autistic children to show socially acceptable communication and behavior, and evidence for its success is often based on reduction of autistic symptomatology (Shyman 2016). While it is often described as the autism intervention with the strongest research base supporting its efficacy (i.e., Foxx 2008; Rosenwasser and Axelrod 2001), there is a great deal of variation in how it is actually implemented in practice (Caffeinated Autistic 2013; Gruson-Wood 2016; Gernsbacher 2003; Jones 2014; Whitt 2014). What is called ABA in one location and time may be very different from what is called ABA in a different context.

Advocates of the technique laud its ability to improve communication, change problematic behaviors, and to teach skills necessary for self-care and independent living (see Matson et al. 2012 for a review). Critics of the technique, however, argue that it is unpleasant and unnatural, to the point of abuse. Children are trained to be compliant and follow orders, and are rewarded for doing so, or they are punished by the withholding pleasures or in some cases the application of aversives. Autistic activists who received ABA as children report the experience was unpleasant and in some cases quite traumatizing. There are many other behavioral approaches as well, such as Floor Time (Greenspan 2006), Sensory Integration Therapy (Ayres 1998) and Treatment and Education of Autistic and related Communication handicapped Children (TEACCH) (Mesibov et al. 2004; Schopler and Reichler 1971), that are less controversial and that many feel are equally or more effective using techniques that are gentle and not coercive. The controversy over ABA therefore highlights some of the major tensions over autism in the United States: Is normalization of behavior, and perhaps the acquisition of certain skills and repertoires, worth compromises to autonomy, spontaneity, and authenticity? What kinds of constraints on behavior are abusive, and what kinds are beneficial? Does the degree of a person's impairment justify treating her in a way that would be considered inappropriate or disrespectful toward the unimpaired?

Autistic people are playing an increasingly powerful role in negotiating these questions. The rise of the autistic self-advocacy movement can be traced back to the late 1980s, when autistic self-advocate Jim Sinclair began working toward the creation of "a mutual aid-self help group for autistic people [...] to share first-hand experiences to counter the uniformly gloomy and pessimistic (and often offensive and insulting) portrayals of autism in the existing literature; and to advocate for improved support services for autistic people" (Sinclair 2005). By the early 1990s, Sinclair, along with fellow autistic self-advocates Donna Williams and Kathy Lissner, had founded Autism Network International (ANI). ANI built autistic community by running a mailing list where autistic people could find and communicate with each other, hosting small gatherings, and eventually developing Autreat, the first conference run exclusively by and for autistic people. ANI members also exhibited and presented at autism conferences that were primarily geared toward parents and professionals, spreading the controversial idea that autistic people had something valuable to say about their own experience (Sinclair 2005). Since then, the autistic self-advocacy movement has grown exponentially in the United States. Today, the Autistic Self-Advocacy Network (ASAN) plays an important role in federal disability policy, while also conducting leadership trainings for the next generation of autistic self-advocates.

Increasingly, autistic self-advocates are working together with peers and family members to educate the population and policy makers how to best appreciate individuals with autism, while seeking to sustain meaningful, socially uplifting and dignified intervention programs. Peer-based delivery models are an emerging area that show promise for mitigating persistent psychiatric disabilities and perhaps autism as well (Castlestein et al. 2015). Peer support happens extensively between autistic adults, though usually not formally or as a form of treatment. Meanwhile, autistic scholars and activists are building bridges beyond autistic communities to create models of understanding and supporting neurodiverse, neurodivergent and neuroqueer individuals (Grace 2013; Walker 2014). Autistic and Mad people are supporting each other in advocating for their inclusion within the design and implementation of new interventions, advisory boards, research, and legislative actions.

Parents of autistic children continue to participate in "forces that challenged psychiatry and combined in the deinstitutionalization and 'normalization' movement" (Eyal 2013, 884) to carve out a new force of expertise. Many innovative programs have been designed by parents whose child's diagnosis was an opportunity to discover that they, too, are on the spectrum. Some examples are Valerie Paradiz, who founded the ASPIE (Asperger Pride in Education) school in Onteorra, New York, starting a trend toward autism-positive services in that region, and Michael-Jon Carley, who started GRASP (the Global and Regional Asperger Syndrome Partnership), the first and largest network of support groups run by and for people on the autism spectrum.

However, the relationship between autistic self-advocacy and parent advocacy is not always so harmonious. As in Brazil, the large and fractious community of people affected by autism often divides among recognizable faultlines. The Autistic self-advocacy movement is often perceived to be in conflict with an alliance between research scientists, many clinicians, and large advocacy organizations initially formed by parents, seeking biomedical causes and cures, and working to ameliorate, rehabilitate, and eradicate disease and dysfunction through somatic and neurologic hegemony. The public rhetoric of such organizations is often characterized by an emphasis on the ways in which autism is antithetical to full participation in society, claiming that both inclusion and independence are contingent upon medical intervention.

For example, in 2011, the NYU Child Study Center released a series of advertisements depicting autism, along with other childhood psychiatric conditions, as kidnappers writing ransom notes to parents. The note signed by "Autism" read "We have your son. We will make sure he will not be able to care for himself or interact socially for as long as he lives. This is only the beginning." The ads encouraged parents not to "let a psychiatric disorder take your child." Instead, they should seek help from the Child Study Center, which (the ad said) would "give children back their childhood" (implying that childhood was something these children, due to their illness, did not currently have) (Kras 2010; Thibault 2014). Similarly, in 2013, a press release from Autism Speaks, written by co-founder Suzanne Wright, described the struggles of families caring for an autistic family member: changing sheets in the middle of the night after a bedwetting incident; struggling to afford doctor's bills; waiting on a waitlist for ABA; not knowing who will care for their child when they are gone. Most controversially, they described these families as follows:

> These families are not living. They are existing. Breathing – yes. Eating – yes. Sleeping – maybe. Working – most definitely – 24/7. **This is autism.** Life is lived moment-to-moment. In anticipation of the child's next move. In despair. In fear of the future. (Wright 2013, emphasis in original)

Autism and the complex and often unmet needs that come along with it are here depicted as by definition antithetical to life—not to mere survival, not to the biological state of being a child, but to a "childhood" recognized as a social role and to a life that is socially recognized as "living." Little attention is given to the possibility of a full life as an autistic social being with particular psychosocial needs and desires.

In part due to the influence of these organizations, the bulk of federal funding for autism is directed toward research into its neurological and genetic underpinnings, thus siphoning resources away from the very psychosocial supports that might make autistic lives easier to live (Singh 2015). Meanwhile, progress in these domains is slow in coming. Though the National Institutes of Mental Health have appeared to be on the verge of a cure for the disease of mental illness for years, no major breakthroughs have occurred in the last two decades. The allocation of resources toward cure and prevention and away from quality-of-life issues has become the subject of critique from many autistic self-advocates (Autistic Self-Advocacy Network, n.d.; Robertson 2010).

More of an affinity exists between autistic self-advocates and scholars in disability and mad studies, who wonder why the experience of disability, autism, and mental health conditions cannot be recognized as part of the authentic spectrum of human experience (Linton 1998; Millet 1990; Silberman 2015). Considering the frameworks created with mental health discourse, they call attention to the processes through which trying to eliminate certain ways of being in the world drives home messages like, *you aren't good enough*, or *you are dysfunctional*, or *you are an anomaly in need of fixing*. As disability scholar Simi Linton articulates, the way societies approach naming and categorizing people has an effect not only upon how we interact and separate people, but also in how we view humanity as a whole. She writes:

> When medical definitions of *disability* are dominant, it is logical to separate people according to biomedical conditions through the use of diagnostic categories and to forefront medical perspectives on human variation. (Linton 1998, 12)

What this means for autistic children and adults and their families is that once they have the diagnosis—once they have the label—their lives are never the same. What historically might have been seen as eccentricity, awkwardness, shyness, suddenly becomes pathologized with the pressure to normalize the errant behavior. Disability studies scholars have tried to unpack this process and understand how diagnosis and difference function as a part of social processes of acceptance and exclusion. Disability rights advocates and madness scholars question what impact concepts like "neurosis," "psychosis," "insanity," "pathological," and "illness" have on being human and continue to encourage others to interrogate the epistemological dimensions of psychiatry and pathology (Canguilhem 1989; Millet 1990; Reaume 2002). Similarly, some autistic self-advocates argue that autism could be part of the spectrum of human variation with not just deficits, but also benefits to the human whole. These ideas are only beginning to be taken up by clinical researchers on autism within the United States. Yet, as autistic scholars, activists, and researchers gain recognition and rise to positions of influence, it seems likely that this perspective will become more prominent in discourse and (we hope) practice.

2.10 Conclusion

Historically, Brazil and the United States alike strained to categorize, name, and legitimize autistic behavior, lumping it into the heap of madness, MR, and later, developmental delay. Once the phenomenon of autism was more distinctly defined, each country went through diverse trajectories in terms of treatment and support. Nowadays, in both the United States and Brazil, there is a push to redefine autism in a way that works within each particular socio-political context. In each country, varied constituencies struggle against each other for different types of perceived gains. In Brazil, this tension involves family associations, in different degrees of partnerships with the disability sector, in conflict with public mental health entities, such as CAPSi, that are closely allied with psychoanalysis and Basaglian psychiatry. In USA, beside the family advocacy and disability rights associations, there are emerging autistic self-advocacy and peer-support groups that often find themselves in conflict with a biomedical mainstream focused on prevention and cure. Ideally, these groups and sectors should collaborate and work synergistically. However, they frequently do not, partly because they have conflicting views of what a person with autism needs.

In the absence of consensus about what autistic people need, we advise listening closely to what the autistic people living in each country want. What do autistic people themselves or the traditionally "neglected voices," as Chloe Silverman (2012, 229) calls them have to say about their experiences receiving services and emerging from childhood into adult roles in their respective societies? What educational and communication approaches are helpful toward their empowerment and well-being? What rights do they feel are still needed to promote their citizenship? In Brazil, self-advocacy groups can be found in relation to other diagnoses and experiences (as in the Psychiatric Deinstitutionalization Movement), but at the present time these groups rarely include autistic people. Greater inclusion of autistic people themselves in policy debates would add an important perspective to questions about how to best preserve their basic human rights and serve their needs.

Meanwhile, attending to the fundamental principles underlying Brazilian psychiatric reform can provide insight into the ways in which individual liberation relies on broader systems of psychosocial support. Mere "dehospitalization"—opening up the doors of the institution and releasing autistic people from inhumane systems of constraint and control—is a deeply important step, but that alone is not enough to allow autistic people to thrive. Attention must be paid to broader social forces, including the ways in which the rights of autistic people are intimately linked to the fortunes of their families and communities. Health and well-being are not simply a matter of fixing the broken body; focusing on causes, cures, and calamities of autism has not proven effective in guaranteeing inclusion for autistic people. Each of these countries thus has something to learn from the other, as we continue to seek to overcome our twentieth-century heritage of "concentration camps" and face the challenge of building a more inclusive and communitarian approach for people diagnosed with developmental disabilities and mental health conditions in the twenty-first century.

Notes

1. America's large state and private asylums were fashioned after European models and came into significant prevalence across the country throughout the late eighteenth and nineteenth centuries. Subsequent sizeable sanatorium asylums mushroomed from California to Massachusetts in the nineteenth century and early twentieth centuries, filling their beds rapidly and then filling their halls and cafeterias with beds or bodies on floors when censuses went beyond maximum capacity (Eisenstaedt 1938; Maisel 1946).

2. In the late 1950s and 1960s, American psychiatrist Thomas Szasz began to speak out against his psychiatrist peers and defined what he called "the myth" or "metaphor of mental illness" (1974). Traditionally, when someone is sick, he argued, they report suffering, disability, and pain. This is a self-defined term. Insanity and mental illness, on the other hand, he noted, is a term assigned by others. Elsewhere, he says cures are also assigned by others through containment (Szasz 1977). For this reason, Szasz argued, society and its psychiatrists cannot be trusted to diagnose mental illness.
3. For advanced analysis of how health, illness and activism are disaggregated in time, see Lisa Diedrich's *Indirect Action* (2016).
4. Liat Ben-Moshe and Tanya Luhrmann (2007 and 2013, respectively) argue that this resulted in transinstitutionalization or *trans-incarceration* (Ben-Moshe 2013), suggesting that instead of making health transitions for people who had been hospitalized against their will, deinstitutionalization had the unintended reality of many individuals ending up in in jails or in and out of jails, on the streets or in nursing homes, and other oppressive sites, none of which was ever intended to be long-term, mental disability treatment centers.
5. However, Liat Ben-Moshe warns "the history of disability is the history of incarceration" (15). Unfortunately, detainment is part and parcel of disability. Ben-Moshe adds that society should be mindful to avoid the prison industrial complex which she feels has become a "continuity of confinement" (2013). Though America's large state asylums and farm institutions have been emptied, humanity must attend to the fact that alternative care systems can still create confining and oppressive spaces.
6. The concepts of 'insanity' or 'madness' inspired by Michel Foucault and Franco Basaglia were used in the context of the Psychiatric Reform as a synonym for a severe mental disorder.
7. The term 'user' has been used in the context of the Psychiatric Reform—and in the whole Brazilian Unified Health System—to replace the term 'patient.'
8. Moreover, the resistance of psychoanalysts and mental health professionals to adopt the term disability is compounded by a language barrier. In the Portuguese language, there is no term that corresponds precisely to the word "disability" in English—the word "desabilidade" has been proposed, but it is a neologism with no current use. The term "deficiência" is currently used to translate both "disability" and "deficiency." We refer the reader to Cascio, Costa & Bezerra Jr., in this volume, for more information on the disability debate in Brazil.
9. According to Article 196 of Brazilian Constitution, "Health is a right of every individual and duty of the state, guaranteed by social and economic policies that seek to reduce the risk of disease and other injuries, and by universal and equal access to services designed to promote, protect, and recover health" (Brasil 1988).

10. Adaptations in regular classrooms to enhance the inclusion of children with autism might range from the presence of a paraprofessional (the so-called "school mediator") aiding the autistic child with classroom interactions, to pedagogical and classroom adaptations.

References

Amarante, Paulo. 1998. *Loucos pela vida*. Rio de Janeiro: Editora Fiocruz.

Amarante, Paulo. 2007. *Saúde mental e atenção psicossocial*. Rio de Janeiro: Editora Fiocruz.

Amarante, Paulo, and Fernando Freitas. 2015. *Medicalização em psiquiatria*. Rio de Janeiro: Editora Fiocruz.

Arbex, Daniela. 2013. *Holocausto brasileiro*. São Paulo: Geração Editorial.

Autism Speaks. n.d. "Applied Behavior Analysis (ABA)." https://www.autismspeaks.org/what-autism/treatment/applied-behavior-analysis-aba. Accessed January 20, 2017.

Autistic Self Advocacy Network. n.d. "Position Statements." http://autisticadvocacy.org/home/about-asan/position-statements/. Accessed February 24, 2017.

Ayres, Anna Jean. 1998. *Sensory Integration and Praxis Tests Manual*. Los Angeles: Western Psychological Services.

Bascom, Julia. (ed.). 2012. *Loud Hands: Autistic People Speaking*. Washington, DC: The Autistic Press/The Autistic Self Advocacy Network.

Ben-Moshe, Liat. 2013. "Disabling Incarceration: Connecting Disability to Divergent Confinement in the USA." *Critical Sociology* 39 (3): 385–403.

Bezerra Jr., Benilton. 1994. "De medico, de louco e de todo mundo um pouco." In *Saúde e sociedade no Braisl: os anos 80*, edited by Reinaldo Guimarães and Ricardo Tavares, 171–191. Rio de Janeiro: Relume-Dumará.

Biehl, João. 2005. *Vita: Life in a Zone of Social Abandonment*. Berkeley: University of California Press.

Block, Pamela. 2007. "Institutional Utopias, Eugenics, and Intellectual Disability in Brazil." *History and Anthropology* 18 (2): 177–196.

Block, Pamela, and Fatima Cavalcante. 2014. "Historical Perceptions of Autism in Brazil: Professional Treatment, Family Advocacy, and Autistic Pride, 1943–2010." In *Disability Histories*, edited by Susan Burch and Michael Rembis, 77–97. Urbana: University of Illinois Press.

Brasil. 1988. *Constituição da República Federativa do Brasil*. Brasília: Diário Oficial da União, 5 de outubro de 1998.

Brasil, Ministério da Saúde. 2002. "III Conferência Nacional de Saúde Mental—Cuidar sim, excluir não. Relatório Final." http://conselho.saude.gov.br/biblioteca/Relatorios/saude_mental.pdf. Accessed January 24, 2017.

Brasil, Ministério da Saúde. 2004. "Saúde Mental no SUS: Os Centros de Atenção Psicossocial." http://www.ccs.saude.gov.br/saude_mental/pdf/SM_Sus.pdf. Accessed February 8, 2017.

Brasil. 2012a. "Portaria n.º 793, de 24 de abril de 2012. Institui a Rede de Cuidados à Pessoa com Deficiência no âmbito do Sistema Único de Saúde." http://bvsms.saude.gov.br/bvs/saudelegis/gm/2012/prt0793_24_04_2012.html. Accessed January 28, 2017.

Brasil. 2012b. "Lei n.º 12.764, de 27 de Dezembro de 2012. Institui a Política Nacional de Proteção dos Direitos da Pessoa com Transtorno do Espectro Autista." http://www.planalto.gov.br/ccivil_03/_ato2011-2014/2012/lei/l12764.htm. Accessed January 19, 2017.

Brasil, Ministério da Saúde. 2013a. "Diretrizes de Atenção à Reabilitação da Pessoa com Transtornos do Espectro do Autismo (TEA)." http://bvsms.saude.gov.br/bvs/publicacoes/diretrizes_atencao_reabilitacao_pessoa_autismo.pdf. Accessed January 19, 2017.

Brasil, Ministério da Saúde. 2013b. "Linha de Cuidado para a Atenção às Pessoas com Transtornos do Espectro do Autismo e suas Famílias na Rede de Atenção Psicossocial do Sistema Único de Saúde." http://bvsms.saude.gov.br/bvs/publicacoes/linha_cuidado_atencao_pessoas_transtorno.pdf. Accessed January 19, 2017.

Brasil, Ministério da Saúde. 2015. "Saúde mental em dados 12." *Electronic Newsletter*, year 10, nº 12. Informativo eletrônico. http://www.mhinnovation.net/sites/default/files/downloads/innovation/reports/Report_12-edicao-do-Saude-Mental-em-Dados.pdf. Accessed January 19, 2017.

Broderick, Alicia. 2010. "Autism as Enemy: Metaphor and Cultural Politics." In *Handbook of Cultural Politics and Education*, edited by Zeus Leonardo, 237–268. Rotterdam: Sense Publications.

Caffeinated Autistic. 2013. "The Good, Bad, and the Ugly: My Assessment of Our Experience with Applied Behavior Analysis (ABA)." https://thecaffeinatedautistic.wordpress.com/2013/01/17/the-good-bad-and-the-ugly-my-assessment-of-our-experience-with-applied-behavior-analysis-aba/. Accessed August 16, 2016.

Campos, Regina Helena Ferreira. 2003. "Helena Antipoff: razão e sensibilidade na psicologia e na educação." *Estudos Avançados* 17 (49): 209–231.

Canguilhem, Georges. (1989). *The Normal and the Pathological*. New York: Zone Books.

Carlson, Licia. 2010. *The Faces of Intellectual Disability: Philosophical Reflections*. Bloomington: Indiana University Press.

Castlestein, S., R. Bruggeman, L. Davidson, and M. van der Gaag. 2015. "Creating a Supportive Environment: Peer Support Groups for Psychotic Disorders." *Schizophrenia Bulletin* 41 (6): 1211–1213.

Cavalcante, Fátima. 2003. *Pessoas muito especiais: a construção social do portador de deficiência e a reinvenção da família*. Rio de Janeiro: Fiocruz.

Couto, Maria Cristina Ventura. 2004. "Por uma política pública de saúde mental para crianças e adolescentes." In *A Criança e a Saúde Mental: enlaces entre a clínica e a política*, edited by Tânia Ferreira, 61–74. Belo Horizonte: Autêntica, FCH-Fumec.

Couto, Maria Cristina Ventura, and Pedro Gabriel Godinho Delgado. 2015. "Crianças e adolescentes na agenda política da saúde mental brasileira: inclusão tardia, desafios atuais." *Psicologia Clínica* 27 (1): 17–40. http://www.psi.puc-rio.br/site/images/psi_puc/publicacoes/Psicologia_Clinica_27-1.pdf.

Delfini, Patricia Santos de Souza, Caroline Dombi-Barbosa, Felipe Lessa da Fonseca, Carlos MendesTavares, and Alberto Olavo Advicula. 2009. "Perfil dos usuários de um Centro de Atenção Psicossocial Infantojuvenil da grande São Paulo, Brasil." *Revista brasileira de crescimento e desenvolvimento humano* 19 (2): 226–236.

Diedrich, Lisa. 2016. *Indirect Action: Schizophrenia, Epilepsy, AIDS, and the Course of Health Activism*. Minneapolis: University of Minnesota Press.

Eisenstaedt, Alfred. 1938. "Strangers to Reason: LIFE Inside a Psychiatric Hospital" [Photo essay]. Time & Life Pictures/Getty Images.

Elia, Luciano, Nympha Amaral, Kátia Wainstock Alves dos Santos, Rosemary Fiães, and N.S. Armoiny. 2010. "Impactos da política de saúde mental infanto-juvenil na clínica do autismo praticada em rede territorial de cuidado no Rio de Janeiro: diretrizes das políticas públicas e estrutura do dispositivo clínico." In *Atenção em Saúde para crianças e adolescentes no SUS*, edited by Edith Lauridsen Ribeiro and Oswaldo Yoshimi Tanaka, 211–229. São Paulo: Editora Hucitec.

Eyal, Gil. 2013. "For a Sociology of Expertise: The Social Origins of the Autism Epidemic." *American Journal of Sociology* 118 (4): 863–907.

Firmino, Hiram. 1982. *Nos porões da loucura*. Rio de Janeiro: Codecri.

Food and Drug Administration, Office of Criminal Investigations. 2015. "May 28, 2015: Seller of 'Miracle Mineral Solution' Convicted for Marketing Toxic Chemical as Miracle Cure." https://www.fda.gov/iceci/criminalinvestigations/ucm448541.htm. Accessed August 16, 2016.

Forman, M. (Director). 1975. *One Flew Over the Cuckoo's Nest*. United States: Fantasy Films.

Foxx, Richard M. 2008. "Applied Behavior Analysis Treatment of Autism: The State of the Art." *Child and Adolescent Psychiatric Clinics of North America* 17 (4): 821–834.

Gerhardt, Peter F., and Ilene Lainer. 2011. "Addressing the Needs of Adolescents and Adults with Autism: A Crisis on the Horizon." *Journal of Contemporary Psychotherapy* 41 (1): 37–45.

Gernsbacher, Morton Ann. 2003. "Is One Style of Early Behavioral Intervention 'Scientifically Proven?'" *Journal of Developmental and Learning Disorders* 7: 19–25.

Grace, E.J. (Ibby). 2013. "Are You Neuroqueer?" http://neuroqueer.blogspot.ca/2013/09/are-you-neuroqueer.html. Accessed August 17, 2016.

Greenspan, Stanley. 2006. *Engaging Autism*. Philadelphia: Da Capo Press.

Gronfein, W. 1985. "Incentives and Inventions in Mental Health Policy: A Comparison of Medicaid and Community Mental Health Programs." *Journal of Health and Social Behavior* 3 (26): 192–206.

Gruson-Wood, Julia F. 2016. "Autism, Expert Discourses, and Subjectification: A Critical Examination of Applied Behavioural Therapies." *Studies in Social Justice* 10 (1): 38–58.

Hidalgo, Luciana. 2011. *Arthur Bispo do Rosário: o senhor do labirinto*. Rio de Janeiro: Rocco.

Hinshaw, Stephen P. 2007. *The Mark of Shame: Stigma of Mental Illness and an Agenda for Change*. New York: Oxford University Press.

Hoffman, Maria Cristina Côrrea Lopes, Darci Neves Santos, and Eduardo Luiz Andrade Mota. 2008. "Caracterização dos usuários e dos serviços prestados por Centros de Atenção Psicossocial Infanto-Juvenil." *Cadernos de Saúde Pública* 24 (3): 633–642.

Johnson, Jenell. 2014. *American Lobotomy: A Rhetorical History*. Ann Arbor: University of Michigan Press.

Jones, Sparrow Rose. 2014. "ABA." Unstrange Mind. http://unstrangemind.com/?s=aba. Accessed October 23, 2017.

Keysey, Ken. 1962. *One Flew Over the Cuckoo's Nest*. New York: Viking Press.

Kliewer, Christopher, and Stephen Drake. 2013. "Disability, Eugenics and the Current Ideology of Segregation: A Modern Moral Tale." *Disability and Society* 13 (1): 95–111.

Kras, J.F. 2010. "The 'Ransom Notes' Affair: When the Neurodiversity Movement Came of Age." *Disability Studies Quarterly* 30 (1). http://dsq-sds.org/article/view/1065/1254. Accessed July 8, 2015.

Lima, Rossano Cabral, Maria Cristina Ventura Couto, Pedro Gabriel Godinho Delgado, and Bruno Diniz Castro Oliveira. 2014. "Indicadores sobre o cuidado a crianças e adolescentes com autismo na rede de CAPSi da região metropolitana do Rio de Janeiro." *Physis Revista de Saúde Coletiva* 24 (3): 715–739.

Lima, Rossano Cabral, Maria Cristina Ventura Couto, Fabiana Pimentel Solis, Bruno Diniz Castro Oliveira, and Pedro Gabriel Godinho Delgado. 2017. "Atenção Psicossocial a crianças e adolescentes com autismo nos CAPSi da região metropolitana do Rio de Janeiro." *Saúde e Sociedade* 26 (1): 196–207.

Linton, Simi. 1998. *Claiming Disability: Knowledge and Identity*. New York: New York University Press.

Lobo, Lilia Ferreira. 2008. *Os infames da história: pobres, escravos e deficientes no Brasil*. Rio de Janeiro: Lamparina.

Lovaas, O. Ivar. 1987. "Behavioral Treatment and Normal Educational and Intellectual Functioning in Young Children with Autism." *Journal of Consulting and Clinical Psychology* 55 (1): 3–9.

Luhrmann, Tanya Marie. 2007. "Social Defeat and the Culture of Chronicity: Or, Why Schizophrenia Does so Well Over There and so Badly Here." *Culture, Medicine and Psychiatry* 31 (2): 135–172.

Maisel, Albert Q. 1946. "Bedlam 1946: Most of U.S. Mental Hospitals Are a Shame and Disgrace." *Life Magazine* 20 (18): 102–118.

Matson, Johnny L., Nicole C. Turygin, Jennifer Beighley, Robert Rieske, Kimberly Tureck, and Michael L. Matson. 2012. "Applied Behavior Analysis in Autism Spectrum Disorders: Recent Developments, Strengths, and Pitfalls." *Research in Autism Spectrum Disorders* 6 (1): 144–150.

Mello, Ana Maria, Helena Ho, Inês Dias, and Meca Andrade. 2013. "Retratos do autismo Brasil. Secretaria de Direitos Humanos da Presidência da República (SDH/PR)." https://www.autismo.org.br/site/images/Downloads/RetratoDoAutismo-20131001.pdf.

Mesibov, Gary B., Victoria Shea, and Eric Schopler. 2004. *The TEACCH Approach to Autism Spectrum Disorders*. New York: Springer.

Millet, Kate. 1990. *The Loony-Bin Trip*. New York: Simon and Schuster.

National Institutes of Health. 2017. "National Institute of Mental Health: Important Events in NIMH History." https://www.nih.gov/about-nih/what-we-do/nih-almanac/national-institute-mental-health-nimh. Accessed October 31, 2017.

National Institute of Mental Health. n.d. "About NIMH." https://www.nimh.nih.gov/about/index.shtml. Accessed October 31, 2017.

Oliveira, Bruno Diniz Castro de, Clara Feldman, Maria Cristina Ventura Couto, and Rossano Cabral Lima. 2017. Políticas para o autismo no Brasil: entre a atenção psicossocial e a reabilitaçãol. *Physis: Revista de Saúde Coletiva* 27 (3): 707–726.

Paim, Jairnilson, Claudia Travassos, Celia Almeida, Ligia Bahia, and James Macinko. 2011. "The Brazilian Health System: History, Advances, and Challenges." *Lancet* 377: 1778–1797.

Reaume, Geoffrey. 2002. "Lunatic to Patient to Person: Nomenclature in Psychiatric History and the Influence of Patients' Activism in North America." *International Journal of Law and Psychiatry* 25: 405–426.

Rembis, Michael A. 2011. *Defining Deviance: Sex, Science, and Delinquent Girls, 1890–1960*. Chicago: University of Illinois Press.

Resende, Heitor. 1987. "Políticas de saúde mental no Brasil: uma visão histórica." In *Cidadania e loucura: políticas de saúde mental no Brasil*, edited by Nilson do Rosário Costa and Silvério Tundis, 16–69. Petrópolis: Abrasco/Vozes.

Rimland, Bernard. 1964. *Infantile Autism: The Syndrome and Its Implications for a Neural Theory of Behaviour*. Upper Saddle River, NJ: Prentice Hall.

Rivera, Kerri, and Kimberly McDaniel. 2013. *Healing the Symptoms Known as Autism*, 1st ed. Chicago, IL: Kerri Rivera.

Robertson, Scott Michael. 2010. "Neurodiversity, Quality of Life, and Autistic Adults: Shifting Research and Professional Focuses onto Real-Life Challenges." *Disability Studies Quarterly* 30 (1). http://www.dsq-sds.org/article/view/1069/1234.

Ronchi, Juliana Peterle, and Luziane Zacché. 2010. "Saúde mental da criança e do adolescente: a experiência do Capsi da cidade de Vitória-ES." *Psicologia: teoria e prática* 12 (1): 71–84.

Rosenwasser, Beth, and Saul Axelrod. 2001. "The Contributions of Applied Behavior Analysis to the Education of People with Autism." *Behavior Modification* (25) 5: 671–677.

Schopler, Eric, and Robert J. Reichler. 1971. "Parents as Co-therapists in the Treatment of Psychotic Children." *Journal of Autism and Childhood Schizophrenia* 1 (1): 87–102.

Shyman, Eric. 2016. "The Reinforcement of Ableism: Normality, the Medical Model of Disability, and Humanism in Applied Behavior Analysis and ASD." *Intellectual and Developmental Disabilities* 54 (5): 366–376.

Silberman, Steve. 2015. *Neurotribes: The Legacy of Autism and the Future of Neurodiversity*. New York, NY: Penguin Random House.

Silverman, Chloe. 2012. *Understanding Autism: Parents, Doctors, and the History of a Disorder*. Princeton, NJ: Princeton University Press.

Sinclair, Jim. 2005. "Autism Network International: The Development of a Community and Its Culture." http://www.autreat.com/History_of_ANI.html. Accessed November 13, 2017.

Singh, Jennifer S. 2015. *Multiple Autisms: Spectrums of Advocacy and Genomic Science*. Minneapolis: University of Minnesota Press.

Szasz, Thomas. 1974. *The Myth of Mental Illness: Foundations of a Theory of Personal Conduct*. New York: Harper & Row.

Szasz, Thomas. 1977. *Psychiatric Slavery: When Confinement and Coercion Masquerade as Cure*. New York: Free Press.

Tenório, Fernando. 2001. *A psicanálise e a clínica da reforma psiquiátrica*. Rio de Janeiro: Rios Ambiciosos.

Thibault, Ronnie. 2014. "Can Autistics Redefine Autism? The Cultural Politics of Autistic Activism." *Trans-Scripts* 4: 57–88.

Tsouderos, Trine. 2009. "'Miracle Drug' Called Junk Science." *Chicago Tribune*, May 21. http://www.chicagotribune.com/lifestyles/health/chi-autism-lupron-may21-story.html.

Visani, Paola, and Silvana Rabello. 2012. "Considerações sobre o diagnóstico precoce na clínica do autismo e das psicoses infantis." *Revista latinoamericana de psicopatologia Fundamental* 15 (2): 293–308.

Wakefield, A.J., S.H. Murch, A. Anthony, J. Linnell, D.M. Casson, M. Malik, M. Berelowitz, A.P. Dhillon, M.A. Thomson, P. Harvey, A. Valentine, S.E. Davies, and J.A. Walker-Smith. 1998. "Ileal-Lymphoid-Nodular

Hyperplasia, Non-specific Colitis, and Pervasive Developmental Disorder in Children." *The Lancet* 351 (9103): 637–641. https://doi.org/10.1016/s0140-6736(97)11096-0. PMID 9500320 (Retracted).
Walker, Nick. 2014. "Neurodiversity: Some Basic Terms & Definitions." *Neurocosmopolitanism*. http://neurocosmopolitanism.com/neurodiversity-some-basic-terms-definitions/. Accessed August 11, 2016.
Weigerink, Ronald, and John W. Pelosi (eds.). 1979. *Developmental Disabilities: The DD Movement*. Baltimore: Paul H. Brookes.
Whitt, Tracy Dee. 2014. "My Thoughts on Applied Behavior Analysis (ABA)—Autism." Lovin' Adoptin' Supporting Adoptive Parents and Families Living with Autism. http://lovinadoptin.com/2014/03/26/my-thoughts-on-applied-behavior-analysis-aba-autism/. Accessed July 22, 2015.
Wright, Suzanne. 2013. "Autism Speaks to Washington: A Call for Action." Originally posted at https://www.autismspeaks.org/news/news-item/autism-speaks-washington-call-action. Accessed February 24, 2017, now accessible at https://unv.is/autismspeaks.org/news/news-item/autism-speaks-washington-call-action. Accessed October 31, 2017.

CHAPTER 3

Psychiatric Reform and Autism Services in Italy and Brazil

M. Ariel Cascio, Bárbara Costa Andrada and Benilton Bezerra Jr.

3.1 Introduction

In the latter half of the twentieth century, psychiatric practices in both Brazil and Italy went through a dramatic period of political reform. These radical reformulations of psychiatric services promoted extensive changes in national mental health public policies as well as professional psychiatric practice, with significant impact both immediately and in the long term on care and services for autism. Today, however, many of the policies and ideals at the heart of Psychiatric Reform (PR) are being challenged by parent

M. A. Cascio—The work described in this chapter was carried out at the Department of Anthropology, Case Western Reserve University.

B. Costa Andrada—The work described in this chapter was carried out at the Institute for Social Medicine, State University of Rio de Janeiro.

M. A. Cascio (✉)
Institut de recherches cliniques de Montréal, Montréal, Canada

M. A. Cascio
McGill University, Montréal, Canada

E. Fein and C. Rios (eds.), *Autism in Translation*, Culture, Mind, and Society, https://doi.org/10.1007/978-3-319-93293-4_3

advocates and self-advocates within autism communities. Post-reform services that operate within the ethos of PR tend to take an ecological approach to human subjectivity that privileges the socially situated experience of suffering, disregarding diagnosis and diagnosis-specific biology as a starting point for health actions. This becomes problematic when meeting the often biologically based and diagnosis-specific politics of autism advocacy groups and their campaigns for specialized services. While these advocates are seeking many of the same goals as PR aimed to serve—social inclusion, respect for rights, and freedom from oppression—they advocate for these goals using some of the scientific concepts PR initially mobilized against: specifically, they emphasize the organic, embodied origins of autism and advocate for diagnosis-specific services. This leads them into particular conflicts with certain post-reform matrices of care.

In this chapter, we provide a brief comparative history of PR in Italy and Brazil, focusing on its implications for those who now would be diagnosed on the autism spectrum. We chart the history, politics, and lived experience of autism[1] in Italy and in Brazil, illuminating key similarities and differences. By observing how the political and clinical intersect through politicized discourse on desired clinical service provision, we analyze some of the contemporary dilemmas around autism, dilemmas which emerge as challenges to well-established public policies from PR processes in each country that have on the whole been considered successful. Following the priorities of cross-cultural autism studies (Cascio 2015b), we demonstrate the impact of local histories of the globalized deinstitutionalization processes on that which is at stake in autism advocacy and organization, and on the tenor of autism politics. We track the ways in which scientific ideas about autism as fundamentally organic or as fundamentally social/relational get mobilized differently in different social and political contexts, and get evoked to serve very different ends. Local and historical particularities, as well as everyday practice, are what make these abstract, globally circulating ideals meaningful in particular ways.

B. Costa Andrada
Institute of Psychiatry, Federal University of Rio de Janeiro,
Rio de Janeiro, Brazil

B. Bezerra Jr.
Institute for Social Medicine, State University of Rio de Janeiro,
Rio de Janeiro, Brazil

3.2 Methods

This chapter brings together ethnographic research conducted in Italy (by Cascio) and Brazil (by Costa Andrada), along with archival and historical investigations. Cascio's research, conducted from October 2012 to August 2013, focused on autism-specific services for adolescents and young adults in a northern region of Italy. Although most Italian disability services are not autism-specific, Cascio explored the growing niche of autism-specificity through participant observation at seven sites (three day centers, two centers that offered both residential and day services, and two social/recreational groups) that aimed specifically, although not always exclusively, at autism. Cascio conducted group or individual interviews with youth using these services ($N = 10$) as well as interviews with parents of such youth ($N = 38$ interviews, 47 individuals), staff ($N = 14$), and other autism professionals in the area ($N = 31$).

Costa Andrada's research involved a period of 24 months (from 2014 to 2016) of ethnographic observations of academic, political, and cultural events related to autism, mental health, and disability; interviews with professionals and parents; and 18 months of participant-observation in two public services that assist children and youth with autism, in a large industrial city in the surroundings of Rio de Janeiro. These services are not exclusive to autism, but attend people with a variety of diagnoses. One is part of the mental health system, deeply steeped in the ethos of PR, and serves only children and youth. The other is part of a municipal foundation, and is more connected to the fields of disability and inclusive education services, and serves people with disabilities from all age groups. Though these projects have slightly different foci, both involved mapping the lay of the land of autism services in these two areas, and thus can be productively compared.

This chapter will first explore the PR movements and their impact on health and human services policies, and then turn to a discussion of autism advocacy movements in post-reform settings. While PR had a tremendous impact on the life experiences of people who would now be diagnosed with autism, these movements were inspired by and tended to foreground the experiences of institutionalized adults. Those who today would be diagnosed in childhood, with autism or other developmental disabilities, tended to receive services through other systems such as education or neuropsychiatry. We will describe the development of these alternative service models and their contribution to the development of strong parent advocacy movements around autism. We will then turn to the present moment, looking at the ways in which discourses of autism as a disability (in Brazil) and autism as a "way of being" (in Italy) articulate dissatisfactions with post-reform mental health services within these autism advocacy communities, through marshalling a biologically based and diagnosis-specific rhetoric.

3.3 Psychiatric Reform in Italy and Brazil

PR movements and deinstitutionalization are keys to understanding the historical and social context of autism. Italian scholars have argued that before deinstitutionalization, people with autism in Italy were placed in mental institutions (Nardocci 2009; Russo et al. 2014). In Brazil, people with autism were indiscriminately institutionalized in shelters, psychiatric hospitals, or addressed to philanthropic institutions; or were outright unassisted (homebound or abandoned) (Block and Cavalcante 2014; Couto 2004; Rizzini 2008). These observations align with Eyal and colleagues' (2010) argument that the autism label emerged after global deinstitutionalization, when specific diagnoses became more important due to the variety of treatments available instead of one treatment—institutionalization—for everything. Eyal and colleagues convincingly argue that deinstitutionalization is responsible for the rise in autism cases worldwide, affecting how autism is defined and managed in the new institutional matrix of outpatient and community-based treatment modalities. However, they do not include data from Italy or Brazil in their analysis, where strong models of deinstitutionalization and universal health coverage led to different outcomes than those in, for example, the USA (Lima et al., this volume).

Deinstitutionalization in Italy and Brazil happened within PR's radical processes, which were much broader than those of USA, UK, France, and other countries (Amarante 2007; Rotelli and Amarante 1992; Scheper-Hughes and Lovell 1986; WHO 1980). Deinstitutionalization involved four dimensions: legal-political changes, epistemological critique of medical and psychiatric rationale, new perspectives on care, and strong efforts to transform the socio-cultural imaginary around 'madness' and mental illness. These strong models of deinstitutionalization[2] sustained a political agenda of profoundly questioning the structure of power relations within and outside the asylum (Scheper-Hughes and Lovell 1986). Besides targeting dehumanization and social exclusion, they fostered a new conceptualization of "madness" as a social identity, one that is embedded in citizenship and social inclusion. This systematic process of deinstitutionalization accompanied the implementation of substitutive community-based services, leaving a legacy of legal and political transformations (Delgado 2013; Goulart 2007; Yasui 2010). Although PR represented a major shift in the psychiatric paradigm, designing new models of assistance in mental health in Italy and Brazil, in each of these places, it involved different key actors and intellectual traditions. This section starts with the origins of Basaglian PR in Italy and moves into the applications of Basaglia's ideas in Brazil.

3.4 Deinstitutionalization in Italy: Democratic Psychiatry and Its Legacy of Inclusion

Deinstitutionalization in Italy started from within the field of psychiatry itself. In the 1960s, a number of psychiatrists, most prominently Franco Basaglia, made a break with previous tradition. Prior to this time, mainstream Italian psychiatry followed organicist approaches and strongly rejected any other. The Italian psychiatric association, *la Società Italiana di Freniatria* (Italian Phreniatric Society), even banned psychologists from membership (Donnelly 1992). Rejecting the positivism and biological determinism that characterized this approach, Basaglia's group aligned instead with interpretivist approaches of phenomenology and existential psychiatry (Donnelly 1992). These approaches valued patients' individual subjectivity and stressed connecting with the patient—something that was not possible in the degrading conditions of psychiatric asylums (Donnelly 1992).

Inspired by these approaches, Basaglia and his colleagues conducted pilot experiments in Trieste and elsewhere, gradually empowering patients, closing institutions, and "socializing" psychiatry. They implemented a series of reforms and experiments within psychiatric institutions, aiming to give patients autonomy in determining the way the institutions would be run. Rather than "dehospitalization" in which measures aim at reducing the use of inpatient beds, Basaglia's "deinstitutionalization" started with the goal of empowering patients *within* the hospitals by creating spaces for patients to meet and discuss how they would like the hospital to be run, and to implement their goals. Democratic Psychiatry focused on deinstitutionalization as liberation from the institutionalizing forces both of the asylum and of pharmaceutical psychiatry (Basaglia 1965), calling not only for the deinstitutionalization of psychiatric hospitals but of psychiatry itself with a focus on collective action and community solidarity that goes far beyond the psychiatric profession (Rotelli 1993). Eventually, this process did lead to the closure of mental hospitals, but as a gradual and patient-centered process, not an abrupt closure. The psychiatrists piloting these PR projects crystallized their ideas into the ideology of *Psichiatria Democratica* (Democratic Psychiatry). Their efforts within the psychiatric associations of the time (their own association called *Psichiatria Democratica*, or PD, and the association of traditional psychiatrists called the *Società Italiana di Psichiatria* or SIP) led to the passage of "Basaglia's Law," the 1978 Law 180 which mandated the gradual closure of psychiatric institutions.

Democratic Psychiatry derived in part from a Sartrean philosophy, seeing the "mental patient" construct as a manifestation of contradictions in society and the asylum as a means of removing these contradictions from view, maintaining the illusion of order (Donnelly 1992). The ideology of Democratic Psychiatry also aligned closely with Italian students' and workers' movements of the 1960s based on the shared experiences of patients, students, workers, and others as *emarginati* (marginalized) (Basaglia and Ongaro 1971; Donnelly 1992; Scheper-Hughes and Lovell 1986). In this way, PR in Italy emerged from within the field of psychiatry but did not see itself as concerned with psychiatry as a limited sphere.

Social and clinical scientists have generally considered deinstitutionalization in Italy to have been successful and a model for other countries, although insiders have pointed out its limitations as well (Burti and Benson 1996; Jones and Poletti 1986; WHO 1980). Deinstitutionalization as codified in Law 180 led to a series of policies aimed at increasing educational and social integration for people who might formerly have been institutionalized, including people with autism. Most important to Cascio's participants was the 1992 Law 104, which established a specific health care program for *aziende sanitarie locali* (local health enterprises—ASLs) to deliver rehabilitative care to people with disabilities (Lo Scalzo et al. 2009). This law established the rights of people with disabilities, formalizing older provisions and setting the ground for future ones (Crialesi et al. 2007, 274). Law 104 also provides for the education of all students (including students with disabilities) in the same public school system—including post-secondary education—in an inclusive education system called *integrazione scolastica* (Educational Integration). Educational integration coincided with deinstitutionalization in Italy and reflects broader national goals of social integration (Canevaro and de Anna 2010). Law 104 is traditionally associated with Basaglia's movement and the Law 180 that bears his name, although Italian scholars have noted that the process of educational integration predates Basaglia and DP (D'Alessio 2011).

Nonetheless, they share some ideological ground and like deinstitutionalization, *integrazione scolastica* has been lauded internationally. English language literature has identified the Italian educational system as a model for inclusive education (Begeny and Martens 2007).[3]

Overall, PR in Italy is widely considered to have been successful and Basaglia's ideas are still greatly respected. However, while Democratic Psychiatry was vital to PR in the 1970s, its ideas do not dominate the landscape of Italian psychiatry in the twenty-first century. The main Italian psychiatric association, *la Società Italiana di Psichiatria* (SIP), descended from the Italian Phreniatric Society described above, which Democratic Psychiatrists so opposed. Democratic Psychiatrists formed their own association, eventually becoming in 1990 the *Società Italiana di Psichiatria Democratica* (Democratica 2011). The two associations have worked together since the 1970s on many issues, but their differences remain important. Although Democratic Psychiatry was vital for establishing community-based mental health care (Rotelli 1993), autism in many ways falls under the purview of SIP (for example, in the *Società Italiana per i Disturbi del Neurosviluppo*, a special section of SIP) (Società Italiana per i Disturbi del Neurosviluppo, n.d.). Yet, it is still another field—*neuropsichiatria infantile* (child neuropsychiatry)—which primarily addresses autism today. This field will be discussed in more detail below.

3.5 Deinstitutionalization in Brazil: Psychiatric Reform and Psychoanalysis in the Context of Political Transformation

Basaglia's ideas were fundamental to Brazilian PR as well, especially in the context of Brazil's liberation from the authoritarian, right-wing military regime that lasted from 1964 to 1985. During the 1970s, the country experienced very harsh political repression, and several pro-democracy activists were arrested, tortured and killed. Basaglia visited Brazil twice, in 1978 and 1979, when the country was under military dictatorship, slowly transitioning to re-democratization, but still with constrained civil and political liberties. Social mobilization was strengthening, as different sectors of civil society associated specific claims with political demands for democracy. In the health sector, social movements combined demands for full citizenship with the idea of *health as a right*, and access to universal health care coverage.[4] The *Sistema Único de Saúde* (Brazilian Unified Health System—SUS) was advanced by one of these early 1980s movements (the Sanitary Reform, which encompassed leftist and socio-democratic movements), and Brazilian PR emerged in this scenario (Atun et al. 2015; Delgado 2013; Lobato and Burlandy 2000; see also Lima et al., this volume). In the late 1970s, an intense mobilization in the mental health sector sprang forth. Mental health professionals clamored for better working conditions and better care for patients, denouncing severe violations of human rights inside of psychiatric institutions. Basaglia's ideas resonated with these local demands, and the experiences of Democratic Psychiatry inspired their struggle (Amarante 2007; Biehl 2005; Goulart 2007; Yasui 2010). What started as a mental health professionals' movement quickly encompassed patients and their families, and consolidated into a bold anti-asylum movement. As in Democratic Psychiatry, its target was not the mental illness itself, nor the individual diagnosis, but the socially situated experience of subjective suffering, and the pursuit of citizenship[5] (Bezerra 1994; Biehl 2005). The consolidation of the Brazilian PR movement as a state public policy came only after several decades, with the approval of the Federal Law 10.216 in 2001. Inspired by Italian Law 180, Law 10.216 establishes "the protection and rights of people with mental disorders and redirects the model of assistance in mental health" toward a community-based/territorial model of care (Brasil 2001).

A distinguishing feature of Brazilian PR is the influence of the psychoanalytic rationale in its epistemic and institutional matrix. This is a major difference when compared to the Italian process, given Basaglia's critique of psychoanalysis (Basaglia 2000; Benvenuto 1997; Goulart 2007; Russo 1997). In Brazil, psychoanalysts collaborated with other mental health professionals in the anti-asylum movement and pro-democracy social movements.[6] (For more detail on the theoretical and clinical perspectives of psychoanalysis in Brazil, see Lima et al., this volume). The historical and clinical influence of psychoanalysis in Brazilian PR marked post-reform services so strongly that even those with no psychoanalysts on staff might echo a psychoanalytical rationale (Lima et al. 2014; Rios and Costa Andrada 2015). Commonly, the clinical services they offer[7] reflect both the psychoanalytic tendency to defend and value subjective uniqueness and the PR rationale of addressing socially situated suffering. This political and clinical role of psychoanalysis in the post-reform matrix of care matters to autism politics and public policies. As described in more detail below, part of the schism around autism politics and care in Brazil is entangled with the psychoanalytic influence in mental health fields.

The shift from psychiatric diagnosis to socially situated suffering, combined with the idea of "health as universal right," fostered non-diagnosis-oriented services. Because of its ideological project, post-reform services operate from an ecological perspective of individual embeddedness—foregrounding socioeconomic and psychodynamic dimensions, family and other social ties—and not from the perspective of the specific diagnosis. This stance does not imply a refusal of the diagnostic dimension. Rather, it removes diagnosis' primacy, turning it instead into one of many dimensions of the "person burdened by mental suffering." Biehl (2005) notes this multidimensional way of addressing service users, writing that "several theoretical languages were deployed at the same time: the patient was thought of as a citizen, as a subject of the unconscious, and as an individual who could be neurochemically regulated" (Biehl 2005, 241). In the case of childhood, scientific arguments about the complex neuropsychological developmental processes that take place in deeply relational contexts support a cautious stance toward early diagnostic labeling. This attention to the particular developmental needs of children was, however, not initially a focus of PR. That initial neglect opened up spaces for child-centered services to be developed separately from the psychiatric mainstream.

3.6 Autism and Children's Mental Health: Challenges and Changes in PR

Initially, PR processes in both Italy and Brazil focused on deinstitutionalization and the development of a network of community-based/territorial services to assist those individuals who had been chronically institutionalized. Children's mental health needs were thus not initially at the foreground of PR. As the reform process advanced, its priorities changed to offer more extended assistance to the community, and to individuals who were not mental asylum survivors (Amarante 2007; Delgado 2013; Goulart 2007). Only after the implementation of community-based/territorial services did children's mental health become the gateway for autism's entrance into PR's agenda. PR reform processes in Italy and Brazil created new matrices of autism care within public mental health assistance. Despite their local distinctions, post-reform services and policies face common challenges regarding autism. In both Italy and Brazil, stark differences exist between children's (develop)mental health assistance and adult services, leading to difficulties in the transition between the two. The following sections will describe the complex relationship, in each country, between programs that support the development of children and programs that serve the mental health needs of adults.

3.7 Italy: Psychiatry, Democratic Psychiatry, and Neuropsychiatry

In post-reform Italy, people with autism are enmeshed in a network of social and educational integration policies, and the institutions (in the broader sense of the word) of community-based (develop)mental health care. However, the current medical specialty that addresses autism in Italy is not psychiatry, but rather *neuropsychiatria infantile*, or child neuropsychiatry (from here on, "neuropsychiatry") (Levi and Bernabei 1997). Part of this divide stems from the simple age group priorities of the different fields. Neuropsychiatry addresses neurological, psychiatric, and developmental problems in children under age 18. *Psichiatria* (psychiatry) treats adults after reaching the age of majority on their 18th birthday. As such, it is tempting to simply distinguish them as child and adult psychiatry. However, neuropsychiatry and psychiatry have distinct origins and practices which make the transition to legal adulthood anything but simple (Nardocci 2009). As the names imply, neuropsychiatry links neurology and psychiatry. Adult psychiatry, however, does not.

While Italian psychiatry has its roots in traditional organic/biology psychiatry and then Basaglia and the ideology of Democratic Psychiatry, neuropsychiatry, on the other hand, has its roots in the figures of Sante de Sanctis (psychiatrist), Giuseppe F. Montesano (psychopedagogue), and Maria Montessori (pedagogue, creator of the "Montessori school" model) and therefore bridges psychiatry and pedagogy (Bracci 2003; Migone 2014).[8] Neuropsychiatry emerged from the work of psychiatrists, psychologists, and pedagogues, initially as a subfield of psychiatry itself (Migone 2014; Storia » Società Italiana Di Psichiatria, n.d.). However, the field became so distinct that ultimately neuropsychiatry created an independent professional association, SINPIA, separate from the Italian psychiatric association, SIP (Storia » Società Italiana Di Psichiatria, n.d.). Neuropsychiatry is also vital in the Italian view on autism. Sante de Sanctis is credited with providing, at the turn into the twentieth century, one of the earliest descriptions of children who would now be labeled "autistic" (Feinstein 2010; Levi and Bernabei 1997). De Sanctis has also been called the "*padre della neuropsichiatria infantile italiana*" (father of Italian pediatric neuropsychiatry) (Cimino and Lombardo 2004)[9] and was also the first chairman of the *Società Italiana di Psicologia* (Società Italiana di Psicologia 2002). Maria Montessori was a student of his; her pedagogy has been important in Italy and the US, including with respect to "special education." Unlike adult psychiatry and Democratic Psychiatry, neuropsychiatry has taken more influence from French psychoanalytic schools (Migone 2014).

The current landscape of autism services post-PR therefore involves a complicated network of services and approaches influenced by the various histories and trajectories of psychiatry generally, Democratic Psychiatry specifically, neuropsychiatry, and related fields such as pedagogy and psychology. Services for Italians with disabilities post-PR are coordinated by regional ASLs and, as in many parts of the world, involve a dizzying range of providers, services, and organizations including the educational system, in- or (more often) out-of-school therapies, recreational opportunities, vocational training, day centers, residential centers, respite services, and more. Before his death in 2011, influential Italian autism psychologist Enrico Micheli classified three main types of treatments: *il gruppo psicodinamico* (the psychodynamic group), *il gruppo psicoeducativo* (the psychoeducational group), and *il gruppo "new age"* (the "new age" group) (Micheli 2005). The first two categories describe major approaches to autism intervention deriving not from neuropsychiatry or psychiatry per se, but from different branches of psychology. These approaches can also be contrasted with the "traditional" approaches of neuoropsychomotor and speech/language therapy. These three approaches (traditional, psychoeducational, and relational) are unpacked in the following paragraphs.

The autism professionals that Cascio interviewed[10] consistently explained that the local health boards directed families of children with autism toward *neuropsicomotricità* (neuropsychomotor therapy)[11] and *logopedia* (speech language therapy), a combination participants referred to as *ufficiale* (official) or *tradizionale* (traditional). They lamented that these treatments were often not tailored specifically for autism. However, there were many therapists who had specific training in autism and collaborated with other professionals in *équipe* (multidisciplinary teams) or worked privately with people with autism. Both *logopediste* (speech language therapists) themselves and staff members at various locations lamented the recent absence of these therapists from public services and the need for parents to pay for them privately.

The vast majority of approaches advocated by professionals in Cascio's study fall under the umbrella that participants called varyingly *psicoeducativo* (psycho-educational), *educativo* (educational), and *abilitativo* ("abilitative," related to "rehabilitative" but without the "re-" prefix); or *cognitivo-comportamentale* (cognitive-behavioral).[12] Participants used these terms to refer to approaches approved by the 2011 National Guidelines for the treatment of autism spectrum disorders (*Sistema Nazionale per le Linee Guida-Istituto Superiore di Sanità* 2011, 2012), which use the terms "*pedogogici ed abilitativi*" (pedagogical and "abilitative") and *educativo* (educational), and specifically recommend interventions such as Applied Behavior Analysis (ABA) and TEACCH (formerly standing for "Treatment and Education of Autistic and related Communication handicapped Children"). Indeed, TEACCH was highly influential in Cascio's fieldsites, though not monolithic. The psychoeducational philosophy encompasses all those approaches and strategies that focus on teaching people with autism and helping them learn, throughout their life. They may include instruments like visual agendas, social stories, and alternative and augmentative communication. The psychoeducational approach may also use pharmaceutical interventions,[13] but to treat symptoms, not to treat or cure autism itself (Micheli 2005).

Some of the professionals Cascio interviewed also described their approach as *relazionale* (relational), synonymous with *evolutivo* (developmental) and *umanista* (humanist). These approaches rarely stood alone but were an important or even central characteristic of their work for some participants (Cascio 2015a). These terms differed from and added to the psychoeducational philosophy by focusing on creating an environment that was adapted to people with autism, but based not so much upon the characteristics of autism but on the characteristics of the individuals themselves and their intrinsic motivations. This focus on connecting with the person with autism draws, explicitly or not, on the phenomenological perspectives that influenced PR in Italy and the psychodynamic and psychoanalytic approaches that also rejected biological/organicist psychiatry.

Some approaches in Italy draw more explicitly from psychoanalysis (see for example Mistura 2006; Wille 1992, 2001, 2012), but share much with cognitive-behavioral approaches including the structuring of the environment and the person-centered approach. All approaches share a rejection of psychogenic theories of autism as derived from poor parenting, although parents may still face these accusations from others. In as much as psychodynamic theory was associated with relational approaches, participants still found it useful. In as much as it was associated with individualist psychotherapies, talking therapies, and treating the family in order to treat the child, they generally did not. In this way, a strong resistance to psychogenic theories of autism coexists with acceptance of some components of psychodynamic theory.

However, the influence of psychoanalysis in the relational camps in Italy contrasts with the Brazilian scene. Psychoanalysis is far less influential in Cascio's fieldsite than in Brazil, as well as in France as reported by Chamak (Chamak 2008; Chamak et al. 2011). Several participants, both parents and professionals, referenced tensions with the psychoanalytic camp. This difference may be due to the distinct trajectories of community-based (develop)mental health care post-PR in these countries. Whereas PR in Brazil involved a political and clinical alliance with psychoanalysis, in Italy, it did not. Today, psychoanalysts have a strong political and therapeutic claim to autism in Brazil and are an important force in the debates about the definition and appropriate treatment of autism. In Italy, psychoanalysis has had influence in some sectors of psychiatry following PR, but this influence waned in the 1980s (Benvenuto 1997) and psychoanalysis today is rather separate from the fields that primarily address autism, especially neuropsychiatry. Psychoanalysis in Italy is more associated with psychologists and "socio-psycho-pedagogical" figures (Benvenuto 1997) and has had a stronger influence in the northern parts of Italy (Feinstein 2010). However, as the above sections describe, the dominant approaches to autism in psychology—affirmed by the national guidelines—are psychoeducational. The influence of psychoanalysis can be seen in the blending of US-influenced cognitive and behavioral approaches to autism, such as TEACCH, with relational approaches that draw on psychodynamic theory. However, psychoanalysis in those words (*la psicoanalisi*) is often rejected in autism-specific circles due to its association with parent-blaming etiological theories.

3.8 Brazil: Pre-reform Ethos, Special Education and Post-reform Mental Health Services

As in Italy, understanding the relationship between PR and autism in Brazil necessitates delving into the broader history of institutional psychiatry in Brazil, prior to deinstitutionalization reforms, and its relationship with the kind of medical-pedagogical interventions directed toward "abnormal" children. From the early to mid-twentieth century, the Brazilian psychiatric ethos balanced eugenic and hygienist influences. Its political mission focused on the nation's progress and aimed to order social life beyond health/disease issues, removing "dangerous" individuals (considered to include the poor, insane, orphans, and other so-called deviants) from social spaces (Ribeiro 2006). Institutionalization therefore had then a double task: both to protect the social realm and to discipline abnormal individuals—either correcting them, or controlling those presumed to be incorrigible (Ribeiro 2006; Rizzini 2008). This system often relied on "extreme technological interventions," such as lobotomy and involuntary sterilization in psychiatric facilities, but not as extensively as was the case in other custodial systems, as in the USA for example (Block 2007; Lima et al., this volume).

However, the Brazilian hygienist model also opened space for milder forms of management of so-called deviants in the medical-pedagogical realm, such as special education classes within psychiatric hospitals. In addition, philanthropic and religious institutions provided care to "abnormal" children, mostly through education. This pedagogical approach later had an important role in restraining Brazil from the massive institutionalization of people with disabilities, in contrast to what happened in USA, for example (Block 2007; Lanna 2010; Lima et al., this volume). It also set several standards for future specialized care of autism outside the custodial matrix (Fonseca 2011).[14]

Philanthropic services from civil society also offered assistance to children with a variety of intellectual and developmental disabilities using non-medical approaches. The most prominent is *Sociedade Pestalozzi*, founded in 1937 by Helena Antipoff, a Russian developmental psychologist. As detailed by Lima et al., this volume, Antipoff's perspective abandoned stigmatizing terms such as "retarded" and "abnormal" in favor of the concept of *crianças excepcionais* (exceptional children)—a category comprising several types of disabilities and severe mental conditions (see also Block 2007; Block and Cavalcante 2014). Antipoff considered the origin of disability to include both organic and socioeconomic conditions. However, the practices of care developed at *Sociedade Pestalozzi* did not totally break with the institutionalization paradigm. The idea of an institution as a special/protected environment was enacted through services organized as boarding schools or other disability-exclusive settings, using educational approaches in segregated settings with a multidisciplinary team of professionals. Such spaces reproduced (even partially) institutionalization's goal of keeping the *crianças excepcionais* apart from general social realm (Gonçalves Mendes 2010; Rafante and Lopes 2008).[15] Over the years, *Sociedade Pestalozzi* founded several branches. Despite uneven distribution throughout the country, as well as problems with funding and human resources, they established a legacy of alternative approaches to psychiatric institutionalization of children, and set standards for parent advocacy movements in Brazil.[16] Recently, these institutions have faced challenges after the adoption of the inclusive education paradigm in national policy, and had to reformulate their activities. Now, they operate mainly as a complementary special educational service for students with disabilities (autism included) enrolled in regular schooling system, and also provide professional training in special inclusive education for teachers (Fonseca 2011; Rios and Costa Andrada 2016).

Initiatives outside the custodial psychiatric matrix, such as these educational options, promoted changes in conceptions of disability, and offered alternatives to institutionalization. They were also the birthplace of several disability rights associations—as they actively included parents as partners in care, displayed an openness to parental expertise, and supported their activism (Lanna 2010). But, despite these positive outcomes, specific transformations in broader federal mental health public policies, services, and legislation did not emerge until the PR process, from late-1970s on.

This history brings us to the current moment, in which two different systems serve people with autism: those within and those outside post-reform public mental health services. Currently, the services from PR matrix that deal most directly with autism are the *Centros de Atenção Psicossocial* (Centers for Psychosocial Attention—CAPS) and *Centros de Atenção Psicossocial Infanto-juvenis* (Centers for Psychosocial Attention for Children and Youth—CAPSi). Divided by age group (CAPSi serve children and youth until the age of 18; CAPS serve adults), they provide interdisciplinary psychosocial assistance to a variety of conditions: psychosis, autism, alcohol and drug abuse, social vulnerability, etc. They operate through a combination of theoretical approaches, counting on families and territorial ties to collaborate with care (Couto 2004). Collective activities are the norm, and their clinical rationale considers uniqueness and diversity as key elements to promote social inclusion and citizenship. But this assistance is not unproblematic: sometimes these services find barriers that compromise effective care—ranging from lack of material resources, to uncommitted families, to unhelpful local political dynamics. As in the Italian context (and the USA—see Lima et al. this volume), the transition from child to adult mental health services is not simple for persons with autism. While CAPSi and CAPS share the same ethos, both political and clinical, CAPSi is perceived as being better equipped to deal with the particularities of autism. There are two main reasons given for this perception: (1) autism first entered mental health public policies as part of the agenda for children and youth, served by CAPSi, and (2) pragmatically, CAPSi tend to group children in collective activities using age group and a loose criteria of "children's profile"—which, in some cases, results in diagnostic-driven groups and activities. This sorting by diagnostic criteria is not common at CAPS, which often becomes problematic in the case of persons with autism in adult services. In her fieldwork, Costa Andrada found professionals and parents facing challenges with the transition of youngsters with autism from CAPSi to CAPS. During a family meeting at a CAPSi, a father of a teenager with autism with high support needs voiced his concern:

> I know my daughter can't stay here for long, but I think CAPS won't do her good. This worries me… They deal with a lot of things there, they don't have this one-to-one dedication. I see here you kind of sort the kids… like, put the special ones, the autistics, in the same group. I know CAPS can do a good job, but I don't think they know how to attend to my daughter's special needs.

CAPSi, although created almost a decade after CAPS, were pioneers in dealing with autism within the mental health field (Lima et al. 2014). Despite CAPSi's relative expertise on autism, they are not specialized centers, nor autism exclusive services. Specialized services are rare within the public mental health network. As autism advocacy became stronger over the years, such specialized services became the leading demand. As we will see in the next sections, this is central to the current controversies around autism care in Brazil.

3.9 Autism Today: Local Controversies in Post-reform Contexts

Around the world, autism has become a major global health and global rights concern (Grossman and Barazzo 2007). It is also a source of great controversy and contestation. These controversies take local form which we argue are shaped—in part—by these local histories of PR which are inextricably tied with and generative of different clinical and political landscapes of autism care. The following sections turn to the local controversies and politics around autism in Brazil and Italy in the early decades of the twenty-first century. In both countries, we focus particularly on the way in which the organic and relational dimensions of autism are conceptualized and the way these conceptualizations are mobilized by parents, professionals, policy-makers, and people with autism. In Brazil, these contests center on the paradigm of "autism as a disability." In Italy, various conceptualizations of "autism as a way of being" play into the organization of autism services. In both contexts, parent advocacy for an organic model of autism and for autism-specific therapies and interventions challenge the diagnosis-agnostic ethos of both PR and psychoanalysis, as the common lack of specificity in community-based (develop)mental health services.

3.10 Autism Controversies in Brazil: Advocacy, Lived Experiences and the Paradigm of "Autism as a Disability"

In recent years, autism has become an object of a contentious debate between advocacy groups[17] and mental health professionals within Brazil's SUS. These groups criticize the treatments offered at public mental health services, such as CAPSi and CAPS, demanding public specialized treatments outside the scope of the mental health services. They generally do not ally themselves with public mental health professionals, refraining from an important feature of PR's legacy. Instead, they argue that autism is better understood as a disability, preferring alliances with disability rights groups, and experts from rehabilitation and education fields. From their perspective, this alliance has a double vantage: (1) identifying autism as a disability dismisses the psychogenic hypothesis, because autism is understood as an effect of neurobiological impairments interacting with hostile socioenvironmental barriers. Also, it reconfigures the role of parents from "inducers" of their children's autism to active actors in their treatments (Ortega 2009b; Silverman 2011); (2) Brazilian legislation regarding rights and benefits to persons with disabilities is more protective than the one concerning people with severe mental disorders[18] (Rios and Costa Andrada 2015). Entailed within the autism-as-disability perspective in Brazil are demands for diagnosis-specific interventions.

The insufficiency of public assistance to autism, especially to children, is a major consequence of autism's late entry into the public mental health sector and has motivated parents of children with autism to take the matter into their own hands.[19] Throughout the 1980s, different parents' associations created services aiming to fill gaps in assistance, and started to consolidate a new paradigm: the notion of autism as a disability in contrast to a form of mental suffering. It was built from the general background of philanthropic special education institutions, described above, combined with the emergence of services provided by parents' organizations, whose first initiatives were based on educational and rehabilitative models. They imported and adapted foreign practices of care (such as ABA and TEACCH) as key components of their activities of advocacy, care, and training (Nunes 2014; Rios and Costa Andrada 2015).

Since the early 2000s, various grass-roots groups have gradually built political influence, lobbying with politicians to advance autism politics from the local to the national level (Costa 2013; Nunes 2014). Their lobby led to the passage of federal law 12.764 in 2012[20] recognizing "autism as a disability for all legal purposes" (Brasil 2012). This law sets wider social protections and access to benefits than would be available were autism not classified as a disability, but it does not define which services are responsible for autism care, despite stakeholders' demands for specialized treatments outside CAPS/CAPSi. From these parents' perspective, social inclusion depends more on the achievement of specific skills or abilities that will come only through structured therapies (such as ABA or TEACCH), and not so much from psychosocial interventions in collective settings. Based on their first-hand experience of post-reform services, they rightly point out the insufficiency of time, infrastructural barriers, and scarcity of resources as common issues in CAPS/CAPSi in attending autism special needs—in practice, several of these services can only provide a couple of hours/week of group therapy, and few individuals with high levels of support needs get to be singly assisted.[21] These stakeholders also take issues with some influences of psychoanalysis in public mental health services (Block and Cavalcante 2014; Rios and Costa Andrada 2015; Nunes 2014).

On the other hand, their criticism loses sight of the scope of these services' interventions that deal with social determinants and intersections of disability and poverty, such as the territorial practices of care. These actions range from home visits to collaborations with different health services and partnerships with other sectors' institutions (justice, social assistance, education, culture, and so on). Their rejection of CAPS/CAPSi and the related understanding of autism as a form of socially embedded suffering de-emphasizes the complexity of autism in the context of social vulnerability—a major issue in autism care and politics given Brazil's stark social inequalities.

Law 12.764 is criticized by the mental health sector and psychoanalytical community, who took issue with the status of autism as a disability. Because most of these professionals are unfamiliar with the Disability Studies field, they tend to resist the idea of autism as a disability, considering the term to be stigmatizing and associating it with a deficit-driven, personal-tragedy model of disability. They consider calling autism a *deficiência* (disability[22]) to be a means of reducing the autistic subject to a position of deficit, worsening the stigma faced by people with autism (Rios and Costa Andrada 2015).

This controversy appears intractable when looked at only through public discourse. However, when approached from local perspectives, this schism is not so sharp. In Costa Andrada's study, services users and their families are far from unanimous in the rejection of CAPS/CAPSi.[23] Although some of them do share the critique regarding gaps in assistance, and even started to organize themselves to demand an autism specialized/exclusive service, their motivations differ from those expressed in the public discourse of advocacy organizations. They consider a "specialized service" an option from a pragmatic perspective, and not because they disagree with the ethos of public mental health services. As a mother of a boy with autism explains:

> We keep going back and forth with these kids... For us, it is very wearing... Can you imagine how it is for the autists?! We take the child to the school in one place, psychologist in another, the speech therapist is far, CAPSi is once a week... Anyway, all these professionals are in different places! So if we had all of them in one place, it would be much simpler.

But this pragmatic approach to treatment and service options can also go the other way: in contexts of extreme social vulnerability, some families embrace the community-based approach as well as more structured therapies. A mother, whose son attends services of both kinds, explains:

> Why not both? There are so few places where I can take my son... you know, in one place they fix one part of my son's problems, and in the other place, they take care of the other problems...

Either way, these mothers realize the territory might offer possibilities of care and social inclusion to their children, and also recognize the gaps in the local management of public health services and intersectoral actions. They found different services that could offer specific types of care to their children (and themselves). Such pragmatic attitude overcomes the dichotomies of the politics and discourses around autism. Most important, it also points to the necessity of a stronger articulation between services and policies—from the local territorial arrangements to the national scenario.

3.11 Italy: Advocacy, Lived Experiences, and the Paradigm of "Autism as a Way of Being"

As in Brazil, parents' associations in Italy play an important role in the landscape of autism services. These associations tend to take an organicist approach to autism—yet, this organicism is very different from that rejected by Basaglia's PD and the deinstitutionalization movement. Just as organicism was harmful in the era of institutionalization, parents find it helpful in the post-PR world. This contrast demonstrates the importance of local and historical context on the mobilization of scientific ideas. Such ideas are not *inherently* helpful or harmful, but rather are *rendered* helpful or harmful in social context.

This section addresses the origins of autism-focused parents' associations and self-advocacy associations, contextualizing them within the broader history of associational movements in Italy. It also addresses the definition of autism not just as a disability but also as a "way of being," as it is mobilized both by professionals and parents. As is the case of "disability" in Brazil, this definition seeks to define autism as an organic, biologically determined phenomenon, while still foregrounding the social and interpersonal nature of the challenges faced by people affected by autism. Defining autism as "a way of being" means seeing it as a consequence of a mismatch between the individual (with innate/inborn autistic characteristics) and a hostilely neurotypical world.

The first autism-specific parents' association in Italy was the *Associazione per le ricerca sulle psicosi e l'autismo* (Association for Research on Psychosis and Autism—ARPA), founded in 1983 in Rome (ARPA, n.d.). As of this writing, the three largest national autism associations in Italy form FANTASIA.[24] Parent and self-advocate organizations undertake many initiatives: fighting for the rights of persons with autism, directing research initiatives (Hanau and Cerati 2005, 74), and initiating experimental projects. The presence of parents' associations was felt in many of Cascio's seven main fieldsites, many of which were created with the heavy involvement of associations, foundations, and/or cooperatives founded or supported by parents.

The current climate of parent–practitioner relationships in Italy is tense, as evidenced by books such as *Disabili, famiglie, e operatori: chi è il paziente difficile* (Vivanti 2006), whose title translates to "people with disabilities, their families, and staff: who is the difficult patient?" Much of this tension may derive from psychogenic etiological theories of autism that place the blame for the condition on poor parenting, most notably (even in Italy), Bruno Bettleheim's (1967) *Empty Fortress*. Indeed, *Associazione Nazionale Genitori Soggetti Autistici* (National Association of Parents of Autistic People—ANGSA) was formed to fight against psychoanalytic parent-blaming which came to Italy largely from France (ANGSA 2016; Feinstein 2010, 111). Bovi and colleagues link the change from psychoanalytic to organicist views of autism in Italy in the late 1980s to a conference organized by parents' groups, which stressed not only the organic basis of autism and the need for specialized treatment, but also "the importance of a collaboration between practitioners and parents, the former experts on autism, the latter experts on the autism of their own children" (2003, 215—Cascio's translation). From their beginnings, associations like ANGSA sought the collaboration of professionals, but they did not find this an easy path. As Bovi et al. (2003, 215—Cascio's translation) explain, these efforts:

> came to a halt precisely because in many levels autism continued to be regarded as a disorder with relational origins. The parents did not succeed, therefore, in getting recognition of the new arguments which, however, they still wielded with difficulty in the face of professionals who were not open to refusing their outdated conceptualizations of autism and how to care for people with autism.

Parent-advocates continued their efforts, in 1988 forming the "Autism and Psychosis Group" within the ANFFAS of Milan, "seeking the welcome of some professionals who were open to new ideas and available to engage with them" (Bovi et al. 2003, 215—Cascio's translation).

With effort and patience, parents were able to find professional collaborations but not the allegiance of all professionals. In contrast to Brazil, the presence of child neuropsychiatry may have helped the parents' approach to take hold, as neuropsychiatrists and parents both argued for a neurobiological basis of autism. These groups also aligned with psychologists who took a psychoeducational, cognitive, behavioral, or cognitive-behavioral approach (in contrast to psychologists who took a psychoanalytic approach).

The situation outlined thus far has involved changing contests between different approaches to disabilities such as autism. Democratic Psychiatry opposed older organicist approaches to mental and developmental disorders generally, which focused on physical and pharmaceutical institutionalization. Decades later, however, autism parents' associates found organicism to be a solution to older psychoanalytic approaches to autism specifically, which focused on relational causes of and solutions to autism. However, the organicism advocated by these parents does not resemble the organicism of institutionalization even though it is similar in theories of etiology. Parents of people with autism and professionals who specialize in autism both described autism as rooted in organic causes, but *also* as a different "way of being" that should be understood and worked with, not against.

Nearly half of professionals ($N = 22$ of 45) in Cascio's study made comments to this effect, defining autism as a way of being, understanding the world, or processing information; a state of being or functioning, an aspect of the human condition, a different perception of the world around the person, and even another culture. Autism can therefore be understood as a mismatch between the way the person with autism exists, and the surrounding world. Defining autism as its own way of being can offer positive valuation, moving away from deficit-focused language. This perspective of autism-as-difference can be seen in all three of the intervention models described earlier in this chapter, as they focus on changing the environment as the first step in facilitating change for people with autism—a sort of social model of neurodisability.

The "different way of being" discourse was also important to parents. Fifteen interviews with parents (39%) included some version of this discourse which described people with autism as having "a different view of the outside;" "a way," "[his] own way," or "manner all his own" of seeing, relating, understanding, being, perceiving, communicating, functioning, socializing; "a very particular world;" and/or a "different real world," a world "where you [the person with autism] understand others, but the others do not understand you." This invocation of "another world" occurred in these statements either to describe autism as itself another world, or as a condition in which the world of others, built by others, is not hospitable. One mother went so far as to tell Cascio, "For me the fact that she has autism is like saying that she has blond hair and blue eyes, it's the same, on the same plane, really. It's a characteristic." This perspective lends itself to a diversity framework with clear parallels to the liberatory message of Democratic Psychiatry. As one parent explains:

> In my own words, autism is… it's not a disease but a way of being […] we should learn from the time we are in preschool that each of us is different from the other, and therefore even people with autism are not to be seen as strange people, but like people different from us. Very different than us, clearly, sure. [….] We need to have respect, you see. Don't take away the respect that each of us on this earth deserves. In the same way they need [it], they have a right to the same respect. (Interview, Parent)

Notably, fewer parents invoked this discourse than professionals, who more commonly included the idea of a different way of being in their definitions. Moreover, parents' use of the different world narrative hinted more at deficit than the different way of being discourse. However, parents talked about potentially bridging these worlds when they talked to their children about their autism. Parents who reported talking about autism with their children commonly described the central message as being that all people have different strengths and weaknesses, and that the characteristics of autism are a part of that common human experience. Summarizing this theme, one mother explained very clearly:

> One thing that I taught [my son], which fortunately he took up very well, I always tell him, "each person has some difficulties. Each person is able to do some things, but is not able to do others. Therefore you aren't good, let's say, in math, like some other people who are very talented in it, but you for example have an exceptional visual memory and therefore you will do something really great using this skill of yours, for example." (Interview, Parent)

Youth drew on the discourse of different strengths and weaknesses as well, suggesting that their parents' conversations with them may have had an impact. Youth drew on some positive language to describe their difference, even if they talked about difficulties as well. They described themselves as "good," "intelligent," "advanced," "better than the others," having "nerd power," and even "a new species of human being." Cascio asked youth what they were afraid of with respect to autism, and one youth encapsulated the difference-not-deficit narrative when he answered: "I am afraid that people think I am different in a negative way but in my opinion I am different in a positive way."

Both reading autism as a way of being and explaining autism in a non-deficit-focused way allude to neurodiversity discourses and the idea of autism as an identity. Although the discourse of neurodiversity[25] had not penetrated the Italian scene of Cascio's 2012–2013 to the extent that it had the English-speaking giants (Baker 2006; Boundy 2008; Brownlow 2010; Cascio 2012; Fenton and Krahn 2007; Hart 2014; Kapp et al. 2013; Orsini 2009; Ortega 2009a; Silverman 2011), the use of the way of being discourse aligns with the ideas of neurodiversity.

However, the discourse of a way of being, in the context of autism-specific services, was not directly opposed to a medical mode of disability. This model still appeared in autism services that could be read as medicalized: services that were often specialized for autism based on a diagnosis made by a medical professional and that followed educational programs such as TEACCH and ABA while often attending to the pharmaceutical needs of the people attending, and sometimes employing the psychiatrists that managed these prescriptions in the first place. The idea behind these interventions, in the context of a definition of autism as a way of being, was not that one should change the environment *instead* of changing the person with autism. Rather, these changes to the environment were made for the purpose of helping the person with autism to learn, grow, and, in a sense, change.

Like the paradigm of autists as "disabled" and "special" in Brazil served the needs of families and professionals to create and obtain specialized services, so the paradigm of autists as qualitatively "different" in Italy served to shape the call for autism-specific services. Both Brazilian parents' use of "disability" and Italian parents' use of the different way of being discourse served to offer non-deficit counter-narratives to the diagnostic narrative of impairments, providing parents a concrete way to interact with both their children and the world of autism services.

3.12 Conclusion

Psychiatric reform, deinstitutionalization, and subsequent community-based care policies have impacted the destinies of people who meet today's criteria for autism spectrum conditions in Brazil and Italy. Such individuals were likely confined to institutions prior to the deinstitutionalization movements of the 1970s–1980s, and are currently served in a network of community-based care that is shaped by the rationale and politics of PR. Contemporary dilemmas around autism take local shapes in Brazilian and Italian contexts, and are intermingled with the rationales of PR in these countries and the policies and practices that emerged as a result.

While both Italian and Brazilian PR took radically emancipatory, democratic, and holistic perspectives, they differ significantly in some respects. For example, psychoanalysis is still deeply integrated with PR in Brazil but less explicit in its influence on psychiatry, psychology, and neuropsychiatry in Italy. Furthermore, in the present moment, we see significant differences between the attitudes of autism parent movements in Italy and Brazil toward the outcome of the anti-asylum and pro-community-care models: Italian autism parents' movements generally favor these movements while Brazilian autism parents' movements tend to contest them.

However, taking a broad historical view of autism politics in Brazil and Italy that goes back to PR and looks at the similarities between these historical trajectories can better inform our understanding of the current situations and the discourses mobilized by various actors. Most notably, in both contexts, the discourses of parents and professionals reveal the flexibility of different concepts to be deployed for different political and clinical agendas. In Brazil and Italy, parents strongly advocate for a view of autism that is organicist—biologically based and diagnostically specific—in contrast to the anti-organicist, anti-positivist, and even anti-diagnostic perspectives of PR. While both the PR movements of the late twentieth centuries and the autism movements of the early twenty-first centuries seek social inclusion, respect for rights, and freedom for people with disabilities like autism, they mobilize nearly opposite discourses to accomplish it. Taking a historically informed view of current autism politics moves beyond the dichotomies and extremities of the current political landscape by demonstrating the contextual nature of these discourses, opening up space for the recognition of common ground and, perhaps, integration.

Notes

1. In this chapter, we use the single word "autism" to encompass a range of diagnoses currently referred to in the DSM-5 as "autism spectrum disorder" (American Psychiatric Association 2013). Most importantly, we use it to mean the term that was most meaningful to our participants.
2. The concept of "deinstitutionalization" varies along with the different processes of reforming psychiatry. For example, in the US Preventive Psychiatry model, 'deinstitutionalization' means "a set of measures to reduce the inflow of patients in psychiatric hospitals, or to reduce the average duration of hospitalization, or, also, the promotion of hospital discharges" (Amarante 2007, 50). It mainly implies changes in the dynamics and in the social role of the psychiatric hospitals, and, therefore, can be better described as a process of dehospitalization. On the other hand, in Basaglia's Democratic Psychiatry, 'deinstitutionalization' carries a wider meaning, and "(…) is not restricted to, much less is to be confused with dehospitalization, insofar as dehospitalization means only to identify transformation with the extinction of asylar/hospital organizations. (…) deinstitutionalization means to understand the institution in its dynamic and necessary complex sense of practices and knowledges that produce certain ways of perceiving, understanding and relating to historical and social phenomena" (Amarante 1998, 53).
3. Although the term *integrazione* is often glossed as inclusion, others (D'Alessio 2008, 57–58) explain that they are not exactly synonymous and advocate for a more inclusive *integrazione*. Full discussion of this issue is beyond the scope of this chapter.
4. Later, the 1988 Constitution defined "health as a right of every individual and duty of the state," with universal health coverage as a fundamental right of all citizens (Brasil 1988). The Brazilian Unified Health System (SUS) was created in 1990 with this purpose, structured by principles of universality, equity, integrality in health care, and decentralization, regionalization, hierarchy, and social participation in its strategies. SUS has, in many ways, been successful in accomplishing many of its goals, but in practice, universal coverage still faces challenges: resistance from private health sector lobbies in Congress, underfunding, barriers to access, and maldistribution of skilled human resources, resulting in gaps in assistance. Autism advocacy is one of several health advocacy movements that evokes 'health as individual right and duty of the state' as legal basis for their claims. They denounce these gaps, demanding specialized assistance through judicialization and local political alliances.
5. The advantage of focusing on suffering is to destigmatize psychiatric conditions, characterizing them as experiences that are simultaneously

singular and universal in human life. Services in the post-reform matrix followed this rationale and operate from non-specialized perspectives. Later, this approach clashed with claims of autism advocacy groups, that decline the "subject burdened by severe mental suffering" as an adequate label to autism, preferring a bioidentity built specifically from a (psychiatric) diagnosis, which sustains their demands of specialized/evidence-based services (Bezerra 1992; Nunes 2014; Rios and Costa Andrada 2015).

6. In Brazil, psychoanalysts commonly work as professors and/or researchers at universities and public health institutions, and often participate as professional staff at a number of public mental health services. However, psychoanalysis presents different profiles in private and public sectors. In the first one, it follows a "classic" ethos of psychoanalytical societies, with transmission through study groups, seminars, clinical supervisions, and didactic psychoanalysis. Dialogues with other disciplines are scarce. In the latter, however, psychoanalysis is embedded in a multi-disciplinary ethos of humanities in universities and research institutes and engaged in political debates in public health.
7. Among the practices commonly used in these settings, one can find children's groups, family therapy groups, craft workshops, group activities with children and parents, and so on. However, this influence does not mean that psychoanalysis is the only therapeutic framework available.
8. Cascio has previously discussed these histories in their dissertation (Cascio 2015a) and a blog post at https://culturemedicinepsychiatry.com/2015/03/25/guest-blog-culture-medicine-and-neuropsychiatry/.
9. Giovanni Bollea has also been given this title (Fiorani 2011; Migone 2014).
10. For more details, see Cascio (2015a).
11. Often shortened as *psicomotricità*. However, the term *psicomotricità* also refers to a specific relational approach, referenced below in the work of Anne-Marie Wille.
12. This term was also used to refer specifically to cognitive-behavioral therapy (CBT). For a full discussion of the nuances of CBT, cognitivism, and behavioralism, see Cascio (2015a).
13. Indeed, many scholars and participants have argued that the primary role of psychiatrists is in prescribing and supervising medication, whereas the work of interventions such as ABA and TEACCH is more associated with psychologists.
14. As Eyal et al. (2010) demonstrate, diagnosis rearrangement and availability of services are intrinsically related. In early to mid-twentieth century's Brazilian psychiatric ethos, the mere existence of alternatives to psychiatric asylums impacted diagnosis: where special education/philanthropic

services were available, the chances of a child be assessed as mentally retarded were higher, and her destiny was likely to be one of these services. However, wherever these alternatives were absent, diagnosis would follow a psychiatric matrix with subsequent institutionalization. In Brazil, systematic diagnosis of autism took place only as recently as the 1980s, and for most of the twentieth century, people with autism would be labeled either intellectually disabled or psychotic. For decades, psychiatrists and educators developed discrete spheres of services, with little theoretical convergence (Block and Cavalcante 2014). This is in direct contrast to Italy where, as described below, neuropsychiatry and education were tightly linked particularly through the educational model of Maria Montessori.

15. This is similar to the perspective of eighteenth century alienism regarding the creation of the first mental asylums; their goals were to protect the insane from the maleficent and sickening conditions of the social environment in order to allow them to be cured.
16. The first parents' association for disability advocacy and assistance was found within *Sociedade Pestalozzi*: *Associação de Pais e Amigos de Pessoas Excepcionais* (Association of Parents and Friends of Exceptional People—APAE), a non-specific disability service provider.
17. Usually, autism advocacy groups adopt a model of activism of public awareness, and political alliances in local and national spheres drawing from the disability rights movement. This differs from the PR's alliance of experts-users-families, whose political actions aim for social participation and empowerment of services' users regarding decisions about their own treatments. There are, though, persons with autism and their families who aligned with this kind of activism that is more engaged in local strategies of care.
18. The mental health legislation is quite protective to former institutionalized patients, but this is not the case of most of the persons with autism nowadays in Brazil.
19. The first autism parents' association—*Associação de Amigos do Autista* (Association of Friends of Autistic Individuals–AMA)—was founded in 1983, as an initiative to provide specialized care when treatment was scarce. It became a model of autism parents' association in Brazilian context. AMA operates a range of activities: advocacy, specialized assistance, public awareness and professional training. As other autism parents' associations, they sought financial support from public and private sectors. They also enhanced their expertise through training at international specialized centers (Mello et al. 2013).
20. It was named "Lei Berenice Piana," after a mother of a youth with autism. She is a leading voice in autism parents' advocacy for specialized/

exclusive services outside public mental health scope, and lobbied for the implementation of a specialized/exclusive center to autism in her city, called *Clínica-escola do autista*—"Autistic's Clinic-school," in a free translation (Nunes 2014). For a first-person account on parental activism in local autism politics, see Costa (2013).

21. Reasons vary for this gap in assistance, from underfunding to high labor turnover due to changes in work contracts.
22. The Portuguese word *deficiência* translates literally as "deficiency." It is a term associated with deficit and rehabilitation, and its semantics don't easily allow the idea of diversity.
23. In a study on parents' evaluation of autism assistance in CAPSi, Lima and colleagues (2014) found that they have an appraisal that is both critical of and more positive about these services than the appraisals of advocacy groups.
24. These organizations are: the *Associazione Nazionale Genitori Soggetti Autistici* (National Association of Parents of Autistic People), founded in 1985; *Autismo Italia*, founded in 1998; and *Gruppo Asperger*, founded in 2000.
25. The usage of the terms *neurodiversità* (neurodiversity) and *persone neurodiverse* (neurodiverse people) as well as the opposite *neurotipici* (neurotypicals) is, however, becoming more common. It is worth pointing out that the discourse of "autism pride" or "Asperger pride," on the other hand, was more often raised during Cascio's fieldwork.

References

Amarante, Paulo, ed. 1998. *Loucos Pela Vida – A trajetória da reforma psiquiátrica no Brasil.* Rio de Janeiro: Editora Fiocruz.

Amarante, Paulo. 2007. *Saúde Mental e Atenção Psicossocial.* Rio de Janeiro: Editora Fiocruz.

American Psychiatric Association. 2013. *Diagnostic and Statistical Manual of Mental Disorders: DSM-V.* Washington, DC: American Psychiatric Association.

Associazione Nazionale Genitori Soggetti Autistici. 2016. "La storia dell'ANGSA." Accessed December 3, 2016. http://angsa.it/chi-siamo/la-storia-dellangsa/.

Associazione per la ricerca sulle psicosi e l'autismo. n.d. "Relazione e Curriculum." Accessed January 21, 2017. http://www.arpaonlus.org/sezione-2-sottosezione-4-id-6-relazione-e-curriculum.htm.

Atun, Rifat, Luiz Odorico M. de Andrade, Gisele Almeida, Daniel Cotlear, T. Dmytraczenko, Patricia Frenz, Patrícia Garcia, Octavio Gómez-Dantés, Felicia M. Knaul, Carles Muntaner, Juliana Braga de Paula, Felix Rígoli, Pastor Castell-Florit Serrate, and Adam Wagstaff. 2015. "Health-System Reform and Universal Health Coverage in Latin America." *The Lancet* 385 (9974): 1230–1247.

Baker, Dana Lee. 2006. "Neurodiversity, Neurological Disability and the Public Sector: Notes on the Autism Spectrum." *Disability & Society* 21 (1): 15–29.

Basaglia, Franco. 1965. "La Distruzione Dell'ospedale Psichiatrico Come Luogo Di Istituzionalizzazione." *Annali di Neurologia e Psichiatria* LIX (1), reprinted in *Primo Convegno Internazionale di Psichiatria Sociale, Londra, Agosto 1964*: 1–10. Available at http://www.fondazionefrancobasaglia.it/images/pdf/BASAGLIA_LA_DISTRUZIONE.pdf.

Basaglia, Franco. 2000. *Conferenze Brasiliane*. Milano: Raffaello Cortina.

Basaglia, Franco, and Franca Basaglia Ongaro. 1971. *La Maggioranza Deviante: L'ideologia Del Controllo Sociale Totale*. Turin, Italy: Giulio Einaudi.

Begeny, John C., and Brian K. Martens. 2007. "Inclusionary Education in Italy a Literature Review and Call for More Empirical Research." *Remedial and Special Education* 28 (2): 80–94.

Benvenuto, Sergio. 1997. "Italy and Psychoanalysis." *Journal of European Psychoanalysis* 5. Electronic Document, available at http://www.psychomedia.it/jep/number5/benvenuto.htm.

Bettelheim, Bruno. 1967. *The Empty Fortress*. New York, NY: The Free Press.

Bezerra, Benilton C., Jr. 1994. "De médico, de louco e de todo mundo um pouco." In *Saúde e sociedade no Brasil: os anos 80*, edited by Ricardo Tavares and Reinaldo Guimarães. Rio de Janeiro: Relume-Dumará.

Bezerra, Benilton C., Jr., and Paulo Amarante, eds. 1992. *Psiquiatria sem hospício: contribuições ao estudo da reforma psiquiátrica*. Rio de Janeiro: Relume-Dumará.

Biehl, João. 2005. *Vita—Life in a Zone of Social Abandonment*. Berkeley: University of California Press.

Block, Pamela. 2007. "Institutional Utopias, Eugenics, and Intellectual Disabilities in Brazil." *History and Anthropology* 18 (2): 177–196.

Block, Pamela, and Fátima Cavalcante. 2014. "Historical Perceptions of Autism in Brazil: Professional Treatment, Family Advocacy, and Autistic Pride, 1943–2010." In *Disability Histories*, edited by Susan Burch and Michael Rembis, 77–97. Urbana: University of Illinois Press.

Boundy, Kathryn. 2008. "'Are You Sure, Sweetheart, That You Want to Be Well?': An Exploration of the Neurodiversity Movement." *Radical Psychology* 7 (1): 1–20.

Bovi, Anna, Anna Riva, and Adele Confalonieri. 2003. "Angsa Lombardia Onlus", ruolo e aspettative dei genitori. In *Autismo: modelli applicativi nei servizi: Realizzazione di un programma psicoeducativo mediante la formazione in service*, edited by Tina Lomascolo, Ascanio Vaccaro, and Susanna Villa. Gussago, Brescia: Società Editrice Vannini a r.l.

Bracci, Silvia. 2003. "Sviluppo della neuropsichiatria in Italia ed Europa. Storia delle istituzioni psichiatriche per l'infanzia." In *L'Ospedale psichiatrico di Roma. Dal Manicomio Provinciale alla Chiusura*, edited by Antonio Iaria, Tommaso Losavio, and Pompeo Martelli, 145–161. Bari: Dedalo.

Brasil. 1988. *Constituição da República Federativa do Brasil.* Brasília: DOU, 5 de outubro de 1998.

Brasil. 2001. *Lei 10.216—Dispõe sobre a proteção e os direitos das pessoas portadoras de transtornos mentais e redireciona o modelo assistencial em saúde mental.* Brasília: DOU, 06 de abril de 2001.

Brasil. 2012. *Lei n8 12.764—Institui a política nacional de proteção dos direitos da pessoa com transtorno do espectro autista.* Brasília: DOU, 27 de dezembro de 2012.

Brownlow, Charlotte. 2010. "Presenting the Self: Negotiating a Label of Autism." *Journal of Intellectual and Developmental Disability* 35 (1): 14–21.

Burti, Lorenzo, and Paul R. Benson. 1996. "Psychiatric Reform in Italy: Developments Since 1978." *International Journal of Law and Psychiatry* 19 (3): 373–390.

Canevaro, Andrea, and Lucia de Anna. 2010. "The Historical Evolution of School Integration in Italy: Some Witnesses and Considerations." *ALTER-European Journal of Disability Research/Revue Européenne de Recherche sur le Handicap* 4 (3): 203–216.

Cascio, M. Ariel. 2012. "Neurodiversity: Autism Pride Among Mothers of Children with Autism Spectrum Disorders." *Intellectual and Developmental Disabilities* 50 (3): 273–283.

Cascio, M. Ariel. 2015a. "Biopolitics and Subjectivity: The Case of Autism Spectrum Conditions in Italy." Doctoral Dissertation, Case Western Reserve University.

Cascio, M. Ariel. 2015b. "Cross-Cultural Autism Studies, Neurodiversity, and Conceptualizations of Autism." *Culture, Medicine and Psychiatry* 39 (2): 207.

Chamak, Brigitte. 2008. "Autism and Social Movements: French Parents' Associations and International Autistic Individuals' Organisations." *Sociology of Health & Illness* 30 (1): 76–96.

Chamak, Brigitte, Béatrice Bonniau, Lila Oudaya, and Alain Ehrenberg. 2011. "The Autism Diagnostic Experiences of French Parents." *Autism* 15 (1): 83–97.

Cimino, G., and G.P. Lombardo. 2004. *Sante De Sanctis Tra Psicologia Generale E Psicologia Applicata.* Milan, Italy: Franco Angeli.

Costa, Ulisses. 2013. *Autismo no Brasil: um grande desafio.* Rio de Janeiro: Wak.

Couto, Maria Cristina Ventura. 2004. "Por uma política pública de saúde mental para crianças e adolescentes." In *A Criança e a Saúde Mental: enlaces entre a clínica e a política*, edited by Tânia Ferreira, 61–74. Belo Horizonte: Autêntica, FCH-Fumec.

Crialesi, R., A. Battisti, L. Salvador-Carulla, R. Martínez-Leal, and A. Rodríguez. 2007. "Deinstitutionalisation and Community Living–Outcomes and Costs: Report of a European Study. Country Report: Italy." In *Deinstitutionalisation and Community Living–Outcomes and Costs: Report of a European Study,* edited by Julie Beadle-Brown and Agnes Kozma, 265–311. Canterbury: Tizard Centre, University of Kent. Accessed January 2, 2013. https://www.kent.ac.uk/tizard/research/DECL_network/documents/DECLOC_Country_Reports.pdf#page=267.

D'Alessio, Simona. 2008. "'Made in Italy': Integrazione Scolastica and the New Vision of Inclusive Education." In *Policy, Experience and Change: Cross-Cultural Reflections on Inclusive Education*, edited by Len Barton and Felicity Armstrong, 53–72. New York: Springer.

D'Alessio, Simona. 2011. *Inclusive Education in Italy.* Rotterdam, The Netherlands: Sense Publishers.

Delgado, Pedro Gabriel G. 2013. "Mental Health Reform in Brazil: Changing Hospital-Centered Paradigm to Ensure Access to Care." *SOUQuarderni* 8, Milan, November 2013. http://www.souqonline.it/home2_2_eng.asp?idpadre=955&idtesto=949#.Wf8MQYZrzUo.

Democratica, Società Italiana di Psichiatria. 2011. "Statuto". Accessed October 31, 2016. http://www.psichiatriademocratica.com/index.php?option=com_content&view=article&id=39&Itemid=165&lang=it.

Donnelly, Michael. 1992. *The Politics of Mental Health in Italy.* London: Tavistock/Routledge.

Eyal, Gil, Brendan Hart, Emine Onculer, Neta Oren, and Natasha Rossi. 2010. *The Autism Matrix.* Cambridge, UK: Polity Press.

Feinstein, Adam. 2010. *A History of Autism: Conversations with the Pioneers.* Chichester, UK: Wiley-Blackwell.

Fenton, Andrew, and Tim Krahn. 2007. "Autism, Neurodiversity and Equality Beyond The 'Normal'." *Journal of Ethics in Mental Health* 2 (2): 1–6.

Fiorani, Matteo. 2011. "Giovanni Bollea, 1913–2011: Per Una Storia Della Neuropsichiatria Infantile in Italia." *Medicina & Storia* 11 (21/22): 251–276.

Fonseca, Maria Elisa G. 2011. *Contextualizando a História da Educação dos Autistas no Brasil: Tendências, Funções e Dinâmicas da Estrutura dos Serviços nas APAEs.* Brasília: FENAPAE.

Gonçalves Mendes, Enicéia. 2010. "Breve histórico da educação especial no Brasil." *Revista Educación y Pedagogía* 22 (57): 93–109.

Goulart, Maria Stella B. 2007. *As Raízes Italianas do Movimento Antimanicomial.* São Paulo: Casa do Psicólogo.

Grossman, L., and P. Barrozo. 2007. "The Next Global Human Rights Issue: Why the Plight of Individuals with Autism Spectrum Disorders Requires a Global Call to Action." *Autism Advocate*, Fourth Edition.

Hanau, Carlo, and Daniela Mariani Cerati. 2005. "Scienze sperimentali e disabilità: Magiche illusioni contro la logica dei numeri." In *Autismo: che fare? Orientersi nella complessità dei trattenimenti e delle teorie*, edited by R. Cavagnola, P. Moderato, and M. Leoni, 60–76. Gussago, Brescia: Società Editrice Vannini a r.l.

Hart, Brendan. 2014. "Autism Parents & Neurodiversity: Radical Translation, Joint Embodiment and the Prosthetic Environment." *BioSocieties* 9 (3): 284–303.

Jones, Kathleen and Alison Poletti. 1986. "The 'Italian Experience' Reconsidered." *The British Journal of Psychiatry* 148 (2): 144–150.

Kapp, Steven K, Kristen Gillespie-Lynch, Lauren E. Sherman, and Ted Hutman. 2013. "Deficit, Difference, or Both? Autism and Neurodiversity." *Developmental Psychology* 49 (1): 59–71.

Lanna, Mário Cléber M., Jr., Comp. 2010. *História do Movimento Político das Pessoas com Deficiência no Brasil.* Brasília: Secretaria de Direitos Humanos/ Secretaria Nacional de Promoção dos Direitos da Pessoa com Deficiência.

Levi, Gabriel, and Paola Bernabei. 1997. "Italy." In *Handbook of Autism and Pervasive Developmental Disorders.* 2nd ed., edited by Donald J. Cohen and Fred R. Volkmar, 973–976. New York, NY: Wiley.

Lima, Rossano Cabral, Maria Cristina Ventura Couto, Pedro Gabriel Godinho Delgado, and Bruno Diniz Castro Oliveira. 2014. "Indicadores sobre o cuidado a crianças e adolescentes com autismo na rede de CAPSi da região metropolitana do Rio de Janeiro." *Physis Revista de Saúde Coletiva* 24 (3): 715–739.

Lobato, Lenaura, and Luciene Burlandy. 2000. "The Context and Process of Health Care Reform in Brazil." In *Reshaping Health Care in Latin America—A Comparative Analysis of Health Care Reform in Argentina, Brazil and Mexico*, edited by Sonia Fleury, Susana Belmartino, and Enis Baris, 79–102. Ottawa: International Development Research Centre.

Lo Scalzo, Alessandra, Andrea Donatini, Letizia Orzella, Americo Cicchetti, Silvia Profili, and Anna Maresso. 2009. "Italy: Health System Review." *Health Systems in Transition* II (6). Copenhagen, Denmark: World Health Organization on behalf of the European Observatory on Health Systems and Policies. http://www.euro.who.int/__data/assets/pdf_file/0006/87225/E93666.pdf.

Mello, Ana Maria, Helena Ho, Inês Dias, and Meca Andrade. 2013. "Retratos do autismo Brasil. Secretaria de Direitos Humanos da Presidência da República (SDH/PR)." https://www.autismo.org.br/site/images/Downloads/RetratoDoAutismo-20131001.pdf.

Micheli, Enrico. 2005. "La scelta dell'intervento. Confusioni, differenze e linee guide." In *Autismo: che fare? Orientarasi nella complessità dei trattimenti e delle teorie*, edited by R. Cavagnola, P. Moderato, and M. Leoni, 77–102. Gussago, Brescia: Società Editrice Vannini a r.l.

Migone, Paolo. 2014. "Storia Della Neuropsichiatria Infantile (prima Parte)." *Il Ruolo Terapeutico* 125: 55–70.

Mistura, Stefano, ed. 2006. *Autismo. L'umanità nascosta*. Turin: Einaudi.
Nardocci, Franco. 2009. "The Birth of Child and Adolescent Neuropsychiatry: From Rehabilitation and Social Inclusion of the Mentally Handicapped, to the Care of Mental Health During Development." *Annali dell'Istituto Superiore di Sanità* 45: 33–38.
Nunes, Fernanda. 2014. "Atuação Política de Grupos de Pais de Autistas no Rio de Janeiro - perspectivas para o campo da saúde." M.A. thesis, Universidade do Estado do Rio de Janeiro.
Orsini, Michael. 2009. "Contesting the Autistic Subject: Biological Citizenship and the Autism/Autistic Movement." In *Critical Interventions in the Ethics of Healthcare: Challenging the Principle of Autonomy in Bioethics*, edited by Stuart J. Murray and Dave Holmes, 115–130. Burlington, VT: Ashgate.
Ortega, Francisco. 2009a. "The Cerebral Subject and the Challenge of Neurodiversity." *BioSocieties* 4 (4): 425–445.
Ortega, Francisco. 2009b. "Deficiência, autismo e neurodiversidade." *Ciência & Saúde Coletiva* 14 (1): 67–77.
Rafante, Heulalia Caralo, and Roseli Esquerdo Lopes. 2008. "Helena Antipoff e a Fazenda do Rosário: a educação pelo trabalho de meninos 'excepcionais' na década de 1940." *Revista de Terapia Ocupacional da Universidade de São Paulo* 19 (3): 144–152, set./dez.
Ribeiro, Paulo Rennes Marçal. 2006. "História da Saúde Mental Infantil – a criança brasileira da colônia à República Velha." *Psicologia em Estudo, Maringá* 11 (1): 29–38, jan/abr.
Rios, Clarice, and Bárbara Costa Andrada. 2015. "The Changing Face of Autism in Brazil." *Culture, Medicine and Psychiatry* 39 (2): 213–234.
Rios, Clarice, and Bárbara Costa Andrada. 2016. "Shifting Notions of Disability in Brazil." *Tizard Learning Disability Review* 21 (2): 75–79.
Rizzini, Irene, ed. 2008. *Do Confinamento ao Acolhimento: institucionalização de crianças e adolescentes com deficiência - desafios e caminhos*. Relatório de Pesquisa. Rio de Janeiro: CIESPI.
Rotelli, Franco. 1993. "8+8 Principi: Per Una Strategia Di Psichiatria Comunitaria, Collettiva, Territoriale (Versus Salute Mentale)." Electronic Document, Accessed November 27, 2017. http://www.triestesalutementale.it/letteratura/testi/13principi.htm.
Rotelli Franco, and Paulo Amarante. 1992. "Reformas psiquiátricas na Itália e no Brasil: aspectos históricos e metodológicos." In *Psiquiatria sem hospício: contribuições ao estudo da reforma psiquiátrica*, edited by Benilton Bezerra Jr., and Paulo Amarante, 41–55. Rio de Janeiro: Relume-Dumará.
Russo, Concetta, Michele Capararo, and Enrico Valtellina. 2014. *A sé e agli altri. Storia della manicomializzazione dell'autismo e delle altre disabilità relazionali nelle cartelle cliniche di S. Servolo*. Milano etc.: Mimesis.
Russo, Jane. 1997. "Os três sujeitos da Psiquiatria." *Cadernos IPUB* 8: 11–21.

Scheper-Hughes, Nancy, and Anne M. Lovell. 1986. "Breaking the Circuit of Social Control—Lessons in Public Psychiatry from Italy and Franco Basaglia." *Social Science and Medicine* 23 (2): 159–178.

Silverman, Chloe. 2011. *Understanding Autism: Parents, Doctors, and the History of a Disorder*. Princeton: Princeton University Press.

Sistema Nazionale per le Linee Guida-Istituto Superiore di Sanità. 2011. *Il trattamento dei disturbi dello spettro autistico nei bambini e negli adolescenti*. Linea Guida 21. Roma, Italy: Istituto Superiore di Sanità.

Sistema Nazionale per le Linee Guida-Istituto Superiore di Sanità. 2012. "Autismo: Quale Trattamento per Bambini E Adolescenti?" Accessible at http://www.salute.gov.it/imgs/C_17_opuscoliPoster_231_allegato.pdf.

Società Italiana di Psicologia. 2002. "Storia della S.I.P.S." Accessed September 4, 2017. http://www.sips.it/sito-vecchio/index.html?includi=storia.

Società Italiana per i Disturbi del Neurosviluppo. n.d. "SIDiN SIRM." Accessed October 31, 2016. http://www.sidin.info/.

Società Italiana Di Psichiatria. n.d. "Storia." Accessed January 19, 2015. http://www.psichiatria.it/chi-siamo/storia.

Vivanti, Giacomo. 2006. *Disabili, Famiglie E Operatori: Chi È Il Paziente Difficile? Strategie per Costruire Rapporti Collaborativi Nell'autismo E Nelle Disabilità Dello Sviluppo*. Gussago (Brescia): Vannini.

Wille, Anne-Marie. 1992. *Il ragazzo nella nebbia*. Bologna: Edizioni Scientifiche CSIFRA.

Wille, Anne-Marie. 2001. *Il gigante silenzioso. Cinque casi clinici in terapia psicomotoria*. Armando Editore.

Wille, Anne-Marie. 2012. *L'inerzia decisionale. La terapia psicomotoria con persone senza iniziativa motoria e con grave ritardo mentale*. Napoli: Cuzzolin.

World Health Organization Working Group on Changing Patterns in Mental Health. 1980. *Changing Patterns in Mental Health Care: Report on a WHO Working Group*. Cologne: World Health Organization. 27 November.

Yasui, Silvio. 2010. *Rupturas e Encontros: desafios da Reforma Psiquiátrica brasileira*. Rio de Janeiro: Editora FIOCRUZ.

CHAPTER 4

Commentary: "Why Not Both?" Negotiating Ideas About Autism in Italy, Brazil, and the US

Francisco Ortega

4.1 Introduction: Autism and Global Mental Health

Autism has recently become a major global mental health (GMH) priority. In 2008 *Autism Speaks* launched the Global Autism Public Health Initiative (GAPH) to enable the development of systematic and sustainable solutions for enhancing awareness, research, training, and service delivery for autism spectrum disorder (ASD) globally. According to GAPH, the 'global burden of disease' attributed to ASD is greater than to several other conditions such as ADHD and intellectual disability.[1] Specifically, in the developing countries, individuals with autism and their families are more vulnerable due to poverty, malnutrition, violence, stigma, and scarcity of services (Rosanoff et al. 2015). Although researchers estimate a global prevalence of ASD of approximately one percent of the population, the condition gets undetected and individuals go without treatment in larger parts of the world. Limited expertise

F. Ortega (✉)
Institute for Social Medicine, State University of Rio de Janeiro, Rio de Janeiro, Brazil

E. Fein and C. Rios (eds.), *Autism in Translation*, Culture, Mind, and Society, https://doi.org/10.1007/978-3-319-93293-4_4

and treatments challenge early detection and intervention for ASD (Wallace et al. 2012). Therefore, the GMH agenda for ASD aims to generate cross-national evidence on prevalence, treatment services, and human resources. Moreover, it claims that the global challenge of autism involves developing culturally appropriate and comparable diagnostic instruments as well as affordable care packages to be used by community health workers (Khan et al. 2012).

GMH initiatives for autism recognize alternative, community-based and culturally sensitive approaches from low- to middle-income countries (LMIC) and reject "one-size-fits-all" approaches for ASD research and interventions. And yet, an editorial in *Autism Research* on Autism and the Grand Challenges in GMH is cautious of "approaches already dismissed by research" (ibid.) such as psychoanalysis, which are still in use in several countries. There is an important tension here between, on the one hand, the need for culturally sensitive and community-based approaches to ASD, and on the other, the dismissal of those approaches when they fail to match the standards of evidence-based practices and interventions. In some countries like Brazil, psychoanalysis constitutes a widely used methodology for ASD within community mental health services. Moreover, as several critics have pointed out, despite GMH's claims that their proposals are "evidence-based," "most of them are highly speculative, bordering sometimes on what psychiatrists themselves like to call 'magical thinking'" (Ingleby 2014, 222), and they exaggerate the benefits of the interventions, thereby promoting the interests of the pharmaceutical industry.

These tensions around culturally sensitive approaches to ASD and GMH claims to 'scale up' and generalize those interventions are evoked in Chapters 2 and 3 commented on in this chapter. By providing a range of views on autism theory and practice, policies relating to autism, and options for treatments in the United States, Italy, and Brazil, these pieces offer insightful perspectives on how global issues and controversies around ASD take local form. The controversies they depict play out across global and local spaces and epistemologies. While the global and the local are often conceptualized as discrete spheres, moving beyond the global/local divide has resulted in rich theorization in anthropology, as in Escobar's notion of "glocality" (2001), Tsing's concept of "friction" (2005) and Ong's notion of "global assemblages" (Collier and Ong 2005), as alternative frameworks. Analyzing the controversies as global assemblages "emphasizes their heterogeneity and perpetual movement and traces their limitations through 'technical infrastructures, administrative apparatuses, and value regimes'" (Bemme and D'souza 2014, 853).

In this chapter I argue that the notorious polarizations around autism might hide important negotiations and spaces beyond such antagonism. Examining systems of care delivery for individuals living with autism in their historical and social context enables us to see how binaries and polarizations (global/local, organicism/anti-organicsm, biological/relational, mental suffering/disability) are challenged and transcended through the pragmatic negotiation and integration of those binaries in the everyday work of those affected by autism, whether that be CAPSi (Centers for Psychosocial Attention for Children and Youth) professionals in Brazil understanding the condition as a disability 'for legal purposes,' parents negotiating etiological conceptions and getting services from multiple sites, or neurodiversity activists arguing for non-individualist cerebral subjects.[2]

4.2 Autism as "Problematic Category"

Controversies around autism's etiology, treatments and polices emerge at least in part because autism constitutes a psychiatric category exposed to public negotiation by medical and non-medical actors. The ontological status of autism, a "problematic category" (Rosenberg 2006), is in ongoing dispute. For some people it is a form of mental suffering, a mental disorder, a brain disease, an intellectual/relational disability or a different way of being based on the brain's natural diversity. Through negotiations of the existence of autism (and other such nosological entities) as social facts, a certain amount of power is gained and lost by individuals affected by the diagnosis (Ortega and Choudhury 2011). The debate surrounding the condition extends out to other public spheres, involving activists (parents and caregivers of autistic children), lawyers, and virtual social networks. Autism is in this sense a "contested illness" (Brown et al. 2011). In the absence of lesions or of a biological root and in the face of uncertainty regarding etiology[3] and the best form of care, status and treatment remain open fields of dispute. These clinical conditions are immersed within debates about their legitimacy and medical, social, epistemic, and ontological status. They generate legal arguments, administrative categorizations, and legislative maneuvers. Those who bear these illnesses and their caregivers thus often become activists, mobilizing facts in favor of the condition's legitimacy and forming groups through which they share their experiences and fight for rights (Ortega et al. 2016).

Controversies around appropriate treatments, service organization, and allocation of resources are often depicted as a conflict between evidence-based, standardizable treatments and interventions designed in developed countries versus alternative, locally developed approaches from developing countries. However, reducing the issues at stake in this way conceals as much as it reveals, occluding the possibility of alternative frameworks and the complexity of conditions on the ground. In the United States, for instance, there is little consensus concerning the appropriate treatments and policies for ASD. Professionals, parents, and self-advocates disagree not only on the appropriate treatments or the best way to allocate resources (on biomedical interventions or on social support initiatives, and the relative amount allocated to each of them), but on whether autism is a disorder to be treated and, if possible, cured, or rather a human specificity (like sex or race) that must be equally respected. In Brazil debates revolve around conceptions of autism as 'disability' or as 'mental suffering' and their implications in policies and services organizations.

The two chapters offer a historically informed and ethnographically grounded account of how such issues are experienced, negotiated, and lived in the United States, Italy, and Brazil. The use of an ethnographic approach enables "careful attention to the effects of the specific contexts within which interventions are embedded; simultaneous awareness of how practices in a particular time and place are connected to larger economic, political, and historical force; and close focus on the experiential dimensions of the clinical encounter" (Jain and Orr 2016, 688). The local and historical particularities of the three national contexts alongside the everyday practice of mental health professionals make the abstract, globally circulating ideas meaningful in particular forms. Moreover, they illustrate how the same outlooks on treatments, interventions, service organization, and mental health policies may be beneficial in some contexts and damaging in others. Responding to these conditions involves more than the adaptation of evidence-based practices to different local realities. It requires the production of "locally relevant evidence" to subsidize "best practices and intervention strategies" (Kienzler and Locke 2017, 293) taking into account "contextually situated experience" (White et al. 2017, 18).

Both chapters display complementary views on the public policies and debates around autism in three countries: Italy, Brazil, and the United States. They put forward a very rich and interesting view on the history of psychiatric deinstitutionalization of autistic individuals as well as on the constitution of policies for autism, autism advocacy, and public and ideological debates around conceptions and treatments. Two of the countries, Italy and Brazil, have a similar tradition of psychiatric reform (PR) and deinstitutionalization. In fact, Brazil psychiatric reform follows the Italian model of PR. Unlike these two countries, in which clinical and mental health agendas largely go hand in hand, public mental health care in the United States conforms to a biomedical model and promotes biomedical and pharmacological treatments for mental complaints. The National Institute for Mental Health (NIMH) foregrounds a clinical agenda, frequently in conflict with advocacy and activist movements' emphasis on social inclusion and citizenship rights for individuals with autism. In each of these settings, we see how conflicts and controversies arise between different biopolitical structures, each with their own set of histories that inform the conceptual frameworks upon which their interventions are grounded. Perhaps more significantly, though, we also gain insight into how we might transcend the terms of these conflicts, instead of continuing to be limited by their dictates.

4.3 Mobilizing Diagnostic Categories to Pragmatic Ends

The main insight from both chapters is the need to move beyond dichotomies and polarizations. Embracing a historically informed view of autism politics on the ground helps to transcend those dichotomies and polarizations and, as Cascio et al. (in this volume) observe, can "open [...] up the space for the recognition of common ground and, perhaps, integration" (p. 77). Both chapters focalize on the local and historical context in which scientific ideas about autism are mobilized, to show that they are not "*inherently* helpful or harmful," but are "*rendered* helpful or harmful in social context" (ibid.). What we see from approaching the autism landscape in the three countries is a pragmatic attitude regarding diagnostic categories, etiology, services, treatments and policies which are negotiated by different actors (medical and non-medical) inside and outside health services. This pragmatic attitude serves to shift the terms of autism debates, taking conceptual binaries and reorganizing, challenging, or integrating them within the everyday practices of the different actors involved: parents, mental health professionals, and individuals living with autism.

Through these pieces, however, we also see how polarizations endure by serving social, political, and personal purposes. Defining what autism *is* in opposition to what it *is not* is frequently a means of advocating for the allocation of particular resources (and sometimes, as a means of rejecting others). In Brazil there is a battle over autism at the level of public mental health discourses and policies, opposing two understandings of autism as 'mental suffering' or as 'disability.' The first view is advanced by the mental health network and resists diagnosis and specific services for autistic individuals. Parent associations champion autism as disability and favor diagnosis-specific services and evidence-based treatments, in the process taking a stand against psychoanalysis. In Italy, where Basaglia and his colleagues largely rejected psychoanalysis, parent associations largely favor deinstitutionalization and community mental health care. Conversely, the highly influential role of psychoanalysis in the Brazilian psychiatric reform and in the organizations of post-reform mental health services is definitely one of the main reasons for the distrust of anti-asylum and community care models often seen among autism parents' movements. In the face of what they called "a series of actions aiming to disqualify psychoanalytic approaches to treat persons with autism," many members of the Brazilian psychoanalytic community insist on the rhetoric of "war" (McGuire 2016), further entrenching a polarized rhetoric. Thus, Luciano Elia, a Lacanian psychoanalyst and professor of psychology at the State University of Rio de Janeiro, believes that "so far only psychoanalysis has proved to be effective. [...] in making important developments in autism care and research" (Elia 2013). He labels behavioral psychologists as "pseudoscientists," who have success with the "managers of the technocratic right wing and of compulsory institutionalization," and with the middle classes that "crave for a hygienist and fascistoid social order" (Elia 2013, cited in Ortega et al. 2016, 49). Taking such explicitly adversarial stances can thus both bolster calls for intervention, and also protect against forms of intervention considered to be oppressive.

In autism debates in the US, polarizations also serve a purpose. Autistic identity politics draw on neurology to justify and naturalize differences between autistics and neurotypicals, de-emphasizing intragroup differences and in doing so, boosting polarized, dichotomous rhetoric. Emphasizing commonality within the spectrum of autism[4] constitutes an important political move that would counter the critiques of several parent and professional groups, who accuse them of speaking in the name of all autistics (Ortega 2013). In many such cases, we can observe how controversies over autism as a contested category actually function to stabilize it.

Still, polarizations have an important epistemic, emotional, political, and economic cost. The polarization between many parents and professionals (who frequently use an aggressive rhetoric, McGuire 2016) and neurodiversity advocates in the United States obstructs meaningful dialogue around the best way to provide for the needs of people living with autism and their families. In Brazil, the antagonistic understandings hamper serious discussions and cooperation between mental health professionals and parent associations; what is worse, it divides already scarce resources, which are designated for the same public, between two different networks (mental health and disability) with almost no interaction.[5]

Of course, not all parent associations in Brazil are against CAPSi, and, what is more important, despite the discourses against diagnosis and specific services, CAPSi gather children together with practical purposes according to criteria of "the children's profile" which in practice frequently leads to diagnostically homogeneous groups and activities (Cascio et al., in this volume). In this sense, parents in Brazil display a pragmatic attitude when they adopt specialized services (a mother refers to the comfort of having all professionals in the same place) or embrace both types of services (mental health and disability) in contexts of extreme social vulnerability. "Why not both?" asks a mother in Costa Andrada's ethnography of autism services in Rio de Janeiro (Costa Andrada 2017, 124). They don't seem to worry too much about whether autism is a mental disorder, a neurobiological disease or an intellectual disability. Etiologic conceptions and public health services are mobilized according to their specific needs.

Parents also exhibit a pragmatic attitude when they ask CAPSi professionals for medical reports and diagnosis in order to get the disability compensation to which they are entitled under the new Autism Law. "I think you have to be careful, yes. You have to do something else before you give the diagnosis, but I also think the team takes too long," declares a CAPSi professional interviewed by Souza Lima (2017, 94). And he adds:

> parents talked a lot about it: "I understand that you do not want to label, but the world requires the labeling. For you to enter a school you need an *ICD*[6] diagnosis. If you do not take the *ICD*, the school will not accept it." So, well, they need it. You cannot be there for a year and keep saying "we do not want to label your child." Okay, you have to be careful, but you have to understand that the school is asking for such things. (ibid.)

We see here that the acceptance of labels with pragmatic ends does not involve any epistemological, ontological, and/or etiological commitment to the 'true' nature of autism. Professionals in Brazil would be well served to keep this in mind, recognizing that medical reports alongside an autism diagnosis are a parent's right (not to mention that most of the parents live in conditions of extreme social vulnerability, frequently residing far away from the CAPSi and with no or very little money for public transportation). The recent 'Autism Law,' a source of so much division in Brazilian autism communities, could be productively seen in that pragmatic spirit as well. The second article of the law determines that "the person with an autism spectrum disorder is considered as a person with disability *for all legal purposes* [emphasis added]" (Brasil 2012). To be precise, what it is essential in the law is that ASD is considered a disability, rather than a mental disorder, "for all legal purposes." Again, it is not about an ontological or epistemological commitment to autism's real nature (in this case, a disability), but a pragmatic understanding of the condition as disability, as a way to "pursue the right to health through alternative channels. [...] adopting an increasingly global discourse of disability rights to marshal new resources for care" (Lima et al., in this volume).

CAPSi professionals could benefit if they adopt this pragmatic attitude as well. At times they do, as when they arrange activities and groups to fit children's profiles of ability and developmental levels. Actually, some professionals welcome the notion of "disability for legal purposes" to get social and educational inclusion among other benefits, as focus groups with CAPSi professionals in Rio de Janeiro illustrate (Souza Lima 2017). However, ontological stances run deep, sometimes contributing to the obduracy of conflicts even between groups committed to an integrative approach. For example, as a recent ethnography with mental health professionals at CAPSis in Rio de Janeiro evinces, even professionals who are not psychoanalysts draw on psychoanalytic terms to describe their work. Or, even more bluntly, some professionals criticize the psychoanalytic discourse that blame the parents, while at the same time they largely draw on that discourse to interpret clinical cases (Feldman 2017). Psychoanalytic approaches thus continue to be extremely prevalent even in settings and among practitioners committed to eclecticism and integration.

In the case of the United States there is at first sight a clash between, on the one hand, autism advocacy professionals which advance a 'militarist' and pro-cure rhetoric and a cultural logic of war together with claims for biomedical interventions, frequently resulting in acts of violence and discrimination against autistic people; and on the other hand, neurodiversity activists opposing genetic and genomic research and biomedical treatments for autism, claiming instead the acceptance and accommodation of autistic individuals (McGuire 2016). However, when we move beyond that polarization ('for' or 'against' autism), we begin to see nuances, chiaroscuros and pragmatic negotiations and integrations that challenge and transcend those divides and tensions. In fact, neither all parents oppose self-advocacy movements, nor do all autistic adults take stances associated with the neurodiversity movement. Some activist parents support neurodiversity and run autism acceptance projects, such as the ASPIE school in New York mentioned in Lima et al. in this volume. Conversely, some self-advocates display a pragmatic attitude toward medical interventions that does not fit neatly within the neurodiversity paradigm. The latter sometimes find it difficult to combine their identities as autistics within the autistic communities, and their identities within the neurotypical world, and this tension can become an important source of anxiety and suffering (Bagatell 2007). In addition, some autistic adults do want to be cured. Sue Rubin, a low-functioning autistic and subject of the documentary *Autism is a World*, claims that whereas high-functioning autistics tend to be against a cure, low-functioning autistics generally hold the opposite position. "As a person with low-functioning autism that is still really awash in autism, I actually am aligned with the cure group," she states, and "the thought of a gold pot of a potion with a cure really would be wonderful" (Rubin 2005; Ortega 2009). Unfortunately, this nuanced landscape is effaced through rhetoric emerging from the neurodiversity movement that tends to homogenize neurodiverse brains and minimize their differences so as to support their claims for the existence of a brain-based autistic identity. Thus, the 'autistic brain' is displayed as ontologically homogeneous and radically different from the also homogeneous NT (neurotypical) brain (Ortega 2013).

Rather than digging into the rhetoric of war and oppositions, it is more productive to investigate carefully the multiple ways different actors engage with autism according to "the position from which they stand and the types of claims they seek to gain" (Singh 2016, 12). In the case of genetic/genomic autism research Jennifer Singh deconstructs genetics and citizenship as "fantasies" of, respectively, a single gene and a single subjectivity. Her insightful examination of the experiences of several adults living with autism evinces, as expected, that those adults displayed a much more ambivalent and less optimistic view on the potential uses of genomic science (which they consider of little value for people living with autism) than the biosocial communities formed by families that either lobbied, raised funds, or influenced research agendas or participated in genetic/genomic research. And yet, although they oppose the idea of erasing autism through genetic technologies, adults living with autism also displayed ambivalence regarding the value of genetic knowledge. A father said he would accept a genetic test if it would lead to the development of medication for the undesired symptoms of Asperger's; and another individual living with Asperger thinks that the identification of a gene for the condition "would have an important role in explaining what made him a person" (Singh 2016, 168). Individuals living with autism do not have just one univocal view of autism genomic research and its implications; they display different attitudes regarding their personal experience, identity negotiations, and advocacy.

In Italy, as well as in Brazil and the United States, parents and professionals pragmatically negotiate ideas about autism for different political and clinical agendas, sometimes doing so in ways that complicate what on the surface look like entrenched ideological oppositions. Despite the shared rejection of psychogenic theories of autism as derived from poor parenting, parents accept some elements of psychodynamic theory associated with relational approaches. And, unlike Brazil, where psychoanalytic and behavioral approaches are opposed, there is in Italy a blending of cognitive and behavioral methodologies with relational approaches that incorporate psychodynamic theories. Additionally, the understanding of autism as both biological and relational, rooted in organic causes but also as a different way of being shared by parents and professionals, helps to transcend disputes between these stances. The comprehension of autism as a biological condition removes the blame from the parents while preserving the relational dimension. Moreover, the idea of autism as a different way of being does not only serve to substantiate the social model of disability and ideas of neurological difference or neurodiversity. It also boosts the call for autism-specific services and the medical model of disability (Cascio et al., in this volume).

4.4 Beyond the Organicism/Anti-organicism Divide

The local and historical context of the three countries examined in the two chapters, Italy, Brazil, and the United States, challenges the assumption that ideas of autism as social/relational or as organic/biological necessarily imply specific public policies and treatments according to each view. Those views are mobilized within different political and clinical agendas according to diverse sociopolitical contexts. The actors in these accounts display a pragmatic attitude regarding ontological and epistemological commitments. They mobilize different etiological and ontological positions according to their utility to pursue the right to health and citizenship.

In Italy and Brazil, autism associations advocate for an organicist view of autism (a brain or neurobiological disorder which is diagnostically specific) that radically opposes the anti-organicist and anti-diagnostic stances of their respective psychiatric reforms. Psychiatric reforms emerged as a radical critique to the organicist view; in the present day, organicist views are taken up with the same aim as PR's original anti-organicist stance, that is, the social, political, and educational inclusion of individuals with autism. Despite the different views around autism ('mental suffering' or 'disability') in Brazil, both professionals at CAPSi and parent associations advance a discourse of citizenship, albeit from opposite premises. While parents embrace an organicist view—autism as an identity marker—professionals reject identity politics, and champion an anti-organicist stance embodied in the notion of 'citizens burdened by mental suffering.' Still, both groups largely share basic assumptions of the social model of disability (Rios and Costa Andrada 2015).

Similarly, the idea of neurodiversity aligns with social constructionism and the social model of disability, while simultaneously presupposing real biological (and neurological) bodies, thus complicating the idea that social constructionist and biological understandings of autism are necessarily incompatible. Organicist views are widely shared by parents, scientists, professionals and self-advocates (neurodiversity activists) in the United States. Unlike autism organizations that claim that autism is a neurological disorder, however, neurodiversity advocates affirm instead that it is a neurological difference. Disorder or difference, the neurological 'reality' of autism remains unquestioned. Yet social meaning still matters; despite widely shared organicist stances, there is very little consensus in the US not only regarding treatments, resources allocation, and services organization, but also regarding the nature of the condition itself: whether autism is a terrible threat, an adversary to be fought or a natural human variation to be respected and even celebrated (McGuire 2016). Similarly, in Italy, the organicist view mobilized by autism associations does not correspond to the organicism of psychiatric institutionalization, but it is associated with the notion of 'autism-as-difference,' a different 'way of life,' or of being. Autism is organic or cerebral, and, simultaneously a different way of being, a different life-form. One may say that this constitutes an illustration of social constructionism substantiating a physicalist view, not just of mental disorders, but of personhood.

The Italian view of autism as cerebral and, at the same time, as a way of being alludes to the discourse of neurodiversity (although, as Cascio, Costa Andrada, and Bezerra Jr., observe in their chapter, this discourse is still very incipient in Italy). Neurodiversity self-advocates' appeal for a "neurological self-awareness" (Singer 1999) allows them to bypass the medical establishment, and provides a substitute to psychoanalytic explanations that are considered unhelpful and even dangerous (Nadesan 2005). One function of embracing the vocabulary of the brain, therefore, is to remove the stigmatizing weight of psychotherapeutic discourses on autism. Turning to the brain-based explanation as an alternative, however, does not lead to the adoption of the deficit model underlying the neurocognitive theories such as 'mindblindness,' 'weak central coherence,' or 'executive dysfunction.' Rather, many autistic self-advocates draw on these theories involving the brain (often imprecisely) to substantiate the notion of a natural difference instead of an evidence for pathology. These individuals embrace the neurobiological explanations of autism, but separate this from the concept of disease, instead associating the neuroscientific basis with a celebrated identity (Ortega 2009).

Interestingly, the case of the autistic self-advocates also challenges the notion that a neuroscientific basis for self-understanding—in this situation, even a brain-based theory that defines individuals as a- or un-social—is necessarily associated with a kind of identity that is alienating or individualizing. Rather, the very acceptance of the neurobiologization of autism is among this group of people the basis for a form of social community of advocates who participate in meetings, discussions, and political formations with the common goal of resisting pathologization. This suggests an alternative to the frequently voiced assumption that neuroscientific explanations go hand in hand with atomized or isolated ways of being. However, it is worth asking if, even though seeing oneself as a "cerebral subject" (Vidal and Ortega 2017) bolsters one's sense of identity and helps erase the social stigma often associated with mental pathology, whether, on the other hand, it somewhat solipsistically narrows the notion of what it is to be a person (Ortega and Choudhury 2011).

Similarly, in Italy ideas about autism as fundamentally organic or as fundamentally social/relational get mobilized differently according to the particular social and political contexts, and get evoked to substantiate multiple types of claims. As in the case of neurodiversity activists in the United States, organicity and sociality are not opposed. The pragmatic integration of sociality and organicity in the same view of autism transcends the dichotomies and polarizations that opposed Italian parents and professionals. They all favor a biological etiology for autism that does not result in reductionist or solipsistic forms of personhood. The biologization or cerebralization of the condition is instead associated to a view of autism as a 'way of being,' a "state of being or functioning, an aspect of the human condition, a different perception of the world around the person, and even another culture" (Cascio et al., in this volume).

4.5 Conclusion

Chapters 2 and 3 offer illustrations of the ways scientific ideas about autism are differently evoked in the three countries for different political and clinical ends. It is precisely the local and historical context and the everyday practice of professionals, families, and individuals living with the condition that render those ideas meaningful. They are not true or false, harmful or helpful in themselves, but are pragmatically negotiated and integrated by clinicians and other mental health professionals, parent associations, and self-advocates in their struggle for better treatments, social and educational inclusion, and other rights. Taking an empirically, ethnographically grounded, and historically informed approach, the two chapters help to understand why the same views on etiology, treatment, service organization, and even personhood have contradictory ends and are rendered harmful or helpful in a given social context. And vice versa, opposing views on etiology, treatment and service organizations, and public policies may underlie the same practical ends. Such an approach offers the potential to move beyond dichotomies and polarizations, which may seem definitive from a distance but which are not so definite when examined through the everyday life and practice of the individuals who are most immediately affected by autism. In addressing the ways in which international discourses get taken up for pragmatic purposes in particular social, political, and historical contexts, these pieces also transcend presupposed divisions between the global and the local. In doing so, these pieces open up possibilities for reconsidering some of the most contested issues in global mental health.

Notes

1. Terms such as Global Burden of Disease (GBD) or disability-adjusted life year (DALY), introduced by WHO in the 1990s and still in use, have undergone harsh criticism from a range of disciplines, from economics, anthropology to global health and disability studies. From an economic point of view, DALYs and GBD would fail to account for the differentials in resource availability. Given that GBD and DALYs are based in measurements from wealthy countries, the differential existing between these populations and those of developing countries measures both burden of disease and underdevelopment. The stronger criticism is advanced by disability scholars, who argue that those metrics devalue the life of disabled individuals and claim that their life should be valued equal to those without disabilities (Anand and Hanson 1997; Becker et al. 2013; Parks 2014; Wikler 2010).
2. I am grateful to the organizers of this volume, Elizabeth Fein and Clarice Rios for the insightful comments on the previous version of this chapter.
3. Psychiatrists, psychologists and neuroscientists primarily describe autism as a neurobiological disorder. Within this tradition there have been a number of cognitive theories proposed since the late 1980s, such as weak central coherence (Frith and Happé 1994), executive dysfunction (Ozonoff et al. 1991), a theory of 'mindblindness' (Baron-Cohen 1995) and a neurophysiological theory of mirror neuron dysfunction (Williams et al. 2001). Lord and Jones note that while there has been great hope for both structural and functional neuroimaging findings, "these approaches seldom provide data on an individual level, do not yet have well-accepted standards or replicability across time or site [...] and have rarely addressed questions of specificity of findings to ASD" (2012, 491). Neither is there consensus

about the methodology to be used in clinical interventions (Feinberg and Vacca 2000; Newschaffer and Curran 2003). In other words, and despite considerable amounts of research, there is still no convincing, well-replicated brain-based autism biomarker with clinical utility (Anderson 2015; Singh 2016; Walsh et al. 2011). However, as Chloe Silverman notes, "although researchers have had trouble finding localized structural changes, autism has retained its identity as a genetic disorder of the brain" (2012, 155). Furthermore, despite the lack of consensus and difficulty in finding brain-based explanations that fully account for autism, the research continues to look for them (O'Dell et al. 2016; Singh 2016).

4. Although autism is considered a spectrum, some self-activists reject the distinction between 'low' and 'high-functioning' autism, and consider differences across autistic populations asvariations of degree not due to fundamental "underlying neurological differences" (Nadesan 2005, 208–209).
5. Focus groups with CAPSi professionals in Rio de Janeiro evinced that the majority of professionals did not know the treatments offered at the specialized centers for autistic individuals associated to the Office of Health Care of People with Disabilities (Souza Lima 2017).
6. *ICD* refers to WHO's *International Classification of Diseases* which is currently in its tenth edition, *ICD-10*.

References

Anand, Sudhir, and Kara Hanson. 1997. "Disability Adjusted Life Years: A Critical Perspective." *Journal of Health Economics* 16: 685–702.

Anderson, George M. 2015. "Autism Biomarkers: Challenges, Pitfalls, and Possibilities." *Journal of Autism and Developmental Disorders* 45 (4): 1103–1113.

Bagatell, Nancy. 2007. "Orchestrating Voices: Autism, Identity, and the Power of Discourse." *Disability & Society* 22: 413–426.

Baron-Cohen, Simon. 1995. *Mindblindness: An Essay on Autism and Theory of Mind*. Cambridge, MA: MIT Press and Bradford Books.

Becker, Anne, Anjali Motgi, Jonathan Weigel, Guiseppe Raviola, Salmaan Keshavjee, and Arthur Kleinman. 2013. "The Unique Challenges of Mental Health and MDRTB: Critical Perspectives on Metrics of Disease Burden." In *Reimagining Global Health: An Introduction*, edited by Paul Farmer, Jim Yong Kim, Arthur Kleinman, and Matthew Basilico, 209–241. Berkeley: University of California Press.

Bemme, Doerte, and Nicole A. D'souza. 2014. "Global Mental Health and Its Discontents: An Inquiry into the Making of Global and Local Scale." *Transcultural Psychiatry* 51 (6): 850–874.

Brasil. 2012. Lei n8 12.764, de 27 de dezembro de 2012, Institui a política nacional de proteção dos direitos da pessoa com transtorno do espectro autista e altera o §38 do art. 98 da Lei n8 8.112, de 11 de dezembro de 1990. Brasília: Diário Oficial da União, 27 de dezembro de 2012.

Brown, Phil, Rachel Morello-Frosch, and Stephen Zavestoski, eds. 2011. *Contested Illnesses: Citizens, Science, and Health Social Movements*. Berkeley: University of California Press.

Collier, Stephen J., and Aihwa Ong. 2005. "Global Assemblages, Anthropological Problems." In *Global assemblages: Technology, Politics, and Ethics as Anthropological Problems*, edited by Stephen Collier and Aihwa Ong, 3–21. Malden, MA: Wiley-Blackwell.

Costa Andrada, Barbara. 2017. "Sentidos e desafios do autism para o território: um estudo etnográfico." PhD thesis, State University of Rio de Janeiro.

Elia, Luciano. 2013. "Psicanalise, ciencia e universidade." In *Psicanalise, autismo e saúde pública*. Available at http://psicanaliseautismoesaudepublica.wordpress.com/2013/04/14/psicanalise-ciencia-e-universidade. Accessed on 6 November 2015.

Escobar, Arturo. 2001. "Culture Sits in Places: Reflections on Globalism and Subaltern Strategies of Localization." *Political Geography* 20 (2): 139–174.

Feinberg, Edward, and John Vacca. 2000. "The Drama and Trauma of Creating Policies on Autism: Critical Issues to Consider in the New Millennium." *Focus on Autism and Other Developmental Disabilities* 15 (3): 130–137.

Feldman, Clara. 2017. "Autismo e rede de atenção psicossocial: Caminhos e desafios de uma rede em construção." PhD dissertation, State University of Rio de Janeiro.

Frith, Uta, and Francesca Happé. 1994. "Autism: Beyond 'Theory of Mind.'" *Cognition* 50 (1–3): 115–132.

Ingleby, David. 2014. "How 'Evidence-Based' Is the Movement for Global Mental Health?" *Disability and the Global South* 1 (2): 203–226.

Jain, Sumeet, and David M.R. Orr 2016. "Ethnographic Perspectives on Global Mental Health." *Transcultural Psychiatry* 53 (6): 685–695.

Khan, Naila Z., Lilia Albores Gallo, Aurora Arghir, Bogdan Budisteanu, Magdalena Budisteanu, Iuliana Dobrescu, Kirsty Donald, et al. 2012. "Autism and the Grand Challenges in Global Mental Health." *Autism Research* 5: 156–159.

Kienzler, Hanna, and Peter Locke. 2017. "The Effects of Societal Violence in War and Post-war Contexts." In *The Palgrave Handbook of Sociocultural Perspectives on Global Mental Health*, edited by Ross G. White, Sumeet Jain, David M.R. Orr, and Ursula M. Read, 285–305. London: Palgrave Macmillan.

Lord, and Jones. 2012. "Annual Research Review: Re-thinking the Classification of Autism Spectrum Disorders." *Journal of Child Psychology and Psychiatry* 53: 490–509.

McGuire, Anne. 2016. *War on Autism. On the Cultural Logic of Normative Violence*. Ann Arbor: University of Michigan Press.

Nadesan, Majia Holmer. 2005. *Constructing Autism: Unravelling the 'Truth' and Understanding the Social.* London and New York: Routledge.

Newschaffer, Craig J., and Laura Kresch Curran. 2003. "Autism: An Emerging Public Health Problem." *Public Health Reports* 118 (5): 393–399.

O'Dell, Lindsay, Hanna Bertilsdotter Rosqvist, Francisco Ortega, Charlotte Brownlow, and Michael Orsini. 2016. "Critical Autism Studies: Exploring Epistemic Dialogues and Intersections, Challenging Dominant Understandings of Autism." *Disability & Society* 31 (2): 166–179.

Ortega, Francisco. 2009. "The Cerebral Subject and the Challenge of Neurodiversity." *Biosocieties* 4 (4): 425–445.

———. 2013. "Cerebralizing Autism Within the Neurodiversity Movement." In *Worlds of Autism: Across the Spectrum of Neurological Difference*, edited by Joyce Davidson and Michael Orsini, 73–95. Minneapolis: University of Minnesota Press.

Ortega, Francisco, and Suparna Choudhury. 2011. "'Wired Up Differently': Autism, Adolescence, and the Politics of Neurological Identities." *Subjectivity* 4 (3): 323–345.

Ortega, Francisco, Rafaela Zorzanelli, and Clarice Rios. 2016. "The Biopolitics of Autism in Brazil." In *Re-thinking Autism: Diagnosis, Identity and Equality*, edited by Katherine Runswick-Cole, Rebecca Mallett, and Sami Timimi, 67–89. London and Philadelphia: Jessica Kingsley.

Ozonoff, Sally, Bruce F. Pennington, and Sally J. Rogers. 1991. "Executive Function Deficits in High-Functioning Autistic Individuals: Relationship to Theory of Mind." *Journal of Child Psychology and Psychiatry* 32 (7): 1081–1105.

Parks, Rachel. 2014. "The Rise, Critique and Persistence of the DALY in Global Health." *The Journal of Global Health*. http://www.ghjournal.org/the-rise-critique-and-persistence-of-the-daly-in-global-health/.

Rios, Clarice, and Barbara Costa Andrada. 2015. "The Changing Face of Autism in Brazil." *Culture, Medicine, and Psychiatry* 39 (2): 213–234.

Rosanoff, Michael J., Amy M. Daniels, and Andy Shih. 2015. "Autism: A (Key) Piece of the Global Mental Health Puzzle." *Global Mental Health* 2 (2): 1–3. https://doi.org/10.1017/gmh.2014.7.

Rosenberg, Charles E. 2006. "Contested Boundaries: Psychiatry, Disease, and Diagnosis." *Perspectives in Biology and Medicine* 49: 407–424.

Rubin, Sue. 2005. "Acceptance Versus Cure." CNN.com. http://www.cnn.com/CNN/Programs/presents/shows/autism.world/notebooks/sue/notebook.html.

Silverman, Chloe. 2012. *Understanding Autism: Parents, Doctors, and the History of a Disorder*. Princeton: Princeton University Press.

Singer, Judy. 1999. "Why Can't You Be Normal For Once In Your Life? From a 'Problem with No Name' to the Emergence of a New Category of Difference." In *Disability Discourse*, edited by Mairian Corker and Sally French, 59–67. Buckingham: Open University Press.

Singh, Jenifer S. 2016. *Multiple Autisms: Spectrums of Advocacy and Genomic Science*. Minneapolis and London: University of Minnesota Press.

Souza Lima, Philipe. 2017. "O autismo como deficiência: impacto sobre o trabalho das equipes dos Centros de Atenção Psicossocial Infanto-Juvenil." MS dissertation, State University of Rio de Janeiro.

Tsing, Anna Lowenhaupt. 2005. *Friction: An Ethnography of Global Connection*. Princeton, NJ: Princeton University Press.

Vidal, Fernando, and Francisco Ortega. 2017. *Being Brains: Making the Cerebral Subject*. New York: Fordham University Press.

Wallace, Simon, Deborah Fein, Michael Rosanoff, Geraldine Dawson, Saima Hossain, Lynn Brennan, Ariel Como, and Andy Shih. 2012. "A Global Public Health Strategy for Autism Spectrum Disorders." *Autism Research* 5 (3): 211–217. https://doi.org/10.1002/aur.1236.

Walsh, Pat, Mayada Elsabbagh, Patrick Bolton, and Ilina Singh. 2011. "In Search of Biomarkers for Autism: Scientific, Social, and Ethical Challenges." *Nature Reviews Neuroscience* 12: 603–612.

White, Ross G., David M.R. Orr, Ursula M. Read, and Sumeet Jain. 2017. "Situating Global Mental Health: Sociocultural Perspectives." In *The Palgrave Handbook of Sociocultural Perspectives on Global Mental Health*, edited by Ross G. White, Sumeet Jain, David M.R. Orr, and Ursula M. Read. London: Palgrave Macmillan.

Wikler, Daniel. 2010. "Cognitive Disability, Paternalism, and the Global Burden of Disease." In *Cognitive Disability and Its Challenge to Moral Philosophy*, edited by Eva. F. Kittay and Licia Carlson. London: Wiley-Blackwell.

Williams, Justin HG, Andrew Whiten, Thomas Suddendorf, and David I. Perrett. 2001. "Imitation, Mirror Neurons, and Autism." *Neuroscience & Biobehavioral Reviews* 25 (4): 287–295.

World Health Organization. 2016. *International Statistical Classification of Diseases and Related Health Problems*. 10th Revision (ICD-10).

PART II

Voice, Narrative and Representation

CHAPTER 5

Music and Autism, Representation and Re-presentation: An Ethnomusicological Perspective

Michael B. Bakan

I am an ethnomusicologist of autism. I am not a music therapist, nor a scientist. I do consider my research to be evidence-based, but the evidence from which I draw is ethnographic, dialogical, and music experience-based rather than clinical, quantitative, or questionnaire-based. I do not aspire to cure, normalize, remediate, change, or improve the functional capacities and skills of the autistic people with whom I work, play music, and collaborate. Nor do I aim to create research designs that are replicable, at least not by conventional measures. I am not interested in developing interventions, though I am interested in facilitating understandings; I am not interested in representing, but I am interested in re-presenting; I don't promote autism awareness, but I do promote autism acceptance.

And that for the most part sums up my epistemological stance, professional aspirations, and personal mission as the thing I am here claiming to be: an ethnomusicologist of autism. In this chapter, I will endeavor to share my conception of just what that is, and from there go on to

M. B. Bakan (✉)
Florida State University, Tallahassee, FL, USA

E. Fein and C. Rios (eds.), *Autism in Translation*, Culture, Mind, and Society, https://doi.org/10.1007/978-3-319-93293-4_5

consider the potential relevance of musical engagement, discourses about music, and ethnomusicological theories and methods to the overarching themes of this volume: autism spectrum conditions in global, local, cross-cultural, and personal perspective.

Before venturing any further, it is important to draw attention to a key structural aspect of this essay: namely, that the chapter as a whole builds toward—and is indeed largely defined by—a separate work of writing contained within it. That work is an autobiographical memoir written in 2014 by the American composer, multi-instrumentalist, and musicologist Gordon Peterson (pseudonym), who has a diagnosis of Autism Spectrum Disorder (ASD), and more specifically of the condition formerly known as Asperger's Syndrome. The memoir is reprinted here with Gordon's permission. It forms part of a series of online dialogues between the two of us that took place over a six-month period from April 2014 to October 2014. These dialogues, in turn, belong to a larger, ongoing project of online dialogical ethnography with autistic musicians and thinkers with which I have been involved since 2011 (see Bakan 2016b, 2018).

5.1 Autism Spectrum Conditions and Neurodiversity

Words matter when we speak or write about autism. As Elizabeth Fein astutely observes elsewhere in this volume with reference to Madeline L'Engle's novel *A Wind in the Door* (L'Engle 1973), "this thing [autism] that this group of us in Rio came a very long way to try to talk about, slips in and out of words - perhaps because they are words that strive to contain it and control it, to render it more tractable or even (as in the case of Asperger's Syndrome), to make its troubling complexities disappear by taking a word away" (Fein, this volume, p. 130).

The word *disorder* is one of those problematically containing and controlling words, and in my view—as well as that of a growing chorus of others working in this area—it is a word that we would do well to slip out of, at least insofar as its inclusion in the master phrase of the lexicon, "autism spectrum disorder," is concerned. Toward that end, I here invoke the word "condition" in its place: autism spectrum disorder, ASD, is recast as autism spectrum condition, ASC.

This terminological shift connects to a larger epistemological one through which I view my position as being essentially in alignment with those of Nick Walker, Elizabeth J. "Ibby" Grace, Amy Sequenzia, and other scholars and activists speaking from within the autistic self-advocacy community, a position that insists on autism spectrum conditions as manifestations of *neurodiversity* rather than of disorder or pathology, with neurodiversity defined by Walker as "the understanding of neurological variation as a natural form of human diversity, subject to the same societal dynamics as other forms of diversity," such as race, gender, ethnicity, or sexual orientation (Walker 2012, 233; cf. Sequenzia and Grace 2015).

Walker calls for a comprehensive epistemological shift from what he terms the pathology paradigm of autism (essentially a subset of the medical model of disability critiqued in disability studies) to the neurodiversity paradigm of autism. It is noteworthy, however, that in doing so, neither he nor other autistic self-advocates who have addressed such issues deny or underplay the significant and often profoundly disabling impact of ASCs on the lives of people who live with them, as well on the lives of those with whom they live, work, and play. That autism can be disabling, or as I prefer to phrase it, disenabling, is not in question. What is in question is, first, what kinds of individual, social, medical, therapeutic, cultural, political, and legislative responses are appropriate and most likely to be fruitful; and second, to what degree might disenablement be effectively assuaged by looking at old challenges in new ways, and especially by listening closely to what autistic people have to say on their own behalves concerning just what it is they need, envision, and desire.

5.2 Autism and Ethnomusicology, Then and Now

Historically and still today, arguments from the mainstream channels of medical and scientific practice and research concerning autism and the autism spectrum have overwhelmingly emphasized priorities of diagnosis, rehabilitation, and cure. Arguments from proponents of autistic self-advocacy and neurodiversity—including activists and scholars in areas such as cultural and psychological anthropology, disability studies, and the philosophy of disability—have contrastingly pushed toward forms of accommodation that acknowledge the expressed wants and needs of autistic people, and also toward engaged and comprehensive acceptance, not mere "awareness," of autistic personhood in its myriad dimensions and manifestations.[1] More specifically, they call for knowing autistic people in terms of who they are rather than what their neurotypical

Others would have them be. Tied to such notions of autism acceptance is a fundamental abhorrence of current initiatives aimed at cure, eradication, prenatal detection, and the like, which are regarded as tantamount to genocidal in intent within certain sectors of the autistic self-advocacy community.[2] Tellingly, these initiatives are closely tied to the missions and programs of organizations like the U.S.-based Autism Speaks, which aggressively promote "autism awareness." Such organizations are vilified by many autistic self-advocates, and thus the phrase "autism awareness" and all that it stands for are likewise targets for derision or worse.

But let me step back for a moment, for among the many other things I am not, bioethicist is one of them, and such debates are beyond the scope of what I am prepared to address here. I am, once again, an ethnomusicologist of autism, and this seems the opportune moment to unpack that 11-syllable mouthful of a job description.

The most enduring definition of my field, ethnomusicology, was coined by Alan P. Merriam in his seminal 1960 article "Ethnomusicology: Discussion and Definition of the Field" (Merriam 1960). In that piece, Merriam defined ethnomusicology as "the study of music in culture," later revising to "the study of music as culture" (Merriam 1977). The potentially varied implications of "in" vs. "as" aside, the key point to bring to bear here is the dialectical inextricability of music and culture that Merriam's definition, along with a host of others that preceded and followed it but never with quite the same impact or wide circulation, achieved. If we are to accept, after Joseph Straus, that autism is "a way of being in the world, a world-view enshrined in a culture [...] a difference, not a deficit" (Straus 2013, 467), then a cultural purview of autistic musical practice and thinking would seem to be an appropriate task of ethnomusicological inquiry, and the mode of that inquiry to be consistent with the larger theoretical aims and methodological approaches of my discipline.

In fields such as ethnomusicology and cultural anthropology, "culture" has of course become a slippery and elusive construct in our theoretical considerations of what we do. Earlier conceptions of cultures as identifiable, singular, and relatively neatly bounded and grounded—geographically, linguistically, musically, and otherwise—have suffered of late under the growing weight of global, transcultural realities and challenges to the very notion that cultures were ever actually as separate or identifiable as scholars of former generations would have had us believe. In spite of such complexities, we can at least say that culture has something to do with shared worldview and shared ideas about ways of being in the world; in other words, it relates to observable or otherwise perceivable manifestations of shared epistemologies and ontologies. Such manifestations constitute a global cultural matrix of near-infinite variation on a fairly set repertoire of standard themes: kinship, religion, subsistence patterns, ritual practice, and so on. Those variations certainly have profound impacts on how people—whether defined at the individual or cultural level or somewhere in-between—turn out. They powerfully direct what Clifford Geertz called "the mechanisms by whose agency the breadth of [a person's] inherent capacities are reduced to the narrowness and specificity of his [or her] actual accomplishments," mechanisms that prompted his claim that one "of the most significant facts about us may finally be that we all begin with the natural equipment to live a thousand kinds of life but end in the end having lived only one" (Geertz 1973, 45).

Bradd Shore's cognitive neuroscience-inspired anthropological work on the interrelationship of mind, brain, and culture expands on Geertz's conception. "[F]ully three-quarters of the human brain develops outside the womb, in direct relationship with an external environment," Shore wrote in *Culture in Mind* (1996, 3). "Evolution has equipped our species with an 'ecological brain,' dependent throughout its life on environmental input" (Shore, 3), and it is in the dialectical interaction that takes shape between that ecological brain and its cultural environment that the individual human mind in a sense emerges, develops, and transforms.

Thus, not just the cognitive dimensions of the mind, but also the physical dimensions of the brain, are in key respects products *of* culture, a theory that much research on neuroplasticity in cognitive neuroscience has supported as well (see, for examples, Doidge 2007). Yet even in acknowledging such malleability and its resultant shaping of minds/brains on an essentially cultural level, scholars such as Shore are quick to emphasize that it has no relationship whatsoever to insidious, debunked theories such as primitive mentality, or by extension racial determinism. Shore writes,

> None of this evidence of psychic diversity throws into question the simplest meaning of 'psychic unity'–that humans all share a common nervous system and the important cognitive entailments follow from this. Nor does it require us to resurrect outworn notions about cultural differences in cognitive capacity or totalizing "mentalities" (the vexing "primitive

> mentality" issue) that are held to distinguish different populations. What it does mean, however, is that the place of cultural models in mind can never be relegated to a kind of window-dressing over some primordial human hardware understood as the "real" meaning of mind. (Shore 1996, 8)

And so we are left with an appreciation for the extraordinary nimbleness of the human brain as a conduit to the diverse formations of actual minds, but also with an affirmation that, at least so far as the starting line of postpartum brain and mind development is concerned, we humans all share, by virtue of our "common nervous system and the important cognitive entailments" which follow from it, a baseline psychic unity that precedes whatever processes of culture-grounded diversification ultimately come to act upon it. The foundational brain hardware we get out of the box, as it were, is pretty much standard issue regardless of whether we happen to be born in Shanghai or Chennai, Bamako or Chicago, and the basic operating system is for the most part the same as well. There is nothing fundamentally different about a "Chinese brain" and a "Canadian brain" other than what happens to each as they become Chinese or Canadian, respectively—or vice versa.

Thus, "the study of culture"—or in the case of ethnomusicology the study of music in or as culture—is an endeavor premised on the assumption of a more-or-less standard model of the human brain. What becomes interesting is how that one basic type of brain can yield such extraordinary variety, say, in musical expression and ability, in the outcomes of its far-reaching journeys as a mind in culture. Whether such journeys yield an American master of Balinese gamelan performance or a Korean piano virtuoso specializing in Chopin is ultimately a matter of available cultural models and selective responses to them. It could indeed be said that virtually the entire modern history of ethnomusicology, certainly from the 1960s onward, may be productively understood in such terms. Even as relatively static models of culture have given way to more dynamic, agency-centered approaches that emphasize negotiation, difference, and the uniqueness of individual actors over cultural norms and regularities ostensibly represented by individual "culture-bearers," that basic line of inquiry remains intact, whether in the presence or absence of the actual term *culture* itself. For example, the epistemological orientation of my recent ethnomusicological work has shifted in accordance with an alternate definition of the field that sidesteps the invoking of that word: "Ethnomusicology is the study of how people make and experience music, and of why it matters to them that they do" (Bakan 2015, 116). This shift, however, does not change the fundamental terms of engagement between available cultural models to which all humans variably respond and the broadly shared human endowments of a common nervous system and attendant cognitive entailments from which such responses emerge. Balinese gamelan musicians and American orchestral musicians certainly bring different cognitive and physical skill sets to their respective crafts, and there is tremendous intracultural variety at the individual level among music makers and music experiencers in both domains as well, but the genesis of such difference and variety does not reside at the level of culturally demarcated brain physiology; rather, it has to do with the play of culture on the musical choices available to and made by individuals (Bakan 1999; Small 1998).

In thinking about the ethnomusicology of autism, though, the basic terms of engagement change. The vantage point of inquiry is transformed, for it *is* at a more baseline neurophysiological, neurocognitive level that "autistic culture"—the particular matrix of worldviews and ways of being in the world that distinguishes autistic subjective experience from other kinds—in essence begins. "One analogy that has often been made" with respect to this distinction, explains the autistic scholar Nick Walker, "is that autistic individuals have a different neurological 'operating system' than non-autistic individuals" (Walker 2014). Related to this idea is Straus's assertion that autism, as culture, is characterized by an identifiable "autistic cognitive style" (Straus 2011), one that is as indexical to ways of behaving, communicating, working, playing, grieving, and joking as are the culturally recognized cognitive styles of, say, people who are identified as Balinese, Kaluli, or Samoan (and indeed with the same liabilities of misguided essentialism that those other cultural identifiers carry).[3] In the autistic case, however, the primary concern is not with how different cultural stimuli acting on an essentially uniform design of physical brain account for cultural diversity—that is, in the sense that we might invoke such a phrase in a comparison of Balinese and Samoan music. Instead, the matter at issue is how cultural stimuli generally—possibly even the *same* stimuli—yield profoundly different results as they act upon differently "wired" brains, that is, brains with divergent "operating systems" that account for the different kinds of cognitive maps and processes that yield distinctive autistic and neurotypical minds, and in turn distinctively autistic and neurotypical ways of making, thinking about, and experiencing music.

Nick Walker offers a useful frame of reference for thinking ethnomusicologically about autistic musicking (Small 1998) in the following passages from his 2014 piece "What Is Autism?" Though he makes no explicit reference to music in this piece, the position he outlines transfers well to musicological considerations. Walker writes:

> Autism is a genetically-based human neurological variant. The complex set of interrelated characteristics that distinguish autistic neurology from non-autistic neurology is not yet fully understood, but current evidence indicates that the central distinction is that autistic brains are characterized by particularly high levels of synaptic connectivity and responsiveness. This tends to make the autistic individual's subjective experience more intense and chaotic than that of non-autistic individuals: on both the sensorimotor and cognitive levels, the autistic mind tends to register more information, and the impact of each bit of information tends to be both stronger and less predictable.... autism has been frequently misconstrued as being essentially a set of "social and communication deficits," by those who are unaware that the social challenges faced by autistic individuals are just by-products of the intense and chaotic nature of autistic sensory and cognitive experience.
>
> Autism is still widely regarded as a "disorder" [...] Ultimately, [however,] to describe autism as a disorder represents a value judgment rather than a scientific fact. (Walker 2014)

5.3 Gordon Peterson, in His Own Words

With Nick Walker's comments and my preceding discussion of the ethnomusicology of autism dually in mind, let us now turn our attention to the promised autobiographical memoir of Gordon Peterson. Gordon came to the exercise of its writing as a gigging musician, composer, early music specialist, and former tenured music professor with a doctorate in early music performance. At the time of our dialogues, he was living in a large city in the U.S. Midwest, was in his mid-40s, and had been diagnosed with Asperger's just a few years prior.

As noted, the memoir (perhaps more accurately a self-reflexive essay) emerged out of a series of online dialogues between Gordon and me; he wrote it in response to a prompt I had sent him. In the course of our dialogues up to that point, questions about how having Asperger's had influenced Gordon's music and his music creation process had come up frequently, but he had not been satisfied with his responses. He felt that he needed more solitary writing and thinking time to do my questions justice, so I encouraged him to take that time, write something up at his convenience, and send it to me when he was satisfied with the result. What follows re-presents the result of that process:

> I've been thinking a lot about your questions regarding how my ASD affects my music. After all this pondering, I have reached the conclusion that I don't think it really does affect it; not the final product, anyway. I don't believe that ASD is at all apparent in the music itself. What ASD does affect is my process, and it affects everything, for better, but mostly for worse. And the more I think about how it affects my process, the more I revisit the question you asked at first, which is if there was a magic wand that could make ASD disappear, would I want it gone [to which I originally answered, "No. It's my superpower when it's working in my favor. But...every superpower has a 'down side.' I'll take the down side because the good is so good..."]. My new answer is yes, I would want it gone. I think it may be much more trouble than it's worth.
>
> In my mind, there is an impossibly complex web of musical and non-musical cultural connections across time and geographic location. I see a ribbon-like time line in my mind, which curves back and forth, doubling back on itself, curling around at other points, as time is not, in my mind, truly linear, but more like David Tennant's 10th Doctor [in the BBC television series *Dr. Who*] says, "wibbly-wobbly, timey-wimey stuff." The ribbon stretches back from today all the way to the beginning of recorded history, and before. There aren't hash marks to note the dates, but the dates hover above general areas of the line, and the side of the ribbon looks like a window, where I see the movers and shakers of the times (that I know of), the way people looked, their food... everything I know about the culture appears through that window, encompassing a day in the life of that era. Each window (though they're continuous and one blurs into the next) can be entered like a portal to that time, and I can walk around in it, looking at the instruments, hearing the sounds, hearing the language... if I go deep enough, it's like I'm there.
>
> But that's all in my mind... it means nothing to anyone that can't get inside my head with me. I draw on this time-ribbon all the time... it's where everything musical, creative, or scholarly comes from. The part of my mind that houses it is the ASD portion of me (there is a portion that's not ASD, that's quite normal, in fact. It just has little control over the ASD side. It's more of an observer. I've already told you about it). But it's where my ideas for original music come from, it's where I go when interpreting other music... it's where I live. But what difference does it make? Other non-ASD artists have their places they go to get what they

need to create, other ways of organizing their inspiration and knowledge. I guess I say that because I love what's in my head… it's an exciting, magical place that amazes me whenever I think about it or spend time there. The contents of that ribbon are so beautiful and highly detailed, and I can get to feeling kind of "special" about it all. But the fact of the matter is that it's only special to me. I can't possibly explain it to you in the detail I'd like. Even if I could, turning that vision into words only detracts from the power and beauty that I perceive in it… trying to tell someone else what it's like doesn't measure up, not even close, to what it's really like. And as for the product I produce using it? Well, I live in poverty and obscurity, so I guess it's not translating to the "real world" very well. So, at least as of today, I don't see that it's a useful or desirable ability outside of keeping my own head entertained. Not quite the superpower I would like it to be.

ASD is also a major stumbling block in my professional and personal life… oh hell, life in general. My inability to maintain good relationships, the way everything HAS to be before anything can be done… if something is done out of "order" I get disoriented at best, totally panicked at worst… I've spent more time trying to create the necessary conditions for consistent production and creation than I have actually producing or creating. I hate that. When I'm on a roll, there's no stopping me, and I think the product I'm able to produce is unique and very good… I base this on actual feedback. My compositions, what few of them actually have been finished, do, I think, sound as I want them to, and are different than anything else out there… but what's unique about that? Of course they're different. Everyone's music is different from everyone else's, even if there are similarities. I don't play my own stuff out much. Why? I don't know exactly, but I do know that it's something in the ASD brain that keeps me from pursuing it…

My biggest ASD-based problem with production of any kind is momentum. It takes me FOREVER to get the "speed" up to write, produce, practice regularly… anything that a good musician should be doing. Once my routine has been broken, I cannot repair it and have to create a new one. I can't tell you how many years I must have lost in this process. Once it's going, though, I experience a usually short-lived bump in creative output until the next external influence comes along to interrupt me and break my stride. Once that happens, practice routines fall away, composition becomes blocked, and I become very depressed. I've set my life up so there is constant musical activity occurring regardless of whether my own routines are in place or not, so I have external motivators that keep me from losing too much time or skill, but I always feel like I'm starting over. This has been a particularly bad problem since the end of my academic career [when I was dismissed from my tenured position] last year.

Rudderlessness, which is what I'm experiencing right now...is just the worst. I need to create routines and "proper parameters" for my work, but if I have no idea what my goals are, I don't know how to set up the routines... routines for what? To go where? In what time frame? I don't know, so I languish and piss about trying to find SOMETHING to latch onto and get going again....

I've been very lucky until recently, as I need a more sheltered environment than some, and I got it [when I was employed as a professor]. It's gone now, but I sure was lucky to have it. My home life sucked, though, and was chock full of stupid interruptions and an uncooperative, insensitive spouse, and I couldn't get my "routine" together because of that....

I think one of the positive effects of my ASD is my ability to compartmentalize. It's why I can go on stage in the midst of a total life crisis and not be affected by it. The second I set foot on a stage, whether it's a literal stage or just standing in front of a lot of people, a switch gets flipped and I'm a different person. I don't even try, it just happens. I'm "on," and I do my job. Then, when it's over, all the anxieties and Aspie crap all come back. But for those brief, shining hours I can function without questioning whether I'm doing the right thing... I am confident in and know my work as a performer, and that comes through when I play. I attribute that to the "superpower" aspect of my ASD. That's as good as it gets, though. All the downsides listed above still apply. I'm really not so sure now that ASD is something I'd want to keep if I had a choice...

5.4 Concluding Thoughts

Gordon Peterson's memoir is the centerpiece of this chapter; the rest is its frame. At this point, I would like to venture some closing thoughts on issues of authorship, ability, re-presentation, representation, and voice that relate to topics and issues raised in the memoir itself, in the earlier parts of the chapter, and also in an insightful response to this piece written by Laura Sterponi (2015).

To make the claim that Gordon's memoir is the central feature of this chapter is to defy conventions of scholarly writing and presentation. Quoting from Laura Sterponi's illuminating response paper to an earlier version of the present essay (which she presented at the workshop that gave rise to this volume), such a claim "puts pressure on the notion of authorship." Ethnographic "subjects" like Gordon, "who would traditionally be merely *represented*, spoken about in a conventional scholarly paper on autism spectrum conditions," Sterponi explains, "are [here] given equal or perhaps even greater status and authoritativeness than [Bakan] himself, i.e., the official author" (Sterponi 2015). Gordon is more properly the co-author of this chapter than its subject, a fact that would be easier to credit were it not for his pseudonymous desire for anonymity in the work.

This begs the question of what *kind* of an autistic subject/author Gordon actually is. He came to the writing of his memoir not just as a highly trained and accomplished musician, but also as a person whose life had centered largely on doing things with language and words: a writer, a scholar, a musicologist, a deep thinker, and an articulate spokesperson for his own views. That reality brings us to a key point of tension in autistic discourse and discourses on autism generally, since people on the autism spectrum differ so dramatically in the extent to which they use language, if at all, to comprehend and engage with the world around them. Some do not use language, others use it very little, still others use it in in highly idiosyncratic ways, and there are also those who employ language only in collaboration with other individuals who serve as facilitators or "translators." Since language so deeply informs multiple dimensions of human experience, such differences are profound in their impact.[4]

Making matters even more complex on this level is the fact that in any given instance, there may not be any correlation between an individual's evident level of verbal/communicative ability and their degree of intellectual ability. Take, for example, the well-known autistic writer and social activist Amy Sequenzia, who does not speak but is most assuredly "verbal" in the extreme on account of the elegant, powerful, and voluminous writings she has produced typing with just a single finger, the support of a full-time aide, and sophisticated assistive technologies (Sequenzia and Grace 2015; Sequenzia 2012). Amy and Gordon, and indeed the vast majority of writers, spokespersons, and activists in the realms of autistic self-advocacy and neurodiversity, belong to this category of people whose lives revolve around doing things with words (Fein 2012). They are unified in some sense by a shared identity captured by Steve Silberman when he writes, "We can speak (or write or sign or type) for ourselves, and it's time to listen" (Silberman 2012, 365). But such a proclamation does not apply universally to individuals across the autism spectrum, not even close, and those falling outside of such parameters of language ability and performance are literally and figuratively muted in the discourse, meaning that as inclusive as works like the present one aspire to be—and as geared toward bringing "autistic voices" to the fore of the discourse—they too are ultimately caught in the politics of exclusion that they endeavor to combat.

So the "voice" of Gordon, as re-presented in his memoir above, must be acknowledged as a privileged kind of voice within the overall range of autistic voices, since Gordon has highly developed language skills upon which he is able to draw in his efforts to communicate with others, his ASC-related social and interactional challenges notwithstanding. Yet another reality must be acknowledged here, too. This reality, as described by Sterponi, is that, generally speaking, "the voices of individuals with autism have long been disregarded," discredited "as either insignificant… or so obscure as to need an expert interpretation, into something meaningful *in and of itself*" (Sterponi 2015).

Thus, whatever limitations Gordon's essay may be deemed to have in terms of *representing* autistic subjective experience writ large, it has tremendous value with regard to framing and *re-presenting* such experience on the granular level where most of life really happens. Reading narratives like his, claims Sterponi, "compels us… to listen to expressions all too often neglected, which in fact could be enriching if we only took the time to listen to them properly" (Sterponi 2015).

Gordon Peterson's introspections and reflections are perhaps too easy of a sell in this regard, given his considerable proficiency as both a wordsmith and musician, but beyond their own interest and revelations, they further have the capacity to open us up to new ways of seeing, hearing, and perceiving the voices and actions of other individuals on the autism spectrum, including people who fall well outside the boundary lines of "highly verbal" classification within which he himself inarguably falls. To exemplify this point, Sterponi makes the following astute observations:

> Peterson's experience and autobiographical memoir reveals that there is only a thin line between blissful creativity and paralyzing chaos. For individuals with an autism spectrum condition, as Peterson points out, there is no choice [between them]. As for the rest of us, we do have choice. So when we see a child with autism incessantly spinning a wheel, we can

> choose to see it as perseverative behavior—[a] characteristic manifestation of autistic obsessiveness and cognitive inflexibility—or we can choose to see it as an experience of sensorial and aesthetic value, pretty much like Marcel Duchamp did when in 1913, here I quote Duchamp itself[, he] "had the happy idea to fasten a bicycle wheel to a kitchen stool and watch it turn"... [thereby creating] an idea and artwork that... challenged and changed the rules and values of artistic tradition. (Sterponi 2015)

Whatever else it may or may not do, and may or not represent or re-present, Gordon Peterson's memoir offers deep insights into how he makes and experiences music, and why it matters to him that he does. In that sense, it is not only an autobiographical piece of writing, but an ethnomusicological piece of writing as well. Moreover, it sheds revealing light on aspects of autistic cognitive processing, cognitive style, and subjective experience that are at once unique and, to some degree, potentially generalizable. Gordon's mid-life transition to his "Aspie" identity has been transformative on many levels, yielding about equal measures of catharsis and struggle and constituting a complex admixture of provisional triumph and wrenching despair. The resulting matrix of ambivalence he presents is certainly specific to his particular situation, but it is also suggestive of larger patterns emergent in a host of recent self-reports by autistic people, as well as elsewhere in the literature (see, for example, Bascom 2012; Sequenzia and Grace 2015; Fein 2012). Foundational to such patterns are statements in which autistic people from various walks of life describe their ASC, to quote Fein's presention at our workshop, as "a thing... both constitutive of their identity, and profoundly disruptive of it." This may seem paradoxical at first glance, but that sense of paradox diminishes when framed by Walker's earlier-cited assertion that autistic subjective experience tends generally to be "more intense and chaotic than that of non-autistic individuals" on both the sensorimotor and cognitive levels.

It is difficult to comprehend such constructs and theories in the abstract, but when they are paired with the kind of evocative and informative account that an articulate spokesperson like Gordon Peterson can provide—and through a compelling narrative rooted in his abiding passion, music and musical experience, in addition—things quickly start making sense. And as they start to make sense, so too do the proverbial workings of "the autistic mind."

Gordon Peterson embodies many qualities that adhere to words which aptly describe him: brilliant, confused, bold, sensitive, creative, complex, conflicted, skilled, confident, insecure, musical, autistic. So with all of that, what might we "Name" him (i.e., other than Gordon) in order to recognize him as most particularly and fully himself? That is actually a trick question, for it is not really our job, right, or responsibility to name Gordon at all. We are better served by truly listening to him, in the broadest sense—reading what he writes, hearing what he says, engaging in dialogue with him, listening closely to his music, listening to it with a well-informed sense of how he experiences it and why it matters to him—if we truly wish to understand who he is and what makes him tick. Gordon identifies himself in relation to his understanding and conception of his own autism spectrum condition; he understands himself as autistic (Asperger's) and he weaves an intricate ontological web around his dual musician/Asperger's identity. That is where Gordon is coming from when he thinks about himself, about autism, and about music, and that recognition should convince us, too, to commence our engagement with him by doing the same.

Is that enough? Probably not, since Gordon's articulate accounts of his ASC-related struggles and modes of suffering suggest that he desires for much about his life to change, both in terms of his ability to more successfully navigate his way through a world that is not very well set up for him and relative to his desire to see changes made in that world, changes which would make it a more accommodating and compassionate place for him to live. I stated at the outset of this chapter that I was not interested in developing interventions, though I was interested in facilitating understandings. In retrospect, I stand by the spirit of that claim, but I also recognize that it rests on a kind of flawed logic. To facilitate understandings is itself a form of intervention, and even when I try to hold to the conviction that the kind of facilitating that I am doing here is fundamentally different than its more conventional counterpart in the "autism intervention" sphere—i.e., since my goal is to modulate how the neurotypical majority views autistic people rather than to intervene in the lives of autistic people themselves—things start to fall apart. I am inescapably an intervener in the lives of Gordon and my other autistic collaborators—for better, for worse, or for both. Through our dialogues, our shared musical experiences, and our public and discursive performances, we are impacting one another, and whether one is promoting autistic self-advocacy and neurodiversity or their opposites, one is inevitably manifesting a form of intervention that pushes one's interlocutors in some direction or another. Gordon was prompted to write his memoir by me: that alone constitutes an intervention on my part.

And there are other complicating factors as well. If there is one thing that seeps through the pores of Gordon's narrative, it is ambivalence. We are left unsure right up to the end of how or whether he might ultimately rectify his attraction to the "superpower" aspects of his ASC and his repulsion toward that ASC's contrastingly destructive impacts. The weight ultimately seems to fall on the side of Gordon's wanting the "magic wand" cure, but even that is left up in the air. Gordon wants help, he wants solutions. Is it enough, then, for us to stand idly by and pat ourselves on the back for having "understood" those desires well? If not, what is the proper role we might adopt, or that given social institutions might adopt, or even societies at large, in accommodating the needs and desires of someone like Gordon, whether in altering the world to accommodate him or helping him to alter himself to accommodate to it?

These are difficult questions and ones that I will not broach here beyond their mention, along with an acknowledgement that the need to press further is never beyond us in this kind of work. Eliciting an "emic perspective" from Gordon Peterson is an important start, but it can and probably should lead well beyond itself and even to the application of "etic" forms of knowledge and action that, if judiciously and sensitively applied, may help him and many other people on the spectrum enjoy better and more fulfilling lives. Concepts such as neurodiversity and autistic self-advocacy are by no means immune from the kinds of flattening, essentializing, and exclusionary proclivities regarding human difference that they inspire in their critique of paradigmatic domains—be those medical, pathological, therapeutic, interventionist, or what have you—and we must remain open to both their critical interrogation and to productive possibilities for their integration with other paradigms, even ones with which they would seem to be at odds at first glance.

Yet placing aside all such caveats and qualifications, I still hold steadfastly to the conviction that understanding autism ought rightly to begin with listening to, communicating with, and learning from autistic people—through their words and utterances, their actions and performances, not ours; on their terms and according to their values, not ours—to the greatest extent possible. This demands creativity, resourcefulness, flexibility, and patience on the part of all parties involved: it may require the recognition or establishment of completely novel modes of communication and interaction; it may push us beyond all kinds of comfort zones, compelling us to distance ourselves from paradigms of legitimacy and identity that we staunchly believe define us to the core; it may even challenge us to dispense with such paradigms altogether.

The challenges inherent in such endeavors are considerable, but the potential rewards justify the effort. If we neglect to listen, and to listen deeply, to what people like Gordon Peterson have to say to us, then we are neglecting our responsibilities as both scholars and compassionate human beings. One skill that any good ethnomusicologist must develop is the ability to listen to unfamiliar musics in ways that allow for the transcendence of pre-established ways of hearing, knowing that such forms of listening go well beyond what that word normally connotes. It compels one to dig deeper, to connect the audible experience of listening per se with a myriad of contextual and relational factors that surround it. It challenges us to hear not just the music or the words that are performed, but to find ways of meaningfully connecting to the unique subjectivities that reflect, embody, and inform their performance. It requires a willingness to embrace new ideas and ideals of engaged listening, to put on "new ears." In listening to the voices of autistic people—whatever form such voices may take—it behooves all of us to do the same.

Notes

1. Among a plethora of representative works that warrant mention in this regard, Prince-Hughes (2004), Biklen (2005), Grinker (2007), Bascom (2012), Fein (2012), Straus (2013), Silberman (2015), and Bakan (2014, 2015, 2016a, b, 2018), as well as a special issue of the *Journal of Autism and Developmental Disorders* dedicated to discourse and conversation analytic approaches to the study of ASD (see O'Reilly et al. 2016) and a special issue of *Ethos* titled "Rethinking Autism, Rethinking Anthropology" (see Solomon and Bagatell 2010), are notable.
2. A number of the essays in the landmark anthology *Loud Hands: Autistic People, Speaking* (Bascom 2012) are reflective of such positions.
3. My selection of Balinese, Kaluli, and Samoan cultures as exemplars is in one sense arbitrary and in another quite deliberate. On the deliberate level,

I am invoking awareness of some highly influential anthropologists and ethnomusicologists who did research in these areas, most notably Clifford Geertz (1973) in Bali; Bambi B. Schiefflein (1990), Edward L. Schieffelin (2005), and Steven Feld (2012) among the Kaluli in Papua New Guinea; and Margaret Mead (2001) and Derek Freeman (1983) in Samoa.

4. I am indebted to one of the anonymous reviewers of a book manuscript based on this same research project for several of the perspectives and ideas explored in this portion of the chapter.

References

Bakan, Michael B. 1999. *Music of Death and New Creation: Experiences in the World of Balinese Gamelan Beleganjur*. Chicago: University of Chicago Press.

———. 2014. "Ethnomusicological Perspectives on Autism, Neurodiversity, and Music Therapy." *Voices: A World Forum for Music Therapy* 14 (3). Online Publication. https://voices.no/index.php/voices/article/view/799/660.

———. 2015. "'Don't Go Changing to Try and Please Me': Combating Essentialism through Ethnography in the Ethnomusicology of Autism." *Ethnomusicology* 59 (1): 116–144.

———. 2016a. "Toward an Ethnographic Model of Disability in the Ethnomusicology of Autism." In *The Oxford Handbook of Music and Disability Studies*, edited by Blake Howe, Stephanie Jensen-Moulton, Neil Lerner, and Joseph N. Straus, 15–36. New York: Oxford University Press.

———. 2016b. "Music, Autism, and Disability Aesthetics." Colloquy: On the Disability Aesthetics of Music (Blake Howe and Stephanie Jensen-Moulton, convenors). *Journal of the American Musicological Society* 69 (2): 548–553.

———. 2018. *Speaking for Ourselves: Conversations on Life, Music, and Autism*. New York: Oxford University Press.

Bascom, Julia, ed. 2012. *Loud Hands: Autistic People, Speaking*. Washington, DC: The Autistic Press/The Autistic Self Advocacy Network.

Biklen, Douglas. 2005. *Autism and the Myth of the Person Alone*. New York: New York University Press.

Doidge, Norman. 2007. *The Brain That Changes Itself: Stories of Personal Triumph from the Frontiers of Brain Science*. New York: Penguin.

Fein, Elizabeth. 2012. "The Machine Within: An Ethnography of Asperger's Syndrome, Biomedicine, and the Paradoxes of Identity and Technology in the Late Modern United States." PhD dissertation, University of Chicago.

———. 2015. "What Do I Study When I Study Autism?" Paper Presented at Autism Spectrum Disorders in Global, Local and Personal Perspective: A Cross-Cultural Workshop, Rio de Janeiro, Brazil, September 2015.

———. in press. "Autism as a Mode of Engagement." In current volume.

Feld, Steven. 2012. *Sound and Sentiment: Birds, Weeping, Poetics and Song in Kaluli Expression*. 3rd ed. Durham, NC: Duke University Press.

Freeman, Derek. 1983. *Margaret Mead and Samoa: The Making and Unmaking of an Anthropological Myth*. Cambridge, MA: Harvard University Press.

Geertz, Clifford. 1973. *The Interpretation of Cultures*. New York: Basic Books.

Grinker, Roy Richard. 2007. *Unstrange Minds: Remapping the World of Autism*. New York: Basic Books.

L'Engle, Madeline. 1973. *A Wind in the Door*. New York: Square Fish/Farrar, Straus and Giroux.

Mead, Margaret. 2001. *Coming of Age in Samoa: A Psychological Study of Primitive Youth for Western Civilisation*. New York: Perennial Classics/ HarperCollins.

Merriam, Alan P. 1960. "Ethnomusicology: Discussion and Definition of the Field." *Ethnomusicology* 4 (3): 107–114.

———. 1977. "Definitions of 'Comparative Musicology' and 'Ethnomusicology': An Historical-Theoretical Perspective." *Ethnomusicology* 21 (2): 189–204.

O'Reilly, Michelle, Jessica Nina Lester, and Tom Muskett. 2016. "Discourse/ Conversation Analysis and Autism Spectrum Disorder." *Journal of Autism and Developmental Disorders* 46 (2): 355–359. Special Issue: Discourse and Conversation Analytic Approaches to the Study of Autism Spectrum Disorder.

Prince-Hughes, Dawn. 2004. *Songs of the Gorilla Nation: My Journey Through Autism*. New York: Harmony.

Schieffelin, Bambi B. 1990. *The Give and Take of Everyday Life: Language Socialization of Kaluli Children*. New York: Cambridge University Press.

Schieffelin, Edward L. 2005. *The Sorrow of the Lonely and the Burning of the Dancers*. 2nd ed. New York: Palgrave Macmillan.

Sequenzia, Amy. 2012. "Non-speaking, 'Low-Functioning.'" In *Loud Hands: Autistic People, Speaking*, edited by Julia Bascom, 159–161. Washington, DC: The Autistic Press/The Autistic Self Advocacy Network.

Sequenzia, Amy, and Elizabeth J. Grace, eds. 2015. *Typed Words, Loud Voices*. Fort Worth, TX: Autonomous Press.

Shore, Bradd. 1996. *Culture in Mind: Cognition, Culture, and the Problem of Meaning*. New York: Oxford University Press.

Silberman, Steve. 2012. "Autism Awareness is Not Enough: Here's How to Change the World." In *Loud Hands: Autistic People, Speaking*, edited by Julia Bascom, 358–390. Washington, DC: The Autistic Press/The Autistic Self Advocacy Network.

Silberman, Steve. 2015. *NeuroTribes: The Legacy of Autism and The Future of Neurodiversity*. New York: Avery.

Small, Christopher. 1998. *Musicking: The Meanings of Performing and Listening*. Middletown, CT: Wesleyan University Press.

Solomon, Olga, and Nancy Bagatell. 2010. "Introduction—Autism: Rethinking the Possibilities." *Ethos* 38 (1): 1–7.

Sterponi, Laura. 2015. "A Commentary on 'Music and Autism, Representation and Re-presentation: An Ethnomusicological Perspective' by Michael B. Bakan." Discussant Remarks Presented at Autism Spectrum Disorders in Global, Local and Personal Perspective: A Cross-Cultural Workshop, Rio de Janeiro, Brazil, September 2015.

Straus, Joseph N. 2011. *Extraordinary Measures: Disability in Music*. New York: Oxford University Press.

———. 2013. "Autism as Culture." In *The Disability Studies Reader*, 4th ed., edited by Lennard J. Davis, 460–484. New York: Routledge.

Walker, Nick. 2012. "Throw Away the Master's Tools: Liberating Ourselves from the Pathology Paradigm." In *Loud Hands: Autistic People, Speaking*, edited by Julia Bascom, 225–237. Washington, DC: The Autistic Press/The Autistic Self Advocacy Network.

———. 2014 (March 1). "What Is Autism?" Posted on Neurocosmopolitanism: Nick Walker's Notes on Neurodiversity, Autism, and Cognitive Liberty (blog). http://neurocosmopolitanism.com/what-is-autism/.

CHAPTER 6

Autism as a Mode of Engagement

Elizabeth Fein

6.1 What Do I Study When I Study Autism?

It started out as a kind of a light. A bright, dancing thing I saw out of the corner of my eye. I couldn't keep from chasing after it, like a cat going after a laser pointer—pouncing on a point that can never be caught and held, caught up in the movement until the movement becomes the point. Or maybe it was more like a sound, sensed with something other than my ears. A sensuous experience, never quite locatable in any one sense.

A boy comes and sits next to me, intent on a list in his lap; he doesn't look at me, but the air crackles with attention. A new friend shows me his room, its walls covered in maps and diagrams. A neighbor gives me a quiet smile from beneath her big hat, and some frantic thing in me stills. There's a hum, at a frequency I learned to recognize. Where does that happen? I feel it inside myself as a heightening shift in my own attention, a sudden sharpening focus, an experience of stimulation and calm that I desire, and seek out.

In those years of seeking, I learned a mass of words to put to this experience, words that I thought would help me locate it. Words like "autism"—a strange word to put around a feeling of connection.

E. Fein (✉)
Department of Psychology, Duquesne University, Pittsburgh, PA, USA

E. Fein and C. Rios (eds.), *Autism in Translation*, Culture, Mind, and Society, https://doi.org/10.1007/978-3-319-93293-4_6

Words like "problem behavior" and "qualitative impairment" and "level of functioning" that carried me farther away from the feeling rather than bringing me closer. These days, I find myself dealing more in words, and less in sensations. And something is lost, something that I'm trying to find again.

I keep trying to answer this question: "what is it that you study? What is this phenomenon that is sometimes called Asperger's Syndrome, and sometimes called autism, and has inhabited so many other names, too, partially and incompletely, in so many other ways?" To Name something, the author Madeleine L'Engle says in her novel "A Wind in the Door," is to recognize it, to help it become most particularly and fully itself (L'Engle 1973). But this thing, that this group of us in Rio came a very long way to try to talk about, slips in and out of words—perhaps because they are words that strive to contain it and control it, to render it more tractable or even (as in the case of Asperger's Syndrome[1]), to make its troubling complexities disappear by taking a word away.

Autism is many, many things to many people; even the fourteen of us who came to the Hotel Novo Mondo to talk about it were talking about many different things. Is autism a disability, a deficiency, a form of estrangement from social expectation, a kind of mental suffering? A child's chronic sleeplessness, an adult's corrosive loneliness, an evolutionary step into a new and desperately needed form of environmental sensitivity?

In this paper, I will try to describe what autism is in the context of my own work. My research began, and in many ways remains, a study of Asperger's Syndrome, and so what I can say about the vastness of the autism spectrum is limited. And still, this thing that draws me in is also the one and only thing I can say that I've experienced with autistic people of all types and stripes. What is this thing that I study, that I chase after, that I dance around, and try in fleeting moments to dance with? The thing I study is more like color than like color-blindness—it's a thing that happens between sensing bodies and sensuous worlds, in all the particularity of each. I have come to think of the thing I seek out as *a mode of engagement with the stuff of the world*—a way of *being with* one's surroundings. In particular, it is a form of permeability, of deep existential vulnerability, to the order of things around us: structured systems, elements in their robust relation, arrangements both deliberate and disavowed. What we say and do about autism, therefore, also tells something about how we relate to these surroundings of ours.

The autistic cognitive style, and particularly the challenges that come with it, have traditionally been depicted as a series of individual deficits in executive function, theory of mind, central coherence. Inabilities to organize, to intuit, to infer, without explicit guidance. Sometimes these qualities are understood less as individual deficits, and more as personal styles (i.e., Baron-Cohen 2000; Happé and Frith 2006; Mottron et al. 2009). But what if we were instead to think of autistic executive function, autistic theory of mind, the creation of autistic coherence, not as internal limitations, but as forms of deep involvement with external ordering systems—systems which are by their nature limited and limiting, as well as generous and generative? Inferences about other minds; planning, organization, and the intentional allocation of attention; the synthesis of parts into a meaningful whole: each of these processes take place in part within the self, but also and inextricably in collaboration with a world of materials and their particular affordances (Ramstead et al. 2016). The autism that I study can be understood as a particularly intimate and co-constitutive relationship with these affordances—and in particular, with culture.

I'm using the word "culture" here as Clifford Geertz defines it in "The Impact of the Concept of Culture on the Concept of Man": as a web of interconnected symbols, "a set of control mechanisms—plans, recipes, rules, instructions (what computer engineers call 'programs')—for the governing of behavior" without which "man's behavior would be virtually ungovernable, a mere chaos of pointless acts and exploding emotions, his experience virtually shapeless" (Geertz 2000, 44). Human beings are

> the animal most desperately dependent on such extragenetic, outside-the-skin control mechanisms, such cultural programs, for ordering their behavior. [...] We are, in sum, incomplete or unfinished animals who complete or finish ourselves through culture. (Geertz 2000, 49)

The people I'm talking about, when I talk about autism, are those who are most dependent upon culture to complete them, for whom organization and planning, the connections from *a* to *b* and onward from there, happen less within the brain, and more between the brain and the world. They are thus profoundly shaped by the patterns, the contours and affordances, of the lived record of human endeavor. The autism I study is a condition within which these extrasomatic arrangements, these existing sets of relationships between particular items, are taken in whole-cloth, and used to provide order, stability and comfort to an unpredictable phenomenological world.[2] As Matthew Belmonte (2008) has aptly said, perhaps the most fundamental human problem is the struggle to create meaning and coherence out of the chaos of existence, drawing on our human heritage of narrative and ritual to defend against the existential threats of perceptual fragmentation, impermanence, entropy, disconnection, and death. If so, autistic people, who do this explicitly and with the greatest intensity and fervor, are human *but more so* (Belmonte 2008).

There is a particular irony in naming such a state "autism"—naming a condition of intimate co-existence with the outside world by a word that means self-contained isolation. It's a kind of un-naming: naming a thing as its opposite. The power in such a move, I think, lies in its ability to discount such modes of relation—to relegate certain forms of sensuality, certain forms of sociality, to the dustbin of not-counting as such. So what's so threatening about this mode of relation, this state of visible symbiosis with the products of human creation, that we would superstitiously come to call it by the name of its absence?

This paper will not answer this question in any definitive way, but I aim to propose some possibilities to think about. In what follows, I will contextualize current understandings of autism spectrum conditions within what Anthony Giddens (2000) describes as a transition from "external risk" to "manufactured risk" within late modern, post-industrial societies. For perhaps the first time in our history, he observes, human beings are living "in a world where hazards created by ourselves are as, or more threatening than those that come from the outside" (Giddens 2000, 52). As the source of the greatest risks we face shifts to "the very impact of our developing knowledge on the world" (Giddens 2000, 44), the products and the byproducts of that human work upon the world come to feel threatening and alien. In its maintenance of the fundamental structure of that which it integrates, the autistic mode of engagement renders particularly visible the inevitable traces of human creations within human being. Autism refracts and performs manufactured material in a way that highlights its form, its robustness, and its power to shape behavior.

In doing so, autism has the power to interrupt broader sociopolitical imperatives that conceal shared social structures by demanding that behavior be explained as individualized and spontaneous, self-determined and unconstrained by externalities.[3] Sociologist Ulrich Beck refers to these imperatives as "institutionalized individualism": the series of "modern guidelines [that] actually compel the self-organization and self-thematization of people's biographies" (Beck 2002, 24) such that all of life's events must be understood and analyzed at the level of the individual. Under such circumstances, autism as a phenomenon is most often located and investigated within the bounds of the individual body. In most diagnostic conceptualizations of autism, engagement with particular extrasomatic content is considered a symptom, not a cause, of the phenomenon autism is considered to be. However, understanding autism as a mode of engagement with such material encourages us to pay more attention to the particular content that people on the autism spectrum engage with, as a constitutive component of their social, emotional, and cognitive development.

In what follows, I will share a few stories, of three young men on the autism spectrum that I have come to know. In each case, their engagement with the particular affordances of the cultural materials around them have shaped them profoundly, within the very cognitive, experiential, temporal, and social domains that are often held to be most definitional of autism. In telling their stories, I will explore what happens when we expand our concept of autism to include the content with which autistic people engage: the blueprints and schedules, the structured narratives and ordered content domains, the mimetic technologies and mass media, the products of human work upon the world that surround us. Doing so may change our understanding of what autism is; I will argue here that this move also poses the risk of a keener and more uncomfortable awareness of the stakes of what we create.

6.2 Trains Just Got Swept Away by These Dynamic Animals

Steve was nineteen when I interviewed him for a qualitative study on the transition from adolescence to adulthood among youth with Asperger's in the United States. Bright and creative, he dreamed of becoming a paleontologist. However, despite his extensive knowledge, I wondered how he would fare in a field that demanded such great competitiveness, discipline, and self-control. For his entire childhood and adolescence, Steve had been troubled by profound difficulties organizing his own behavior to meet the demands of his environment. He was taking several potent medications—an antidepressant, a mood stabilizer, an antidepressant—in an only somewhat effective attempt to keep his explosive anger under control; his meltdowns were so severe that he couldn't function in mainstream classrooms and had been educated predominantly within programs for students with emotional and behavioral disabilities. His mother proudly informed me that Steve was learning to make sandwiches in the school cafeteria as part of his school's job skills training program; shame-faced, he reminded her that he had not yet mastered that skill and so was still filling the ice buckets.

When he talked about dinosaurs, however, Steve came alight, and the room lit up with his evocation of their majesty. Dinosaurs were a constitutive element of Steve's personal cosmology. His encounters with contemporary representations of ancient megafauna had re-organized his felt sense of time, space, and sociality. As he told me the story of his life, as I investigated his troubled transition out of high school into an uncertain future, he told me about another transition that he felt was highly significant in his overall development: the transition from an intense, circumscribed focus on scheduled machines to an engulfment by the world of dynamic living creatures.

> Originally, I was really into trains. I was into Thomas the Tank Engine and all this—which train fares, et cetera, et cetera. I was nuts about trains. And then—I'm not exactly sure what it was [...] It was around the same time a couple of different things happened—they had that Storybook [show] on ABC, had a story about a dinosaur—a Stegosaurus. And my dad took me to the Field Museum for the first time, and I saw a movie about Earth's history. And it briefly refers to dinosaurs. So all these things sort of coalesced in my young, fertile imagination [...] And all of a sudden, this whole—other world! It just engulfed my little brain, and to this day, I haven't been the same since! Y'know? Trains just got *swept aside* by these *dynamic animals.*

There is something particularly *autistic*, in the sense of the word as I'm using it here, about the fertility of Steve's imagination, the depth of his availability to *this whole other world.* Most of his friends, he told me, were also diagnosed on the autism spectrum. This was partly because there were a lot of other students with autism classifications in his classroom, but also because he shared with them the experience of being deeply touched by the structures of the world, even as their particular interests take different forms.

> Me and Robert, we'll go to a museum, he'll get all excited and I'll just stand there in, in *reverence*. Of a dinosaur skeleton. Because that structure itself is just so compelling. And Michael is the physics guy. There's just something about—*knowing* the *universe*. That even if you're not totally into that, and it doesn't strike a chord with you? There's still something deep and meaningful. That touches—it touches us. I think for *all* of us.

Being touched in this way catalyzed a transformation in Steve. Through dinosaurs, he developed a passion for not only structure but also context, movement, and embodiment.

> The skeletons *themselves* are just so compelling, just that structure, the sauropods, they're like great bridges. But for me, I want to go beyond just *bones*, and speculation. I wanna know *exactly* what these animals were like. I wanna *see* them fleshed out, actually moving along in their natural habitat.

For Steve, the shift in his attentions from the simplicity of trains to the dynamic world of dinosaurs and prehistoric life brought about a profound shift in his view of time and the universe:

> Y'know, it's like every time I go start thinking about dinosaurs, I'm not even in the same universe as other people [...] For most people, a long time is what they had for *breakfast*. For me, it's like, a long time is like, a hundred years. A *really* long time is a million years. And deep time—y'know, for archeologists, it's like, a thousand years is deep time. For me, that's not even scratching the surface of what's come before. For me, it's hundreds of millions of years, of vertebrate evolution; that really fascinates me. And the more I learn about dinosaurs, the more I got into the other avenues of prehistoric life. Mammals, fish, and then slowly but surely, this whole other universe, this other time, that we are separated from by a great distance—not in space, but in time.

Shifting from trains to dinosaurs transformed the horizons of Steve's cognitive, social, temporal, and experiential world. And it did so in ways that are inseparable from the core symptom domains of autism spectrum disorder: restricted, repetitive behaviors, and limitations in sociality. The fascinations that shape his conceptualization of the universe have moved from mechanized and scheduled to dynamic and interactive. And—at least according to Steve himself—the availability and affordances of this particular content domain drove aspects of that developmental process. Steve's autism is inextricable from the cultural materials through which his modes of sociality have taken form.

6.3 The Numbers Do Not Lie, They Tell a Story

The idea of the autistic "special interest" as constitutive of dynamic, relational processes may at first seem counterintuitive. Previous research on the special interest tends to depict this obsessive focus on systems as a deviant alternative to engagement with the social and emotional world—as Simon Baron-Cohen puts it, a focus on systemizing instead of empathizing (Baron-Cohen et al. 2003). The tendency of individuals with Asperger's to focus on mechanistic systems rather than people is frequently remarked upon, to the point of having become a bit of a humorous cliché (i.e., Atwood 2007). However, these distinct realms of systems and sociality are not mutually exclusive, nor, often, fully separable. Instead, they come to inform each other in complex ways.

I interviewed twenty-year-old Dave via email, as part of the same study described above. Dave's particular obsessions were driving, the laws of physics and—above all—the rules of compound interest. As he told me the story of his life, he framed the narrative—full of interpersonal disappointments and unmet needs—as a story about financial knowledge and inheritance.

> I really despise my parents. They got divorced when I was 17, and now look where they are. Middle income with lots of bills, debt, and liabilities. What a joke. I am totally against the idea of buying anything on credit, except for real estate. I would want nothing more in life than to NOT turn out like most people these days. I don't think I could ever get married after what I saw my parents put themselves through. I could never get to sleep because they were always screaming and hitting each other late at night long after I should have gone to sleep. They did this every night. I did nothing about it because I thought it was normal for married people then. I still do. I really despise my parents for not being billionaires or at least millionaires.

Per his own report, Dave had an IQ of 146, which falls in the Very Superior range. He lived on his own in an apartment and described himself as a reliable, punctual employee. He considered himself, he told me, to be superior to most people. But he was agonizingly lonely.

> I have taken tests on the internet that conclude I am severely depressed. This is no surprise to me. I guess I always have been in some ways. Just now that I am older and out of school it has gotten much worse. I am alone 95% of the day. I was always teased and picked on in school a lot. It was very hard on me. I have never had any friends. Never any girl friend, or anything like that. Can you imagine what that would be like?

Dave spent all day alone, mostly sleeping and listening to Marilyn Manson, and all night driving a forklift at a Home Depot. The only people he talked to were his co-workers, occasionally, and not by choice. He felt they did their jobs sloppily, and they made jokes about him and his perpetual single status—he didn't understand the humor, but had learned, over time, to recognize the cruelty. As he told me his story, his feeling of being poorly prepared for adult life continued to return to the theme of money, even though it became clear from his story that there are more interpersonal losses involved as well:

> My parents never taught me the things a person needs to get ahead in this world today. The things a person needs to know to be successful. The things a person needs to know to be rich. You know there is one talk every parent has to give their kids to prepare them for adulthood. That talk is the talk about the birds and the bees. This is a talk I never got... Like I said I have never had a girl friend. I am still a virgin, which I am proud of in some ways and ashamed of in others [...] I am still angry about it to this day and I have not talked with my dad for many years. He is everything I don't want to be. This will not change. He is an insurance claims handler for a major insurance company. And he will die poor just like all the rest, and I don't feel one bit sorry for him.

As he planned his own life, Dave explicitly rejected traditional life trajectories based around marriage and family, planning his expectations of his own future instead according to investment principles. Returning to the theme of being poorly prepared by the previous generation, he described his new favorite book, "Rich Dad Poor Dad: What the Rich Teach Their Kids About Money—That the Poor and Middle Class Do Not!" (Kiyosaki 2000):

> It's about what the rich teach their kids about money that the poor and middle income do not. This is very interesting stuff to me. It offers hope. I don't have to worry about making a high income (which will be taxed

> high as well too) because now I know an easier way. It's called compound interest and it will work very well for someone starting to invest at such a young age as twenty. I have no doubt I will be a millionaire before 50, if not 40 [...] I am willing to make sacrifices now other people can't. I have run the numbers on calculators, and numbers do not lie, they tell a story. My future financial story is looking very good from the numbers I have seen. I would rather be rich than have a family, and I will save a lot of money with this belief.

It became clear, listening to Dave reconstruct his past and imagine possibilities for his future, that his appreciation for the systematic laws of finance did not exist in isolation from his experience of the interpersonal world and its traumatic vicissitudes. Rather, he used these laws like a genre, or a master-narrative, structuring causal and temporal relationships between events and formulating his own expectations and sense of personal identity through their promises. Sociolinguist Charlotte Linde has written that the particular "coherence systems" we use to organize our life stories assist us in creating a sense of coherence about our lives as a whole (Linde 1993). For Dave, these precise and predictable calculations did, indeed, tell a story—and through that story, he imagined the future trajectory of his life.

6.4 He Will Come Out with Something from TV to Give Him the Words

Steve's "engulfment" by the prehistoric and Dave's "future financial story" highlight the many ways in which autism is constituted in significant part by the cultural materials with which it engages. If cultural forms shape autistic development, this suggests we consider the possibility of a cultural contribution to the particular forms of what has come to be seen as autistic symptomatology. Under conditions of mass production, standardization and routinization, many cultural symbol systems are produced in such a way that the relationship of component parts to one another and the relationship of the whole to the perceiving audience will be as constant as possible across all consumers and circumstances, transcending the particularities of a particular place and time. The easy availability of such systems can serve as a means of socialization for those who are most dependent on stable, external organizations of meaning to structure their experience and teach them how to be in the world.

When I met Eric, he was eleven years old, and attending a private school in a major East Coast city, for higher functioning kids on the autism spectrum. I met and interviewed Eric as part of a two-year ethnographic study that looked at how the shifting diagnostic category of the autism spectrum is being interpreted by people diagnosed with these conditions, their families, and the professional communities that surround them. As part of that research, I was helping to run a drama club at Eric's school, and he was a member.

When I came to his house to interview him and his family, Eric emerged from his room wearing a Groucho Marx mask—with the glasses, and the nose, and the mustache—and demanded that I speak all my interview questions into his toy microphone. I was momentarily disoriented by the way he inverted the interview frame, utterly compromising its polite invisibility. Eric spoke in an exaggerated, stylized sing-song, like an old-fashioned circus showman. His parents called him "the director," because his favorite thing to do was to make them act out routines he's seen on YouTube. Over, and over, and over.

He didn't have many friends. The other kids at school liked him, but he didn't like to hang out with them, because he couldn't predict their behavior. Something might happen that he didn't expect, and he wouldn't know what to say or do if they went off-script. So instead, unless his parents were forcing him to go to tennis camp or our drama club or something like that, he stayed at home and watched his videos. Over and over and over. And through this process, he was socialized into a particular way of being in the world.

> "When a DVD comes out" his father explained to me, if it's a movie that he liked, he gets it the day it comes out and he will watch it 30 times. He will learn every line, every word; he will ask what expressions on people's faces mean, about colloquialisms he hasn't heard before. What he will very often do is—totally appropriate, totally on point, totally on subject, totally scripted—he will come out with something from TV to give him the words. We know that without video, without Sesame Street, without his ability to go back and review things over and over, and I mean it can be 30, 40 times [...] he wouldn't have learned half his language because nobody can do the repetition he needs.

Eric, like many individuals now diagnosed with autism spectrum disorders, had an underlying difficulty with auditory processing. It took him a while to understand what he heard, and by that point, the rapid-fire conversations around him had usually long moved on. But the DVD player was a patient teacher, showing Eric ways to organize words into sentences, parts into wholes, disparate concepts into chains of meaning. Through these narratives, he could reach out to others and show his deep care and concern for their welfare. His father went on to tell me:

> He saw a commercial the other day for Life Alert. You know: *I've fallen, and I can't get up!* My mother has been a widow for 25 years. He called my mother and got the answering machine and of course said, "Grandma, I want you to get Life Alert." And then proceeded to do the straight 30 seconds right out of the commercial: *Every senior citizen should have one, if you live alone—but then you won't be alone and I won't worry about you.* And totally on his own, I mean, he never asked what a senior citizen was, he never talked about that grandma lives alone. He put all these things together himself. This just happened this week, we're thrilled.

When I was first reviewing this material, I saw this incident, as his father had intended me to, as teaching me something about Eric: about how his brain works, and how he learns about the social world. But what if we were to look instead at what this story could teach us about the social world that he is learning, and how that content and context affects his process of socialization? Consider the following summary of what Eric has learned from his study of the Life Alert commercial: Grandma is a *senior citizen*; Grandma *lives alone*; senior citizens living alone is *commonplace* but also *something he should worry about*; there is a *machine that will take care of this problem for them.* These givens of Eric's social world—the classification of persons according to large-scale bureaucracies, the weakening of traditional social and familial ties with geographic dispersal of families and communities, and technology and consumer goods rushing in to fill that void—have shaped Eric's mode of sociality. I don't mean to say that Eric's family, those immediately around him, have failed in any way in their efforts to teach him about the world around him. As his father says, no person can provide the amount of repetition he needs to learn the complexities of his social environment. But the DVD player helps. Some part of Eric's socialization has taken place through video, through Sesame Street, through the ability to go back and review things over and over. And each time, things go exactly the same. This mimetic quality, its consistency, has shaped the tightly scripted nature of Eric's mode of sociality. How much of what we now call autism—the repetitiveness and the rigidity of its routinization—is resulting from the availability of these sorts of cultural materials, the unprecedented technological capacity to make things go the same way every time?

In asking these kinds of questions, I'm inspired by the work of sociologists studying what they consider to be a second phase of post-industrial modernity, sometimes referred to as "late modernity" (i.e., Beck 1992; Beck and Beck-Gernsheim 2002; Giddens 1991, 2000). Scholars of "late modern" or "high modern" societies suggest that such societies are going through a shift away from shared, stable, explicit systems of social organization and towards forms of social participation characterized instead by individual choice accompanied by uncertainty, ambivalence, and risk. The fading away of manifest social organization in its traditional forms has not meant that all people in fact operate as unique, free agents; rather, our seemingly free choices are now shaped and governed by bureaucracies, mass culture, and other such standardizing forces. Beck (1992) gives television as an example of what he calls "institutionalized individualism":

> [I]ndividualization delivers people over to an *external control and standardization* that was unknown in the enclaves of familial and feudal subcultures [...] Television isolates *and* standardizes. On the one hand, it removes people from traditionally shaped and bounded contexts of conversation, experience, and life. At the same time, however, everyone is in a similar position: they all consume institutionally produced television programs, from Honolulu to Moscow and Singapore. The individualization—more precisely, the removal from traditional life contexts—is accompanied by a uniformity and standardization of forms of living. (132)

At the same time, Beck observes, this process also mandates an emphasis on the individual as the sole unit of action and analysis, resulting in an obscuring of social and structural forces.

> Your own life—your own failure. Consequently, social crisis phenomena such as structural unemployment can be shifted as a burden of risk onto the shoulders of individuals. Social problems can be directly turned into psychological dispositions: into guilt feelings, anxieties, conflicts and neuroses. Paradoxically enough, a new immediacy develops in the relationship between the individual and society, an immediacy of disorder such that social crises appear as individual and are no longer—or only very indirectly—perceived in their social dimension. (Beck 2002, 24)

Herein lies the double impact of institutionalized individualism upon the people I'm talking about in this paper. They are more symbiotically reliant than most upon culture to complete themselves, yet the culture they find is one that denies the very impact of shared social structures in favor of explaining all phenomena on an individual level of analysis. And the process itself is described by medical and scientific knowledge production systems as arising exclusively from the inherent qualities of their individual brains.

6.5 That Was from Something

I got to observe this process in action when I went through training on the ADOS (Autism Diagnostic Observation Schedule), one component of the assessment system that has been the gold standard for autism diagnosis during autism's extraordinary rise in diagnostic prominence (Akshoomoff et al. 2006; Gotham et al. 2007; Oosterling et al. 2010).[4] The ADOS is a sustained, structured social interaction between an examiner and an examinee, during which the examinee is assessed on his or her interactional style and approach to tasks.

Successful social behavior on the ADOS modules is behavior that appears to be specific to the particular situation, specific to the particular people involved, and not ordered or organized by any sort of identifiable external form or task demand. Participants, for example, gain points towards a classification of autism for being determined to finish a task, to do things in a particular order, or to otherwise organize their behavior or circumstances according to some extrinsic form not explicitly demanded by test administrators. The irony, of course, is that the ADOS is a standardized diagnostic assessment of sociality, and so the entire interaction is thoroughly standardized, externally structured, and designed to be similar, in fundamental ways, across administrations. As the authors wrote in a 1989 article introducing the instrument:

> The general format of the schedule is to encourage an interaction that appears natural, during which preplanned "occasions" for certain behaviors arise, with the imposed structure as invisible to the subject as possible. However, in reality, this structure has been carefully determined in terms of social tasks that are defined in detail by variations in cognitive demands, in the type of materials, and in the behavior of the interviewer. […] These standard situations thus provide comparable social stimuli for all subjects. (Lord et al. 1989)

The burden is thus on test participants to occlude the artificiality of the interaction; for those who cannot or do not do so, their deviation from this imperative is pathologized as developmental disability.

I began my training by watching two videotapes, of two children being assessed on the ADOS (Western Psychological Services 2000). The first was a little boy who used few words, squealed and hummed, and appeared basically oblivious to the examiner's attempts to engage him in play. The little boy received a diagnosis of autism. The second was a little girl, who was chatty and cooperative with the examiner, gamely going along with the various activities proposed and carrying them out with a certain amount of verve and flair. But in the end, the little girl, too, received a diagnosis of autism. Here is why: She had made several different comments in the identical tone of voice, with the same phrasing and inflections each time: *Hey, the blocks fit! Hey, a hot dog! Hey, look, a piece of bread!* There was something exaggerated in how she talked ("REALLY? That's SO COOL!"), her voice lilting in a way that made her sound stilted, artificial. When asked who her friends are at school, she rattled off an alphabetized list of all her classmates, talking about what desks they sit at rather than who they were as people. When the examiner tried to interrupt her, she just kept talking until she was done with her list. She was more interested in investigating the camera in the corner and the one-way mirror on the wall next to her than she was in chatting, anyway. Her eyes wandered around the room while the examiner was talking. It was these quirks that got her the points that added up to her autism classification. Mia's social behavior, overall, appeared *stereotyped* rather than *spontaneous*, and only the latter is counted as legitimate social behavior.

At the training, we spent the bulk of our time learning what kinds of interactions to code as genuine and appropriate social behavior, and what kinds do not meet those criteria. The distinction that gets repeatedly drawn, when scoring the ADOS, is between a behavior that is explicitly elicited by *someone else* (i.e., a child volunteering a personal story only after being asked to do so) or that clearly comes from *somewhere else* (i.e., an examinee answering a question in a way that appears to have been memorized or to emerge out of his or her own preoccupations) versus a behavior that emerges *sui generis* from the subject him- or herself, in direct relation to the immediate context (i.e., a child spontaneously telling the examiner about his recent trip to the beach in response to being shown a picture of a beach scene). Only the latter is counted as true social behavior.

In some cases, this distinction is easy to draw. At the training I attended, the trainer administered a module 3 to a little boy, Jay, who was more interested in playing with the frame of our interaction than the toys and activities that were its official content. He addressed, rather than ignored, the assembled audience of observers, singing us a song about the alphabet into a microphone clipped to his neck. "I want to sing the movie song!" he insisted, as the administrator gently tried to guide him from one activity to the next. "That was *from* something" she inferred about the "movie song," and scored him a 2 for "stereotyped or idiosyncratic use of phrases." But at other times, drawing this distinction is more difficult. At one research lab where I observed, two staff members disagreed by one point in their scoring of a young boy, and this one point would make the difference in whether or not he met criteria for autism spectrum disorder—and thus for inclusion into the research study. The main point of contention was whether he had shown age-appropriate insight into social relationships. At one point during the administration, he had asked the examiner if she knew the story of Martin Luther King Jr. "We don't treat our friends like that anymore" he announced. But when asked "what is a friend?" he fumbled, said the question was hard, asked for an easier one. So did he show insight into friendship? "The Martin Luther King thing sounded rehearsed," the research assistant conceded, and adjusted his scoring so that he met criteria for autism spectrum disorder.

This distinction, between the genuine and the staged, also extends to judgments about the genuineness of the subjects' pleasure and enjoyment of the examiner and of the activities themselves. The activities have been designed to be fun: stuffed animals, funny stories about monkeys and coconuts, a very cool plastic bubble gun. And the examiners, almost exclusively people who have made professional careers out of working with children, have carefully honed their appeal, squatting down next to kids and speaking in an ingratiating, playful way. Given this standardization of fun, if a subject does not show "definite pleasure" in the interaction with the examiner, the assumption is that there must be something wrong with the subject, that he or she is deficient in his or her capacity for "appropriate social pleasure." "I don't think they [the signs of pleasure] were clear or definite. He didn't show 'definite pleasure' to me," our trainer told us after her ADOS with Jay. By the end of the test, tired and cranky, Jay had resorted to giving a little bow and thanking us gathered observers after every test item, then attempting to head offstage, only to be gently redirected back time and time again by assistants waiting in the wings. It had started to feel uncomfortably like watching an actor's nightmare. "Remember, we're coding him in relation to his average nonverbal mental age" she continued. "He should be able to do things at that ability level. The best fit is 'shows some appropriate pleasure in the examiner's actions' [among the criteria for a score of 1]. I think a zero is being too generous, too generous."

In difficult cases, we are instructed to attend to whether the subject invokes in us a sense of personal connection, a sense of being genuinely enjoyed. "I didn't get a sense that he was enjoying *me*" our trainer explained her scoring after we watched her administer a Module 2. "I might as well have been a bubble-blowing machine." Mia's faux-pleasure, her artificial-sounding cries of "cool!" in response to the appearance of yet another toy she does not want to play with, are insufficient.

In many ways, what is being measured here is a participant's ability to perform what Anthony Giddens (1991) calls the "pure relationship." A pure relationship is "one in which external criteria have become dissolved: the relationship exists solely for whatever rewards that relationship as such can deliver" (6). Such a relationship is pure because it is "not anchored in external conditions of social or economic life—it is, as it were, free-floating" (89). Participants engage in the relationship not because they have to, but by free individual choice based on their own desires and the degree of intrinsic satisfaction the relationship provides, and they can leave at any time on that same basis. The catch in this context, of course, is that the ADOS subject is usually not here by choice. Also, Giddens notes that the successful cultivation of such a relationship requires the labor-intensive building of mutual trust; ADOS participants are strangers to each other, meeting for the first time in a doctor's office or research lab. But participants are still expected to enact the ideal of a pure, spontaneous, voluntary, pleasurable social interaction as a condition of social health.

The ADOS appears to be measuring the extent to which subjects spontaneously produce genuine responses, unconstrained by rules or routines or pre-fabricated repertoires. What it is actually measuring is a task somewhat more complicated and far more difficult: the ability to comply with a complex and minutely prescribed set of social demands, while making it *appear* to an observer as though these perfectly appropriate behaviors originated purely within the individual in response to the interlocutor. It is the responsibility of test subjects to occlude the broader context of the interaction, its power imbalances and its standardization, acting as if they were merely meeting with the examiner to play together for the pleasure of it.

The Autism Diagnostic Observation Schedule both exemplifies contemporary pressures toward the routinization and standardization of social life, and enforces the imperative to render those pressures invisible by manifesting social behavior that appears sufficiently "spontaneous" and not inappropriately "scripted." As such, it equates social health with a particular contemporary form of authenticity, characterized by a linked pair of cultural imperatives: the requirement to adjust one's behavior to a precise set of social norms, while simultaneously making it appear as though one were acting purely out of one's own immediate, spontaneous, and internally generated inclinations. An autistic mode of engagement is incompatible with these imperatives, because the cultural products that structure behavior remain obdurately visible as such, thus confronting us with the rigid, repetitive, routinized forms that populate and order our social lives. We are inevitably shaped by the ways in which we have shaped our surroundings.

6.6 My Child Is a Toxic Waste Dump

Concerns about the autistic mode of engagement are inextricable from concerns about the impact of our human work upon the world. This became most clear to me when I started spending time with people who sought to "recover" their children from autism, which they defined as a whole-body disease resulting from exposure to man-made toxins. As they struggled to separate the autism from the child (both conceptually and concretely), parents and practitioners often identified autism as the result of injudicious human intervention upon the body or the broader world. In a historical moment when our transformation of our environment may be rendering that world less hospitable to human life, the permeability of autism becomes a source of alarm about human industry more broadly.

"Our children live in a physically and emotionally toxic world!" pediatrician Anju Usman announced at the 2008 meeting of the National Autism Association. The slides behind her listed "genetic predispositions, mother's burdens, heavy metals, environmental pollutants, electromagnetic fields, excess sensory input, stress/internal conflicts, dietary factors, microbial/biofilm, immune/inflammatory burden, chronic infections, clostridia, strep, viruses, glutamate, ammonia, mercury, aluminum, lead, pesticides, [and] vaccine adjuvants (viral fragments)" as contaminants, both physical and emotional, that build up in children's bodies and cause them to sicken (Usman 2008).

Parallels are often drawn, at these events, between pathologies of the body, pathologies of behavior, and pathologies of the broader sociocultural and physical environment. For example, clinical nutritionist Liz Lipski's (2009) talk at the Defeat Autism Now! conference described the intestines of autistic children as full of fungal overgrowth (clostridia, candida), then compared these bodies to the monoculture of post-industrial agriculture. "It's like a rainforest," she declared.

> Where you decide you could make a lot more money by clearcutting and raising soybeans! They are like a rainforest, an ecosystem that's full of dyes. Preservatives. Metal toxicity. So they have a rainforest that's been clearcut and people are growing soybeans—soybeans that look like clostridia! Like candida! Like things that should be there in small quantities. (Lipski 2009)

The replacement of nature's biodiversity with an imbalanced, unhealthy sameness plays out in parallel, on the globe and in the gut. The consequence is routinized, repetitive, and restricted behaviors on the part of the child, who both embodies and enacts this artificial overgrowth.

A major theme at these conferences is the novelty of these toxic exposures. At a Defeat Autism Now! conference in 2009, an essay reprinted in the conference booklet refers to autism as a "Disease of Modernity":

> Toxins have become ubiquitous and can penetrate our defenses from every corner. From the air we breathe outdoors, which is more likely than not to be contaminated with industrial pollutants, to our in-door or in-vehicle air, which is almost certainly contaminated with vinyl off-gasses. Foods can be contaminated with pesticides, hormones, and non-stick coatings from cookware. Water can suffer contamination from a host of pollutants; even the disinfectants used by most municipalities produce by-products which are felt by many to be unsafe to drink and can be absorbed through bath-water as well. Whether through the digestive tract, the lungs, or the skin, we did not evolve with the defenses to protect us from the host of man-made toxins in our current environment. (Levinson 2009, 25)

The author goes on to advise that there is "more involved" in creating a non-toxic environment "than avoiding plastics, heavy metals and industrial pollutants. [...] Stress, poor eating habits, poor-self care, and limited creative outlets, exercise, and pastimes affect the well-being and lifespan," adding that "there is largely no margin for error in the household of an affected child" (Levinson 2009, 26).

I'm not a toxicologist, and my aim here is not to evaluate the accuracy of each of these specific concerns. Rather, what I am struck by again and again is the way in which the byproducts of human work upon the world—both material and sociocultural, physical and emotional—have come to evoke intense fear and distrust. The repetitious cultural outputs of mass production and mass media that are such robust fodder for the autistic style can also be understood as a form of manufactured risk. When a child shows affection for a friend through dialogue out of a Disney movie, or shows love by reciting a commercial, his body and his being become sites at which this anxiety is negotiated. "If your kid's a stimmy kid—flapping hands, verbally perseverative, scripting, rewinding videos, obsessed with things—we think of that as a viral child," one of the presenters at the 2009 AutismOne conference observed in her presentation, her use of the word "virus" effectively indexing a rich node of association between information technology and biological illness. "There's a whole pile of viruses" (Hintz and Rankin 2009).

As can be seen in the notorious conflicts between those in this so-called "biomedical community" and autistic self-advocates, it can be difficult to square respect for autistic personhood and autistic ways of being with these anxieties. *Our children are being poisoned,* I heard a parent say at one of these conferences. *Their brains are destroyed.* At another presentation, a photograph of human corpses piled in a pit was used as a metaphorical illustration of the brain cells of autistic children (Blaxill 2009). On several occasions, I heard parents say: *my child is a toxic waste dump.* In the years since I first heard those words, I've never really stopped grappling with what to *make of* that statement. How do we consider the possibilities to which this phrase refers and its implications without denigrating the kinds of subjectivities that emerge under those conditions, without catastrophizing them as damaged or devalued? Perhaps the troubled coexistence of our selves and our creations is so salient in the case of autism because it is so fraught—with peril, with contention. Perhaps also because it is passionate—and here I mean passion in the sense of love, and also passion in the sense of suffering. Autism places us squarely in the vulnerability of our incompleteness, and the terrifying range of its potentiality.

As a result of my having done the work I have done, I have become more of an environmentalist. I have become more deeply aware of the permeability of our insides by our outsides, of the way we are always consuming what we create, even and especially those "byproducts" of our creation that we try to render invisible. At our Rio conference, Bárbara Costa Andrada contextualized her presentation on autism services in the Baixada Fluminense region of Brazil by showing us pictures of the legal and illegal dumping grounds that surround the industrial city where she conducted her ethnography. Thick with both toxins and treasures, the massive landfills provided a living for a local economy of thousands of people who picked through them for recyclables (Costa Andrada 2015). It is impossible to understand autism without understanding the environments that autistic people inhabit—these dangerous ecologies, and the gifts they offer.

Scripted comments, routinized play, industrial chemicals and vinyl off-gasses, clear-cut forests and dangerous electromagnetic fields: though they are different in their medium and mechanism of action, they share certain key characteristics. They are particular arrangements of elements—words, concepts, molecules, materials—that are assembled as such via human action, and that have become necessary for our current mode of functioning. They are discarded and occluded, but are then taken up and made visible as robust forms by the autistic mode of engagement. The autistic incorporation and performance of these arrangements compromises our ability to disavow them. By pathologizing the autistic mode—and in particular, pathologizing it by collapsing it onto the individual body and thus denying its fundamentally extrasomatic dimensions—we perpetuate our ability to *trash:* to keep unwanted byproducts of human production well out of sight.[5]

But this concealment comes at a cost. To over-value the impossible ideal of a pure individual self, uncorrupted by material of human making, devalues many aspects of being human. Because of the fertility (to use Steve's term) of autistic subjectivity, its permeability by the stuff of human making, respect for autistic self-expression especially requires respect for selves and social relations that are so constituted. It also requires that we recognize the full range of our productions—both those we would value and those we might rather send away—acknowledging the ways in which such human creations are inextricable from human development. To do so requires that we grapple with the consequences of our work upon the world, and the ways in which our intertwinement with each other transcends and permeates our own skins—even when the consequence is a terrifying sense of impingement. But the consequences of not doing so may be worse yet.

In her remarks on the earlier version of this paper that was presented at our workshop, discussant Dawn Prince-Hughes suggested that autistic sensitivity—and even autistic withdrawal—can be a much needed invitation into a deeper awareness of our interconnectedness with our threatened environment.

> If you can imagine standing in a hula hoop that you can't get out of, no matter what, and there's a godawful high school marching band going around you constantly, someone's making you eat and smell limburger cheese, and you're being pricked by needles by people that are coming in at random intervals, just pricking you at different places in your body—now imagine living like that for seven years without a break, or 35 years, or 52 years, now, which I'm coming up on—and then you're supposed to—*let's see, what are the rules*—you're supposed to *be spontaneous!* and *show joy in interacting with people!* And it's just the craziest thing! When you know [autism] from the inside out, you think, *well, nobody's gonna do that.* And to me, that is the case. Nobody's doing that. When I think of the spectrum—and I think of myself as far over on the spectrum but I see everybody on that spectrum—and when you mentioned the toxic waste dump idea, I think that in the case of autism, it's almost as if evolution is anticipatory. So the kind of toxic environment, culturally and physically, that we're being born into actually needs people like us to be the canaries in the coal mine, that say:
>
> *This is too much.*
> *We can't deal with it.*
> *It's painful.*
>
> What you said about the environment really resonates with me, because even though I'm so much better now, every day I can feel the sadness of people around the world. I can feel the dying of the planet. I can never get away from it. And I think other people are feeling it too. But they find their own different ways to seize on culture to limit the kind of stimuli that they're feeling.
>
> We do it as academics all the time. We saw it yesterday when we were trying to have our discussion. Our impulses to cling to the familiar. To repeat patterns that aren't necessarily going to do us any good in the long run. We hold on to methodology, or onto our field of study. We hold on to our professorship. And to me this is all just the same thing. It's just a matter of degree rather than kind. (Prince-Hughes 2015)

I hope that in this preliminary set of thoughts I have taken some small step outside of familiar patterns, and into a slightly different way of attending to the world around us.

Notes

1. Asperger's Disorder as a distinct term was removed from the most recent revision of the Diagnostic and Statistical Manual of Mental Disorders (American Psychiatric Association 2013), subsumed under Autism Spectrum Disorder.
2. For further accounts of this process, see Badone et al. (2016), Fein (2015), Prince-Hughes (2004) and Solomon (2004).
3. Furlong and Cartmel (1997) refer to this process of occlusion as the "epistemological fallacy of late modernity," observing that "although social structures, such as class, continue to shape life chances, those structures tend to become increasingly obscure as collectivist traditions weaken and individualist values intensify [...] People's life chances remain highly structured at the same time as they increasingly seek solutions on an individual, rather than a collective, basis" (2–5).
4. Since the time of this training, a revised version of the ADOS, the ADOS-2, has been released. Though the ADOS-2 is similar in many ways, the following discussion should nonetheless be understood as a snapshot of a particular historical moment rather than a description of current practice.
5. Joe Masco (2013) gives a chilling account of a similar process in his essay "Side Effect."

References

Akshoomoff, Natacha, Christina Corsello, and Heather Schmidt. 2006. "The Role of the Autism Diagnostic Observation Schedule in the Assessment of Autism Spectrum Disorders in School and Community Settings." *California School Psychologist* 11: 7–19.

American Psychiatric Association. 2013. *Diagnostic and Statistical Manual of Mental Disorders.* 5th ed. Arlington, VA: American Psychiatric Publishing.

Attwood, Tony. 2007. *The Complete Guide to Asperger's Syndrome.* London: Jessica Kingsley.

Badone, Ellen, David Nicholas, Wendy Roberts, and Peter Kien. 2016. "Asperger's Syndrome, Subjectivity and the Senses." *Culture, Medicine and Psychiatry* 40: 475–506.

Baron-Cohen, Simon. 2000. "Is Asperger Syndrome/High Functioning Autism Necessarily a Disability?" *Development and Psychopathology* 12: 489–500.

Baron-Cohen, Simon, Jennifer Richler, Dheraj Bisarya, Nhishanth Gurunathan, and Sally Wheelwright. 2003. "The Systemizing Quotient: An Investigation of Adults with Asperger Syndrome or High-Functioning Autism, and Normal Sex Differences." *Philosophical Transactions of the Royal Society B* 358 (1430 Autism: Mind and Brain): 361–374.

Beck, Ulrich. 1992. *Risk Society: Towards a New Modernity*. London: Sage.
———. 2002. "A Life of One's Own in a Runaway World: Individualization, Globalization and Politics." In *Individualization: Institutionalized Individualism and Its Social and Political Consequences,* Ulrich Beck and Elizabeth Beck-Gernsheim. London: Sage.
Beck, Ulrich, and Elizabeth Beck-Gernsheim. 2002. *Individualization: Institutionalized Individualism and Its Social and Political Consequences.* London: Sage.
Belmonte, Matthew. 2008. "Human But More So: What the Autistic Brain Tells Us About the Process of Narrative." In *Autism and Representation*, edited by Mark Osteen. New York: Routledge.
Blaxill, Mark. 2009. "Intellectual and Moral Failures in Autism Science." Presentation at Autism One, Chicago, IL, May 2009.
Costa Andrada, Barbara. 2015. "Paradigms of Autism and Local Practices of Care: Challenges to Social Inclusion." Paper presented at Autism Spectrum Disorders in Global, Local and Personal Perspective: A Cross-Cultural Workshop, Rio de Janeiro, Brazil, September 2015.
Fein, Elizabeth. 2015. "Making Meaningful Worlds: Role-Playing Subcultures and the Autism Spectrum." *Culture, Medicine and Psychiatry* 39 (2): 299–321.
Furlong, Andy, and Fred Cartmel. 1997. *Young People and Social Change: Individualization and Risk in Late Modernity*. Buckingham: Open University Press.
Geertz, Clifford. 2000. "The Impact of the Concept of Culture on the Concept of Man." In *The Interpretation of Cultures.* 2000 ed. New York: Basic Books.
Giddens, Anthony. 1991. *Modernity and Self-Identity: Self and Society in the Late Modern Age*. Cambridge: Polity Press.
———. 2000. *Runaway World: How Globalization Is Reshaping Our Lives.* New York: Routledge.
Gotham, Katherine, Susan Risi, Andrew Pickles, and Catherine Lord. 2007. "The Autism Diagnostic Observation Schedule: Revised Algorithms for Improved Diagnostic Validity." *Journal of Autism & Developmental Disorders* 37 (4): 613–627.
Happé, Francesca, and Uta Frith. 2006. "The Weak Coherence Account: Detail-Focused Cognitive Style in Autism Spectrum Disorders." *Journal of Autism and Developmental Disorders* 36 (1): 5–25.
Hintz, Sonja, and Sym Rankin. 2009. "How to Get Your Mainstream Physician to See Beyond Autism." Presentation at Autism One, Chicago, IL, May 2009.
Kiyosaki, Robert T. with Sharon Lechter. 2000. *Rich Dad, Poor Dad: What the Rich Teach Their Kids About Money—That the Poor and Middle Class Do Not!* New York: Warner Business Books.
L'Engle, Madeline. 1973. *A Wind in the Door.* New York: Square Fish/Farrar, Straus and Giroux.

Levinson, Andrew. 2009. "The Road To Recovery: Walking with Patience, Peace, and Perseverance." Essay Printed in Conference Booklet for Defeat Autism Now! Conference, Atlanta, Georgia, April 2009.

Linde, Charlotte. 1993. *Life Stories: The Creation of Coherence*. Oxford: Oxford University Press.

Lipski, Liz. 2009. "The Autism-Digestion-Brain Connection." Presentation at the Defeat Autism Now! Conference, Atlanta, Georgia, April 2009.

Lord, Catherine, Michael Rutter, Susan Goode, Jacquelyn Heemsbergen, Heather Jordan, Lynn Mawhood, and Eric Schopler. 1989. "Autism Diagnostic Observation Schedule: A Standardized Observation of Communicative and Social Behavior." *Journal of Autism and Developmental Disorders* 19 (2): 185–212.

Masco, Joseph. 2013. "Side Effect." *Somatosphere: Science, Medicine, and Anthropology*. December 2, 2013. http://somatosphere.net/2013/12/side-effect.html.

Mottron, Laurent, Michelle Dawson, and Isabelle Soulières. 2009. "Enhanced Perception in Savant Syndrome: Patterns, Structure and Creativity." *Philosophical Transactions of the Royal Society B* 364: 1385–1391.

Oosterling, Iris, Sascha Roos, Annelies de Bildt, Nanda Rommelse, Maretha de Jonge, Janne Visser, Martijn Lappenschaar, Sophie Swinkels, Rutger Jan van der Gaag, and Jan Buitelaar. 2010. "Improved Diagnostic Validity of the ADOS Revised Algorithms: A Replication Study in an Independent Sample." *Journal of Autism & Developmental Disorders* 40 (6): 689–703.

Prince-Hughes, Dawn. 2004. *Songs of the Gorilla Nation: My Journey Through Autism*. New York: Harmony Press.

———. 2015. Discussant Remarks Presented at Autism Spectrum Disorders in Global, Local and Personal Perspective: A Cross-Cultural Workshop, Rio de Janeiro, Brazil, September 2015.

Ramstead, Maxwell J.D., Samuel P.L. Veissière, and Laurence J. Kirmayer. 2016. "Cultural Affordances: Scaffolding Local Worlds Through Shared Intentionality and Regimes of Attention." *Frontiers in Psychology* 7: 1090. http://doi.org/10.3389/fpsyg.2016.01090.

Solomon, Olga. 2004. "Narrative Introductions: Discourse Competence of Children with Autistic Spectrum Disorders." *Discourse Studies* 6 (2): 139–146.

Usman, Anju. 2008. "Excitotoxicity in ASD." Presentation at the National Autism Conference, Fort Lauderdale, FL, November 2008.

Western Psychological Services. 2000. "Autism Diagnostic Observation Schedule: Workshop Video (DVD 1)." Torrance, CA: Western Psychological Services.

CHAPTER 7

Autism and First-Person Accounts: The Cognitive Problem

Jurandir Freire Costa and Roy Richard Grinker

7.1 Introduction

In their recent edited volume *Worlds of Autism: Across the Spectrum of Neurological Difference* (2013), Davidson and Orsini draw attention to the extreme diversity of human thought and experience now included under the label "autism." The authors underline the growing desire to learn about autism from self-advocates, in large part because autistic individuals' representations of themselves challenge many of the assumptions about autism that scientists, clinicians, and educators continue to reproduce. These assumptions derive from the search for commonalities along the wide-ranging spectrum of autism and revolve mainly around absence and deficit: for example, the lack of a theory of mind (including empathy), impairment in executive functioning, and "weak central coherence," a particular cognitive processing style in which individuals exhibit a bias towards details or local information, and have difficulty integrating

J. F. Costa (✉)
Institute for Social Medicine, State University of Rio de Janeiro, Rio de Janeiro, Brazil

R. R. Grinker
George Washington University, Washington, DC, USA

E. Fein and C. Rios (eds.), *Autism in Translation*, Culture, Mind, and Society, https://doi.org/10.1007/978-3-319-93293-4_7

those details into a larger context. Whereas in the past it was thought that most people with autism could seldom understand themselves through the abstract framework of autism, nor author many insights to the scholarly study of autism, there are today dozens of first-person accounts by adults and children who self-declare as autistic; parents who recount the experiences of autistic children as involving both deficits and abilities; and also by some caretakers and scholars who published in a variety of forms (such as blogs, poetry, essays, and books) who contribute to furthering a narrative genre that helps us rethink this deficit model.[1]

We seek to compare some of these first-person accounts with ideas commonly held by experts on the subject.[2] First of all, we must make five preliminary observations. First, we sought to avoid the quarrel over the authenticity of accounts written with the aid of facilitated communication. The hypothesis of fraud regarding the texts' authorship remains, but this does not negate the value of what was written about the lived experience.[3] Second, we do not intend for these accounts to faithfully mirror the "intrinsic nature" of autism. To us, there is no "essence" or "intrinsicality" in this form of subjectification. This work seeks merely to better understand psychological expressions that bear a "family resemblance," in Wittgenstein's sense of the expression, by which we mean phenomena that may overlap, but as a group may share nothing in common. Third, the narrated cases are far from representing all subjects who participate in the autism spectrum. Many of these do not acquire the ability to communicate through personal linguistic expressions.

The fourth observation concerns the limits of this type of narrative. Many first-person accounts have a similar structure in terms of their basic constituent elements: recounting the experience of the disquiet and suffering of parents, relatives, and the subjects when faced with the first signs of what would later be diagnosed as autism; initial contacts and obstacles with educational and therapeutic professionals and equipment; the disappointment, in most cases, with the routine way with which the problem is treated; the discovery of more creative and emotionally rich means of expression than those described or prescribed by the experts' body of knowledge; et cetera. Additionally, in nearly all accounts, subjects revisit narratives of previous experiences, adding new observations. Obviously, a "first person" account is itself a particular kind of style, constructed as a convention in writing, a style that marks, delimits, and simultaneously enables the enunciation of the psychological peculiarities of this modality of human experience. However, we could say that similar styles are enacted across multiple frameworks for communicating psychological experiences in societies that possess similar concepts of the individual and individualism. In all of them, there is a cultural imprint of the historical matrix; of the many ethnic, religious, social, professional, gender (etc.) cultures or subcultures; of academic specialties; and so on. All are inescapably present. We believe there is no way to escape the theoretical shadow of the vocabularies used to describe the autistic experience and we acknowledge that the descriptions are grounded in the long-standing ideology in Western civilization that societies are constituted by individuals, and that each individual is a discrete and complete being. Even the person suffering from psychotic delusions draws on his or her knowledge and experience in the world to create them. Thus, the fact that the study of first-person accounts requires a perspectival approach to autism does not mean that these accounts lack refined and original observations of psychological processes.

Finally, our goal is to illustrate, through the language of people with autism, how people construct their subjectivity and interpretative vocabulary. And in doing so, we are perhaps not far from much of psychiatric and psychoanalytic practice, which often relies on first-person accounts as evidence, even if clinicians also often deny that patient narratives can validate a diagnosis. We are approaching first-person accounts differently, however, to the extent that we draw on a non-medical vocabulary—namely, literature in phenomenology and philosophy of mind. Ironically, in using philosophical perspectives to think about the language of people with autism, we are performing our own estrangement from "normal" disciplinary practices in psychiatric research, and in autism research in particular.

7.2 Meanings of Autistic Experience

Understanding the meaning of the autistic experience depends largely on understanding the unusual way in which subjects communicate lived experiences to one another within their shared environment. These experiences are, in short, intentional states, processes or occurrences; that is, they represent needs, desires, thoughts, sensations, feelings, beliefs, judgments, actions, et cetera.

The meaning of autistic expressions may, for the purposes of argumentative clarity, be divided into four major dimensions: *cognitive*; *sensory-motor*; *affective* and *communicational*. We chose these four topics due to their tacit dialogue with conventional interpretations of the autistic experience or, in more scientific parlance, the broader autism phenotype: in conventional psychiatric nosology, so-called cognitive, affective, sensory, and communicational deficits are viewed as pathognomonic signs of autism.

By communicational performance, we designate the set of physical-mental resources that enable the subject to render intentional acts comprehensible to another subject. These resources may also be described as the linguistic and pre-linguistic competence that is necessary for the agent to produce, in the interlocutor, satisfactory or unsatisfactory responses to their demands, which may be conscious or unconscious; clear or confusing; simple or complex, et cetera. This includes cases described as "social communication deficits," one of the most highly researched aspects of autism, and the subject of numerous psychometric tests, including difficulty expressing oneself, social reciprocity and turn-taking, and inability to develop meaningful friendships (Tager-Flusberg et al. 2011).

By sensory-motor performance, we designate the physical expression of the body concerning the capacity to discern internal or environmental stimuli, ordering them in "types" or "instantiations of types" with cognitive-affective value, and also the heightened sensitivities (Baranek et al. 2014). Sensory-motor performance enables us to selectively cope with things and events, due to different inclinations, needs, beliefs, desires, aspirations, et cetera.

By affective performance, we designate subjects' ability to manifest emotion, feelings or affections that are appropriate to different life circumstances. This includes all aspects of the debate on the "empathy deficit" that is supposedly characteristic of autistics. Deficits in affective performance refers to the observations that people with autism exhibit flat or neutral emotional expressions and, moreover, exhibit emotional expressions that are unusual or socially inappropriate in given contexts (Hobson 2014).

Each of these topics is extraordinarily wide-ranging and complex, and we do not wish to oversimplify them as features of autism. Nonetheless, they do represent major areas of behavior that clinicians construe as impairment and deficit, and are already codified (and, one might argue, simplified) in diagnostic tests, and in the American Psychiatric Association's *Diagnostic and Statistical Manual of Mental Disorders* (*DSM-5*) (2013). We should also add that in the examples we will analyze, the four elements were isolated for didactic purposes. In intentional human conduct, they are inextricably connected.

Given both the current stage of our research and the limits imposed by the scope of an article, we will focus on examples of cognitive actions. In future research, the other aspects will be analyzed.

7.3 Cognitive Performance

We chose to analyze and, with the help of examples, question the hypothesis of a central coherence deficit. This hypothesis typically refers to the tendency in people with autism to focus in their cognitive processing on details rather than the "big picture" or integrative gestalt (Happé et al. 2001). Central coherence is a term coined by cognitivist theories to describe a supposed autonomous instance responsible for the subject's capacity to follow rules, based on systems of compulsory inferences. As Douglas Biklen critically observed, this thesis is based on the idea that the autistic subject is incapable of: (a) constructing categories, based on similarities and differences of the members of a logical set; (b) showing interest in the whole and not only in a part of a phenomenon, ultimately; and (c) deriving a gestalt of observed facts from individual occurrences (Biklen 2005, 40–43).

Scientific assumptions about a lack of central coherence continue to influence the way autistic individuals think about themselves—witness the large number of blogs and other writing in social media created by autistic individuals who identify weak central coherence (WCC) as a common deficit, even if they also sometimes challenge the assumption. There is considerable complexity and nuance in the psychological literature on WCC. Scientists debate whether WCC is distinctive to people with autism. They show elements of WCC in, for example, artists, and people with eating disorders. Moreover, scientists have also noted that WCC and other frameworks (e.g., systematizing and executive function models) are not mutually exclusive. Note, however, that considering WCC in its pure form as an ideal type, as first articulated by Frith (1989), subjects' spontaneous capacity to structure the world, based on the embodied action of perceptive interactions and sensory reactions, is reduced to an almost theoretical-epistemological operation. This unsuccessful operation would be the bedrock of their supposed inability to deal with the logic of means suited to ends or to correctly infer satisfactory logical conclusions from consistent premises.

In the psychological literature, experimental work has complicated WCC as a model that explains or essentializes individuals with autism. In this chapter, we seek to demonstrate how the hypothesis is challenged in first person narratives by subjects' capacity to offer acceptable justifications for their actions, whether manifest or merely imagined. The ability to justify satisfactorily one's own conducts is proof of subjects' rational integrity. Rationality is obviously not explicitly addressed by most studies on cognitive deficit within the autism field. However, the rational justification of conduct is the very expression of the integrity (1) of the logic of classifying things and events in the world, and (2) of the logic of valid and plausible inferences between premises and conclusions. By defining (1) X things or events as types or instances of Y things or events, or by saying (2) that A events have a logical connection with B conduct, which justify their role as motives for the latter, subjects show that their cognitive processes may be atypical,[4] but not necessarily evidence of a deficit in "central coherence."

For these reasons, in their accounts, autistic writers strive to make others understand that cognition is not a disembodied process to be judged in terms of a shared rationality derived from the consensus of "neurotypicals." As we note below, first-person accounts of autism show that autistic subjects know and seek to communicate about what they are thinking and feeling in an atypical way which is nonetheless rationally/cognitively coherent.

This view is not foreign to anthropology. Anthropologists have long validated a relativist perspective, beginning with Evans-Pritchard's classic account of Azande witchcraft beliefs as rational *in context*. Nor is this view foreign to Freudian psychoanalysis in which the reasons a person gives to explain a behavior cannot be evaluated by shared cultural expectations about what is rational or reasonable but must be understood in terms of how the ability to explain oneself structures one's psychological life.

As first-person accounts illustrate, autistic individuals not only wish to explain themselves to others but also to explain why they behave in a way that others interpret as strange—that is, they want to communicate their empathic understanding of the relationship between Self and Other. This ability is not trivial. Translating one's own subjectivity into and out of the hegemonic mental vocabulary of those who, from the autistic person's perspective, are the atypical requires an enormous cognitive effort. We will emphasize this last aspect of cognitive performance, that is, the rational justification of conducts, desires, beliefs, et cetera, because we believe it is frequently underestimated in discussions of autism.

7.4 Fragments of Accounts

7.4.1 Attfield

Richard Attfield was one of Douglas Biklen's collaborators in his well-known work on autism. In one part of his account, Attfield says:

> I am not retarded ... All my life I have been considered stupid. I understand that autistic people are intelligent and if you people admitted that you cannot understand us then perhaps we could try in a way to understand each other as fellow human beings. (Biklen 2005)[5]

The fragment speaks for itself. Attfield is not only capable of understanding what "understanding" means, he is also capable of "understanding" the reasons why he is not understood by most people around him. He knows his expressive means, the expressive means of others and can grasp, in a broad gesture of moral openness, the value in human beings' efforts to understand one another. Preconceived ideas of a central coherence deficit, as the logical ability to justify rationally the meaning of what is done, said or thought, are seriously called into question by accounts of this sort.

7.4.2 Mukhopadhyay

In his 2011 autobiographical account *How Can I Talk if My Lips Don't Move: Inside My Autistic Mind*, Tito Mukhopadhyay, a poet on the autism spectrum, states that once he was shown a toy tiger and, when asked to name the object, encountered difficulty. He thought of many things associated with the tiger, such as "carnivore, stripe, ferocious, forest, hunt, etc." but could not come up with the name of the animal until he arrived at a method of naming it: "A striped animal, which is not a zebra, is a TIGER" (115–116). Mukhopadhyay uses the object's defined description, first in its positive form—a striped animal—then in its negative form—which is not a zebra—to then use the common noun as an index of singularization. He thus shows he can resort to an atypical logical procedure that is nonetheless perfectly intelligible both to himself and to others. He is therefore competent to generalize based on singular phenomena and to construct categories formed by elements with similar characteristics.

At other moments, he describes a peculiar way of defining common nouns. For example, "a soft petaled part of a plant is a FLOWER" (ibid.); he also adds that "a very big animal, which evolved from a mammoth, is a ELEPHANT" (ibid.). In this case, what draws our attention is not just the logic of classification and naming, but the creation of new metaphors and metonymies. Describing a flower as "a soft petaled part of a plant," and an elephant as "a very big animal, which evolved from a mammoth," shows the integrity of cognitive functions and the creativity of the definitions. The originality of the definitions is even more remarkable when we consider his ability to move to another level of abstraction and stress the importance, in his mode of comprehension, of understanding the context in which words and expressions "gain meaning" and then including a description of that process in the act of definition. He wrote:

> The story behind an object is far more important to me than the object. That is why a description of a situation becomes more important to me than the situation itself. (ibid., 54)

Such background thinking, perhaps more common than most people realize, or are willing to admit, often goes unnoticed, as if the "common noun" were a tag affixed to a product, as a matter of cognitive convenience or availability. In their everyday thinking, Mukhopadhyay and other autistic individuals excel at making a version (though non-binary) of de Saussure's classic semiotic argument that signs have significance only in relationship to other signs (1998). For most of us, the context that originates a meaning is brought to the foreground and subjected to analytical deconstruction only when the meaning is disputed. But Mukhopadhyay spontaneously carries out this process.

7.4.3 Fleischmann

Carly Fleischmann, in a biography written with her father Arthur Fleischmann, shows, like Mukhopadhyay, an admirable capacity for creating unusual metaphors, in addition to interrogating the idea of a categorical thought deficit in autism. For example:

> "What do you want to do in New York?" [Arthur Fleischmann, Carly's father] asked Carly. "The lady with the torch," she replied.(Fleischmann 2012, 173)

In another section, the dialogue is richer:

> *Caretaker*: Then if you get it, let's do a pop quiz. Name three types of birth control.
> *Carly*: Pill. Condom. Diaphragm.
> *Caretaker*: How does the birth control pill work?
> *Carly*: It tricks your body into thinking it's pregnant. (ibid., 179, 183–184)

Lastly, consider these two sentences, simple yet rich in psychological and moral resonance: "You know how people talk behind people's back? With me, they talk in front of my back" (ibid., 125).

In these examples, Fleischmann exhibits the capacity to categorically distinguish objects between types and examples—birth control as type, and pill, condom, and diaphragm as examples. Additionally, the metaphor of the Statue of Liberty and the way in which birth control acts "tricking" the body show her intellectual creativity, as she uses unusual images to describe usual things and events. The use of the expression "in front of my back" is painful. It illustrates the disregard with which we may treat people who express themselves differently from the majority and the feeling of belittlement felt by those treated disrespectfully. The majority is perceived as having a "front" and "back"—a metaphor for the rules of decorum that compel us to respect the feelings of others. The autistic subject, however, is often perceived as not entitled to the same respect. Anything can be said in front of them, even that which may come to offend or humiliate them.

7.4.4 *Tammet*

Daniel Tammet, in his autobiography, says he is most widely known as "an autistic savant," an unusually gifted learner who speaks numerous languages and has an extraordinary memory for numbers (once reciting more than 22,000 digits of pi in a single 5-hour period). He also has a form of synesthesia, in which numbers and letters are associated with colors. However, his remarkable intelligence for numbers and language acquisition is not a mechanical activity. This is notable, among other things, in the justification he formulated to explain synesthesia. He states that synesthesia is a natural phenomenon that is potentially available to most people. In his case, the synesthetic potential is nearly fully developed. In support of this opinion, he turns to neuroscientist V.S. Ramachandran. He writes of a mid-century psychological test for the human disposition towards onomatopoeia in which research subjects were given artificial words and then asked to associate them to particular feelings:

> Recently, Professor Ramachandran's team has replicated the results of this test using the invented words bouba and kiki. Ninety-five percent of those asked thought the rounded shape was a bouba and the pointed shape a kiki. Ramachandran suggests the reason in that the sharp changes in the visual direction of the lines in the kiki figure mimics the sharp phonemic inflections of the word's sound, as well as the sharp inflection of the tongue on the palate. Professor Ramachandran believes this synesthetic connection between our hearing and seeing was an important first step towards the creation of the word in early humans. (Tammet 2006, 166)

Tammet suggests that his own synesthesia is just a permutation of a human capacity that exists on a wide continuum, with himself at one extreme. The propriety of this reading of Ramachandran on synesthesia is irrelevant. What is important is the improvization displayed in Tammet's cognitive operation. By naturalizing synesthesia, he creatively subverts his sensory-perceptive atypicality. His kinship with so-called "neurotypicals" is evident. There is nothing in his way of feeling and thinking that is "deficient." His abilities are typically human, only more so.

7.4.5 *Higashida*

Naoki Higashida, in his autobiographical account, discusses a relatively frequent behavior among autistics, repetition of the same question. About this kind of perseveration, he says:

> It's true; I always ask the same questions. "What day is it today?" or "Is it a school day tomorrow?" … I don't repeat my question because I didn't understand—in fact, even as I'm asking, I know I do understand. The reason, why? Because I very quickly forget what it is I've just heard.

> Inside my head there really isn't such a big difference between what I was told just now, and what I heard a long, long time ago … . I imagine a normal person's memory is arranged continuously, like a line. My memory, however, is more like a pool of dots. I'm always "picking up" these dots—by asking my questions—so I can arrive back at the memory that the dots represents. (Higashida 2013, 10)

Let us observe three characteristics of his account because they are reproduced by almost all authors of the accounts we analyze. Firstly, he diagnoses the cause or reason of his expressive particularity and leads us to see that the supposed "echolalia" or "linguistic stereotyping" is a meaningful act. Secondly, he explains the peculiarity of the mnemic functioning, linking together the image of a container, the storing of memories, and the usual image of a path, a progressive line in time, which is a normative image of recollection. Higashida's cognitive performance is undoubtedly exceptional, though atypical. Higashida additionally notes that, for him, language is not only about memory but is, in the simple terms, about playing with, experimenting with, sound and rhythm. The sound of certain questions is pleasurable enough to warrant being repeated. Repetition in speaking is thus not entirely dissimilar, then, from the repetition of, say, playing catch with a baseball or a Frisbee.

7.4.6 Blackman

Lucy Blackman, in her autobiographical book, explains the meaning of the echolalia in her behavior and shows the efficacy of the cognitive activity that is implicit in atypical communication forms. Speaking about the verbal habit, she says:

> … I used echolalia not as much as more fluent autistic children, but still enough to confuse the issue. I use to repeat single words to say that I agreed, because I did not use the 'y-e-s' word then. A second reason for echoing was that I did not understand. I still do that, not with a nice questioning lilt, but with a panicky flutter in my voice which is the forerunner to real stress. These days background sound in quiet places is less disorienting, so I can see this panic starting up and control it, but in places like city streets of offices full of computers and air conditioners it erupts without warning. The third reason for my echolalia has gone, thank goodness. This urge to speak spontaneously was always preceded by a patch of

> internal silence and I simply dared not leave a vacuum in the sound that I felt within my head, because I felt the word as if it were part of me and not something said by me. (2001, 42–43)

Observe Blackman's ability to distinguish between several referents of a single term and the acuity with which she operates this distinction. In the first case, echolalia appears as a substitute for words not yet learned. It therefore works as a sort of idiosyncratic synonym of the word "yes." In the second case, it is used as a defense against affect disorientation in the face of a meaning Blackman does not control, particularly the flow of intense sounds in noisy places. It is a defense, therefore, against the excess of noises and information that are onerous to her sensoperception. In the third referent, echolalia has a near opposite goal, to fill with a thought vacuum with sounds. In other words, the meaning of that which, at first glance, seems to be a pure repetition of sounds deprived of a semantic load is the effect of a similar verbal act with diverse pragmatic functions. Blackman not only uses words as we have all learned to use them, that is, in context and with diversified communicative functions. She is also able to explain the subtle difference between psychological states that justify or do not justify the idiosyncratic use of language sounds. Her ability to articulate this difference contradicts conventional notions of cognitive deficit in autism.

7.4.7 Mukhopadhyay and Barron

Both Tito Mukhopadhyay (2011) and Sean Barron, who wrote an autobiographical book with his mother Judy Barron, through these examples once again show the authors' ability to rationally justify the meaning of behaviors they recount. Mukhopadhyay and Barron both used to turn light switches and electrical appliances on and off repeatedly, which disoriented and sometimes annoyed their parents.

In Barron's account, he states that:

> I loved repetition. Every time I turned on a light I knew what would happen. When I flipped the switch, the light went on. It gave me a wonderful feeling of security because it was exactly the same each time. (Barron and Barron 2002, 20)

Mukhopadhyay offers more than one explanation for a similar behavior. He explains the compulsion for turning light switches on and off as follows:

> As I did my work with the switches, it gave me a feeling of great triumph, as if I was holding the reins of those bright dark moments in my hands. And those moments comforted me by their predictability. (Mukhopadhyay 2011, 52)

He then states that the switch's rhythmic movement enables him to better understand what is happening in his environment and asks the following question:

> And why should comprehending the environment become less fragmented if I turned the switches on or off? […] I would just see one aspect of the environment. The illuminating aspect, with a controlled probability of either bright or dark. After controlling my visual senses I would be able … to eliminate other visual distractions like shadows, reflections, and the movement of the blades of the fan. (ibid., 54)

On another occasion, he answers the question about the role of rules and routines in his everyday life, stating that:

> Rules are somewhat the very proof to an Autistic person that he exists. […] I am no exception and I get a sort of self-existing sense when I have followed a routine set of activities. […] But if I decide to switch on the lights at midnight and wake the whole house up by playing my tape recorder, just because I want to find my identity, I need to be stopped. (Biklen 2005, 126–127)

Observe their capacity to offer diverse causes and reasons to behaviors that, at first glance, are nearly indistinguishable. Barron associates the repetition of flipping the light switch on and off with the desire to find everything around him in exactly the same place. Undoubtedly, the behavior is atypical, but it cannot be classified as "stereotyped," if by stereotyped we mean mechanical movements with no meaning. A movement that seeks to create conditions for the subject to have the experience of constancy, permanence, of the vital environment is anything but "meaningless."

Mukhopadhyay also offers two other justifications for the impulse to repeat. First, the repetitive gesture is interpreted in an extremely inventive way. By controlling the light, he controls his horizon of vision in order to only see an "aspect of the environment," eliminating "other visual distractions." This cognitive strategy is similar to the "scenic rhetoric" of theater spectacles. Through the use of spotlights, the director manipulates the gaze of the viewers, fixing their attention on the aspect of the plot he hopes to highlight. Second, he does not explain the function of repetition as filtering the environment's sensory stimuli. The behavior's meaning is not to order the environment's elements, but to strengthen the experience of recognizing his identity. Additionally, even though he understands how important it is to attain this goal, Mukhopadhyay agrees that at times others should stop him. His cognitive performance is thus more complex than meets the eye since his explanation incorporates the variable of "inconvenience to others."

7.4.8 Shore

In Stephen Shore's text, *Beyond the Wall: Personal Experiences with Autism and Asperger Syndrome*, the cognitive device is used in an original way. In discussing his compulsive tendency to mimic his brother's gestures and ways of speaking, he says: "Perhaps I had difficulty seeing myself as an autonomous being, separate and distinct from my brother" (Shore 2003, 35). He acknowledges his behavior as strange and then justifies it with an argument that is logical and makes cultural sense. Being aware of the possible lack of distinction between Self and Other and articulating this phenomenon in relation to the compulsion to mimic shows intellectual dexterity. Indeed, configuring, and communicating about, the Self as an object to be described demands a complex cognitive effort. Experiences of "agency," "authorship," "self-awareness," "self-knowledge," et cetera, all implied in everyday actions, have to be broken down so they can be cognitively transmitted. Expressions such as "seeing myself," "autonomous being," "separate and distinct," et cetera, presuppose a level of abstraction that is incompatible with the "central coherence deficit."

7.4.9 Barron

Barron had two compulsive habits that annoyed his mother. The first was repeatedly throwing pencils at the home's radiator; the second was throwing objects at a tree, without bothering to find out if the objects belonged to people who may not have wished them to be thrown. In both cases, Barron was satisfying his curiosity about ballistics. His interest consisted in discovering repeated patterns of flight behavior by observing the time and speed of ascent and descent of objects thrown against a rigid target, situated at different heights and distances from the thrower. Barron's aggressive reaction to his mother's reproach is not easily defensible, but is nonetheless intelligible if we look at it from the perspective of his self-interest. Barron claimed that, in repeating this gestures, he felt great satisfaction, because

> This was my world and I had control over it. I controlled the object. It went up to the top of the tree because I made it happen. And if the thing I threw belonged to someone, that didn't concern me and I had nothing to do with it. When I was called names and punished, I felt invaded. I was no longer in control; someone had control over me. (Barron and Barron 2002, 45)

The conduct's intelligibility is evident. The context of meaning may seem extravagant, but, once re-described, becomes absolutely justifiable. The desire for pattern, routine, and repetition becomes understandable when we consider them as mechanisms to stabilizing the identity and the environment.

7.5 Cognition Revisited

In other words, cognition is not equivalent to mere "intelligibility," if by intelligibility we mean the capacity to competently use abstract arguments and thoughts in the dominant and ordinary language. The cognitive activity of autistic individuals, both in categorically distinguishing between things and events and in plausibly justifying intentional acts, is irreducible to the idea of a central coherence deficit or executive function deficit. As Brendan Hart (2014) has shown, communication between caretaker adults and autistic subjects occurs through the use of "prosaic technologies" such as "radical translation," "joint embodiment," and "prosthetic environment" (287). In "radical translation," caretakers translate subjects' behavior in order to signal and index what happens in the subject's internal worlds. In "joint embodiment," parents and child together create "an improvised choreography whereby parents and child prompt each another, verbally, gesturally and physically" (288). Thus, autistic subjects come to have a "prosthetic environment" in which they can express cognitive, affective, sensory-motor, and communicative functions that are necessary to developing their personalities.

What Hart describes at a socio-anthropological level corresponds to what authors such as Robbins and Aydede (2009), Gallagher (2009), and Lakoff and Johnson (1999), for example, understand to be the requirements for the expression of a "situated cognition." Robbins and Aydede break this expression down into three main notions: "embodiment, enactivism, and extended mind" (2009, 3). In their words:

> First, cognition depends not just on the brain but also on the body (the embodiment thesis). Second, cognitive activity routinely exploits structure in the natural and social environment (the embedding thesis). Third, the boundaries of cognition extend beyond the boundaries of individual organisms (the extension thesis). (ibid.)

Gallagher (2009), in turn, cites Bergson, Merleau-Ponty, Dewey, Heidegger, and Wittgenstein in his reading of the philosophical antecedents of "situated cognition" in order to show that cognition is not an isolated act of the body, the language and of other components of the physical and human environment that circumscribes the subject. To Bergson, Dewey, and Merleau-Ponty, he says, "cognition is a form of action and not a relation between a thinking that goes on in the mind and a behavior that goes on in the world" (ibid., 37). Continuing, he shows that, according to Heidegger, the subject's situationality in the world precedes and founds the conditions of cognition:

> By the time we think about things, or explicitly perceive them as what they are, we have already been immersed in their pragmatic meaning. To be pragmatically immersed in worldly contexts is to have a certain knowing relation to the world, which Heidegger calls "circumspection" (*Umsicht*) and distinguishes from theoretical knowledge. (ibid., 39)

However, in Wittgenstein's formulation, Gallagher continues,

> the meaning of a concept, and the significance of verbal and gestural actions are inseparable from the setting of actions … In a well-defined situation, a practice can be well defined not by the existence of a rule book that is consulted, or by an explicit understanding of the rules, but by the physical and socially defined situation itself … . A language and a set of concepts are created by the particular purposes involved in the situation. Thus, in contrast to traditional approaches that make concept use a matter of detached and deliberative judgment, Wittgenstein maintains that concept use is more like a practical skill. (ibid., 46)

As for Lakoff and Johnson (1999), both show that the significance or meaningfulness of a cognitive act is more than its intelligibility; it is a way of being in the world, an embodied experience of coping with the environment. Meaningfulness is the vocabulary abbreviation of a gestalt structure that gives coherence, regularity and intelligibility to the subject's action and perception. If, in positioning themselves in the world, subjects use unusual image schemata, metaphorical projections, or rational justifications they usually produce reactions of unfamiliarity in the environment.[6] This is an argument that warrants repetition and further research. As Olga Solomon (2010) points out, the subjective, the sensory, and the perceptual, are always susceptible to the power of systems of governance, such as psychiatry and psychology to order, regulate, and pathologize ideas and actions. Indeed, to some extent, autistic discourses such as those analyzed here are forms of resistance to hegemonic discourses and authority, whether specific models, such as weak central coherence and impaired theory of mind, or even science in general.

The theoretical discussion of this topic could extend far beyond what is possible within this format and the examples could be multiplied in order to illustrate the diverse facets of *cognitive integrity* present in the conduct recounted by the authors of the accounts. We would thus prefer to end this text with this eloquent poem by Birger Sellin (1998):

Je veux aussi montrer les absurdités autistiques
Mais je les interpréterai et les expliquerai aux gens
Car chaque absurdité a un sens profond comme tout
Tout chez nous revêt un sens
Notre monde n'a pas sombré pour toujours dans
L'insensé comme on le suppose
Notre monde au contraire est pareil à un système
D'antennes de sécurité né d'îles fabuleuses. (61, 62)

I also want to highlight autistic absurdities
But I will interpret and explain them to others
For each absurdity, like everything, has deep meaning
And because everything in our world has meaning
Our world has not sunk forever into the darkness
As the fool assumes
Our world is a system
Alarms, born from fabulous islands.[7]

Notes

1. Most of the accounts analyzed here are in English because the literature we are discussing largely comes from English-speaking countries where the lay movement that debates the "nature" of autism began. Since the study's objective is not the transcultural expression of autism, but rather its phenomenology, this restriction of the universe of analysis is not especially relevant. The Brazilian literature is much more scarce. It will probably be the object of investigation in a latter stage of the study.
2. We thank Elizabeth Fein and Michael Orsini for their careful reading of this text. Their critiques and suggestions have decisively contributed to the work.
3. On this discussion, see: Michael Klonovsky's 1998 "Postface" in Birger Sellin's *La Solitude du Déserteur* (229–263).
4. We will use the terms "atypical" and "atypia" in the sense of perceptive-linguistic variants of "cultural prototypes," in Rosch and Mervis's definition. The authors define prototypes as the "abstract representation of a category" (Rosch and Mervis 1975, 575). That is, a group of individuals—in the logical sense of discrete units, whether things, living beings or persons—is prototypical when its members possess family resemblances to each other. A prototype need not have a property in common with all the members of the group it represents. Its function as a representative of the category's "normalcy" or "typicality" is accepted and naturalized in everyday communication pragmatics, which always depends on contextual cultural habits. Thus, we consider that a subject is perceived as "typical" in their way of existing or expressing themselves if they present features that make them similar to the prototype's abstract imagetic or conceptual figure. On the other hand, applying terms such as "atypical," "atypicity," etc., to certain subjects means highlighting the wealth of variation of human conduct with regard to the dominant prototype, and not evaluating its forms of expression as "abnormal," "deficient," "pathological," "ill," "dysfunctional," etc. Additionally, regarding the difference between "abnormal" and "pathological" or "functional and dysfunctional," see Canguilhem's (1972) indispensable classic on the normal and the pathological, and regarding the contestation of the difference between a species' "proper function" and supposed "dysfunctional" individual variants, see the enlightening studies by Ruse (2002), Boorse (2002), Millikan (2002), Hardcastle (2002), and Cummins (2002).
5. Attfield, Richard. In Biklen (2005, 58).
6. See Johnson (2008, 1987), Lakoff and Johnson (1999).
7. Translated by Roy Richard Grinker, 2017.

References

American Psychiatric Association. 2013. *Diagnostic and Statistical Manual of Mental Disorders: DSM-V*. Washington, DC: American Psychiatric Association.

Baranek, Grace T., Lauren M. Little, L. Diane Parham, Karla K. Ausderau, and Maura G. Sabatos-DeVito. 2014. "Sensory Features in Autism Spectrum Disorders." In *Handbook of Autism and Pervasive Developmental Disorders*, vol. 1, edited by Fred R. Volkmar, Saly Rogers, Rhea Paul, and Kevin A. Pelphrey, 378–407. Malden, MA: Wiley.

Barron, Judy, and Sean Barron. 2002. *There's a Boy in Here: Emerging from the Bonds of Autism*. Arlington, TX: Future Horizons.

Biklen, Douglas. 2005. *Autism and the Myth of the Person Alone*. New York: New York University Press.

Blackman, Lucy. 2001. *Lucy's Story: Autism and Other Adventures*. 2nd ed. London and Philadelphia: Jessica Kingsley.

Boorse, Christopher. 2002. "A Rebuttal on Functions." In *Functions: New Essays in the Philosophy of Psychology and Biology*, edited by André Ariew, Robert Cummins, and Mark Perlman, 63–112. Oxford: Oxford University Press.

Canguilhem, Georges. 1972. *Le normal et le pathologique*. 2nd ed. Paris: Presses Universitaires de France.

Cummins, Robert. 2002. "Neo-teleology." In *Functions: New Essays in the Philosophy of Psychology and Biology*, edited by André Ariew, Robert Cummins, and Mark Perlman, 157–172. Oxford: Oxford University Press.

Davidson, Joyce, and Michael Orsini, eds., 2013. *Worlds of Autism: Across the Spectrum of Neurological Difference*. Minneapolis: University of Minnesota Press.

Fleischmann, Arthur with Fleischmann, Carly. 2012. *Carly's Voice: Breaking Through Autism*. New York: Touchstone.

Frith, Uta. 1989. *Autism: Explaining the Enigma*. Oxford: Basil Blackwell.

Gallagher, Shaun. 2009. "Philosophical Antecendents to Situated Cognition." In *The Cambridge Handbook of Situated Cognition*, edited by Philip Robbins and Murat Aydede, 35–51. Cambridge: Cambridge University Press.

Happé, Francesca, Jacqueline Briskman, and Uta Frith. 2001. "Exploring the Cognitive Phenotype of Autism: Weak 'Central Coherence' in Parents and Siblings of Children with Autism: I. Experimental Tests." *Journal of Child Psychology and Psychiatry* 43 (2): 299–307.

Hardcastle, Valerie Gray. 2002. "On the Normativity of Functions." In *Functions: New Essays in the Philosophy of Psychology and Biology*, edited by André Ariew, Robert Cummins, and Mark Perlman, 144–156. Oxford: Oxford University Press.

Hart, Brendan. 2014. "Autism Parents and Neurodiversity: Radical Translation, Joint Embodiment and the Prosthetic Environment." *BioSocieties* 9 (3): 284–303. https://doi.org/10.1057/biosoc.2014.20.

Higashida, Naoki. 2013. *The Reason I Jump*. New York: Random House.

Hobson, R. Peter. 2014. "Autism and Emotion." In *Handbook of Autism and Pervasive Developmental Disorders*, vol. 1, edited by Fred R. Volkmar, Saly Rogers, Rhea Paul, and Kevin A. Pelphrey, 332–353. Malden, MA: Wiley.

Johnson, Mark. 1987. *The Body in the Mind: The Bodily Basis of Meaning, Imagination, and Reason*. Chicago: The University of Chicago Press.

Johnson, Mark. 2008. "Philosophy's Debt to Metaphor." In *The Cambridge Handbook of Metaphor and Thought*, edited by Raymond W. Gibbs, Jr., 39–53. New York: Cambridge University Press.

Lakoff, George, and Mark Johnson. 1999. *Philosophy in the Flesh: The Embodied Mind and Its Challenge to Western Thought*. New York: Basic Books.

Millikan, Ruth Garrett. 2002. "Biofunctions: Two Paradigms." In *Functions: New Essays in the Philosophy of Psychology and Biology*, edited by André Ariew, Robert Cummins, and Mark Perlman, 113–143. Oxford: Oxford University Press.

Mukhopadhyay, Tito Rajarshi. 2011. *How Can I Talk If My Lips Don't Move? Inside My Autistic Mind*. New York: Arcade Publishing.

Robbins, Philip, and Murat Aydede. 2009. "A Short Primer on Situated Cognition." In *The Cambridge Handbook of Situated Cognition*, edited by Philip Robbins and Murat Aydede, 3–10. Cambridge: Cambridge University Press.

Rosch, Eleanor, and Carolyn Mervis. 1975. "Family Resemblances: Studies in the Internal Structure of Categories." *Cognitive Psychology* 7 (4): 573–605.

Ruse, Michael. 2002. "Evolutionary Biology and Teleological Thinking." In *Functions: New Essays in the Philosophy of Psychology and Biology*, edited by André Ariew, Robert Cummins, and Mark Perlman, 33–59. Oxford: Oxford University Press.

Saussure, Ferdinand de. 1998. *Course in General Linguistics*. London: Duckworth.

Sellin, Birger. 1998. *La solitude du déserteur*. Paris: Robert Laffont.

Shore, Steven. 2003. *Beyond the Wall: Personal Experiences with Autism and Asperger Syndrome*. 2nd ed. Shawness Mission, KS: Autism Asperger Publishing.

Solomon, Olga. 2010. "Sense and the Senses: Anthropology and the Study of Autism." *Annual Review of Anthropology* 39: 241–259.

Tager-Flusberg, Helen, Lisa Edelson, and Rhiannon Luyster. 2011. "Language and Communication in Autism Spectrum Disorders." In *Autism Spectrum Disorders*, edited by David Amaral, Geraldine Dawson, and David H. Geschwind, 172–185. Oxford: Oxford University Press.

Tammet, Daniel. 2006. *Born on a Blue Day: Inside the Extraordinary Mind of an Autistic Savant*. New York: Free Press.

CHAPTER 8

Commentary: Words, Voice, Silence

Laura Sterponi

8.1 Words

> These days, I find myself dealing more in words, and less in sensations. And something is lost, something that I'm trying to find again. (Elizabeth Fein)

The relationship between words and meaning is complicated and paradoxical. The very moment a linguistic symbol brings into being an element of reality it also indicates its absence. With language, an irreversible rupture is produced: on one side, the reality, on the other, words; on one side, sensations, on the other, concepts; lived phenomenal experience and linguistic form. Arguably, philosophy of language has developed as an attempt to articulate as well as come to terms with this estrangement.

Analytic philosophy, culminating with Wittgenstein's *Tractatus Logico-Philosophicus*, has painstakingly endeavored to demarcate the limits of language and characterize the relationship between language and reality in the idiom of mathematical logic. Desire, emotions, and sensory experience fall outside the scope of the propositional calculus. Hence Wittgenstein's famous assertion: "Whereof one cannot speak, thereof one must remain silent" (Wittgenstein 1922, 189).

L. Sterponi (✉)
Graduate School of Education, University of California, Berkeley, CA, USA

E. Fein and C. Rios (eds.), *Autism in Translation*, Culture, Mind, and Society, https://doi.org/10.1007/978-3-319-93293-4_8

The lively discussions that developed over our time together in Rio, and the three essays to which I have the privilege to respond, represent ways to engage with the silence, strategies to complicate the spoken and to interrogate the unspeakable. I suggest that two main strategies are leveraged in this semiotic enterprise. I would characterize them as *denotational layering* and *non-referential signification*.

Not dissimilar to Derridean drift—which challenges the idea of a stable, final, authorized, and authentic meaning (Derrida 1976)—denotational layering seeks to expand meaning through ad infinitum successions of referential characterizations articulated in relations, associations, and reverberations. As such, denotational layering defeats the purposes of the referential process the very moment it enacts it. Denotational layering is predicated on a fundamental principle of Peircian semiotics—"a sign is something by knowing which we know something more" (Peirce 1974, 8.332). At the same time, denotational layering eschews delimiting and limiting signification, and along with it the containment of meaning in a univocal, unambiguous definition.

Freire Costa and Grinker's analysis of the ways individuals with autism account for their engagement with words attests to this process of denotational exploration. The authors highlight how the definitional practices of Mukhopadhyay and other individuals with autism transcend the denotational conventions by incorporating into word definition the contextual connections that a definition normatively effaces. Put another way, autistic denotational practices unveil language's inherent relation to context, which entails polysemy and can never be entirely bracketed off or limited to the pretense of literal meaning. Autistic accounts of meaning-making thus reveal, as Freire Costa and Grinker suggest, engagement with the potential of language to expand experience, to deepen our connection with the world of others and cultural artifacts.

A most insightful reflection on autistic engagement with the world is articulated by Fein, in Chapter 6. Fein unearths forms of engagement with the world, which are deeply sensorial and symbiotic, for which autistic individuals display a penchant. By way of thought-provoking inversion, Fein invites us to think of what conventionally is interpreted as autistic deficits—for example, impairment in self-other differentiation, difficulty in abstracting from the particular to the whole—in terms of more acute permeability to the surrounding. It is thus ironic, Fein points out, that "a condition of intimate co-existence with the outside world" ended up being labeled "by a word that means self-contained isolation" (this volume, p. 132).

Engagement with language, in autistic experience, is also profoundly sensorial. Autistic engagement with language is often experientially attuned to sound and form, in excess of semantic content, thereby revealing of dimensions of significance that tend to be overlooked in autism research. Non-referential signification refers to and affirms the possibility of linguistic expressions to be meaningful without denoting. Conjuring up realities through referential operations is undoubtedly a chief semiotic capacity of language. There is also semiotic potential, however, in the musicality of phrases and their articulatory texture—as they are experienced in ear and in mouth. Autistic modes of engagement with language subvert the referential hegemony to uncover additional dimensions of significance and experience of language (see also Ochs 2012).

The early work of Julia Kristeva provides theoretical grounding to this strategy. Kristeva theorizes a fundamental distinction between the semiotic and the symbolic. These are two dimensions of meaning: the symbolic can be roughly described as encompassing the referential functioning of language—utterances with propositional content, signifiers standing for signifieds, language mobilized to predicate upon the world. The semiotic dimension, on the other hand, includes the non-referential aspect of linguistic signification—notably tone, rhythm, prosody, the musicality of language (so to speak). Kristeva refers to the symbolic and the semiotic as two distinct logics of signification, the former "based on a zero-one sequence (true-false, nothingness-notation)" (Kristeva 1980, 40), and the latter on the *0–2 interval*, which embodies the *power of the continuum*, "a continuity where 0 denotes and 1 is implicitly transgressed" (ibid., 41).

To the semiotic Kristeva associates poetic language. While never dispensing entirely with the symbolic, poetry makes room for the expression of the semiotic potential of language. The poetic word, Kristeva claims, is polyvalent and multi-determined, adhering to a logic exceeding that of codified discourse.

Autistic attunement to sound, rhythm, and form, to the articulatory makeup of words and phrases, adheres to the semiotic logic of signification. It is a profoundly embodied form of engagement with the sensuous attributes of linguistic signification. In their own way, Freire Costa and Grinker give credit to semiotic signification. Drawing from the first-person account of Naoki Higashida, they acknowledge echolalia as a meaningful act, motivated by the pleasurable experience of playing with sound, in excess of meaning.

8.2 Voice

toward bringing 'autistic voices' to the fore of the discourse. (Michael Bakan)

There is more to echolalia than the pleasurable engagement with rhythm and sound. In my own work on the topic (Sterponi and Shankey 2014), I have demonstrated that when we approach echoic utterances with an attunement to the phenomenological dimensions of language, we do not find automatic or self-stimulatory regurgitations of past strings of words. In those echoes, voices can be heard—that is, the animation of subjective expressions, one's own or others'. Therefore, I have suggested to consider echolalia as *revoicing*. As such, echoes can articulate and negotiate—actively and creatively—social, interpersonal, and affective experiences, navigating the complexities of perspective-taking and emotional processing (see also Sterponi et al. 2015).

Borrowing from anthropologist Greg Urban (1989), we can thus reframe echoes as "de-quotative speech": indexical cues (e.g., voice quality, pitch, and volume) allow different voices to be animated while the absence of a quote-framing clause affords a maximal projection of the speaker into another self. Drawing further from Urban, it can be emphasized that insofar as a quoted utterance is an icon of the utterance it purports to re-present, the speaker is also engaged in "iconic otherness" or, put a slightly different way, in "a subjective experience of otherness" (Urban 1989, 46). My work has thus invited to reappraise echolalia with a sensibility toward the experiential affordances that language yields: the repetition of another's utterances can be thought of as mechanism to experience the other, or to access the experience of the other. In this sense, echolalia can be interpreted as a form of perspective-taking.

The notion of voice features centrally in Bakan's essay, which advocates for the autistic voices to be re-presented rather than represented in scholarly discourse. In other words, the author argues that too frequently the autistic experience is investigated from an outside perspective, made object of representation, as if autistic individuals lack the reflective capacity to understand and account for themselves. While both Freire Costa and Grinker's and Bakan's chapters offer correctives to this misconception, Bakan's paper places this issue further in the foreground. Bakan not only petitions to bring autistic voices to the fore, he also enacts this move by making space in his pages for the voices of individuals with an autism spectrum condition, by letting them inhabit no less than half of the pages of his text, directly, in quotation marks, without the filter of rephrasing or editing and with minimal side commentary. The autistic voice is re-presented on the page and we hear it with its distinctive tonality and texture. But voice as semiotic dimension of signification, as subjective expression of being, is present in silence too.

8.3 Silence

> What they thought was silence, because they didn't know how to listen (John Cage)

In 1952, in Woodstock, New York, in an open-air theater, with a rustic style that matched with the surrounding natural environment, one of the most surprising and influential musical works of the last century was premiered. It was 4' 33" by American composer and music theorist John Cage. The composition was popularized with the name "Silent Piece" since it comprises three movements during which a performer—or performers—are instructed to produce no intentional sounds for 4 minutes and 33 seconds.

It was a radical gesture, a paradigm-shifting move that upended the traditional structure of music and subverted conventional expectations about what music is. The purpose of the silent piece was to make people listen, attune their ears to phenomena that would have typically been considered nonmusical (Kostelanetz 1988). Cage's composition opened up a space—4 minutes and 33 seconds long—to experience sounds that we habitually do not listen to, or might perceive as noise or interference, and to experience them with the same ear with which we listen to music.

Each in distinctive ways, Fein's, Bakan's, and Freire Costa and Grinker's papers have accomplished a similar move of opening and transformation. They have expanded our capacity to perceive signification and meaning; they have discerned significance and value where traditionally there was meaninglessness or chaos; and they have engaged the silence. So do I, now.

180 L. STERPONI

This page was intentionally left blank by the author.

References

Derrida, Jacques. 1976. *Of Grammatology*. Translated by Gayatri Chakravorty Spivak. Baltimore: Johns Hopkins University Press.

Kostelanetz, Richard. 1988. *Conversing with Cage*. New York: Limelight.

Kristeva, Julia. 1980. "Word, Dialogue, and Novel." In *Desire in Language: A Semiotic Approach to Literature and Art*, 64–91. New York: Columbia University Press.

Ochs, Elinor. 2012. "Experiencing Language." *Anthropological Theory* 12 (2): 142–160.

Peirce, Charles Sanders. 1974. *Collected Papers of Charles Sanders Peirce*. Cambridge, MA: Harvard University Press.

Sterponi, Laura, Kenton de Kirby, and Jennifer Shankey. 2015. "Subjectivity in Autistic Language: Insights on Pronoun Atypicality from Three Case Studies." In *The Palgrave Handbook of Child Mental Health*, 272–295. London: Palgrave Macmillan.

Sterponi, Laura, and Jennifer Shankey. 2014. "Rethinking Echolalia: Repetition as Interactional Resource in the Communication of a Child with Autism." *Journal of Child Language* 41 (2): 275–304.

Urban, Greg. 1989. "The 'I' of Discourse." In *Semiotics, Self, and Society*, edited by Ben Lee and Greg Urban, 27–51. Berlin: Mouton de Gruyter.

Wittgenstein, Ludwig. 1922. *Tractatus Logico-Philosophicus*. London: Kegan Paul.

PART III

The Autism Concept

CHAPTER 9

Expert on Your Own Child, Expert on Your Own World—Reinventing Autism Expertise(s)

Clarice Rios

9.1 Introduction

"Parents are the real experts on their child", says Maria, a speech therapist at *Círculo da Esperança*, a parents' association that has acted as a service provider for lower income families and their autistic children for over fifteen years. When Inês, who co-founded the association with Maria, first heard the word "autism" as a possible diagnosis for her seven-year-old son, she was no expert at all. In fact, she did not even know what the word meant. On asking the doctor for an explanation, she heard that there was no point in trying to explain it to her because she would not understand it.

Inês was a high school dropout when she moved to Rio de Janeiro, coming from one of the poorest regions in Brazil. The eldest of her two children, Ivan, showed signs of autism early on, but it took her years and many consultations with all kinds of professionals to find an adequate diagnosis. The definitive diagnosis came through a neurologist working

C. Rios (✉)
Department of Social Psychology, Federal University of Rio de Janeiro,
Rio de Janeiro, Brazil

E. Fein and C. Rios (eds.), *Autism in Translation*, Culture, Mind,
and Society, https://doi.org/10.1007/978-3-319-93293-4_9

in the public hospital where she also met Maria. Maria had been interning at the hospital, learning about autism by observing the neurologist during his consultations, and applying screening tools to help him with the diagnostic process. Concerned with the destiny of the many children who got a diagnosis through that doctor, but had nowhere to go after leaving his office, Maria decided to organize a support group for parents of autistic children. In a time when there was very little specialized literature in Portuguese about autism, Maria would translate English material she found on the Internet and bring it to the group for discussion. Inês' persistence and commitment to the group turned into a long-lasting friendship and working partnership with Maria. The support group eventually turned into a parents' association that acts as a service provider, *Círculo da Esperança*. The story of this association is both representative of the larger historical process of establishing a network of expertise in autism in Brazil, and unique in the combination of professional and experiential knowledge enabled by Ines and Maria's long-lasting friendship and partnership.

With that in mind, I explore the notion of autism expertise in this specific context—a parents' association founded at a time when there was very little literature and professionals specialized in autism in Brazil. I argue that what makes them "experts on their own child" is a combination of credentialed knowledge about autism and situated experiential knowledge about their child and the local worlds they live in. In that sense, autism expertise is never simply about autism alone, but instead, about autism in context. In addition, more than the simple adaptation of therapeutic strategies to local contexts and to the needs of specific autistic individuals, such expertise also involves a specific type of translation work—that of turning tacit knowledge about local social worlds into explicit knowledge that can be used both to improve the whole family life and to teach the autistic child to better navigate these worlds. In the following pages, I would like to focus on the different kinds of knowledge and epistemic translation work involved in becoming an expert on autism, and propose a model of autism expertise that takes into account both local social worlds and a way of being in the world that is described in the scientific literature as Autism Spectrum Disorders (ASD).[1] In doing that I challenge the uncritical adoption of autism therapies developed in different social, material and cultural worlds, while acknowledging their important role in developing context sensitive forms of expertise.

9.2 The Research

The material presented in this chapter is part of a larger ethnographic research project that I conducted as part of a postdoctoral fellowship in Collective Health at the Institute for Social Medicine of the State University of Rio de Janeiro (UERJ) with the help of two graduate students from the Institute, Bárbara Costa Andrada and Clara Feldman. While the initial project was to map the biopolitics of autism in Brazil overall, the ethnographic work took place in Rio de Janeiro. The methods included bibliographic research (including official documents, and Internet and printed media related to autism) and participant observation in a number of autism related public events as well as at several sites that provided services for autistic people. By the time we started the project there was a heated public debate about autism in Brazil, which led us to choose these services based on the perspectives of the different social actors involved in the debate. As outlined in two other chapters of this book (Cascio et al., Lima et al., this volume) the controversy involved parent activists and mental health professionals from the public system. Among other things, parent activists demanded specialized treatment for their children within the public health system, claiming that services were virtually non-existent.

For these parents, the demand for specialized treatment basically meant that their children should be treated in places exclusively designed for autistic children, where they would have access to evidence-based therapies exclusively designed to treat autism. Although these parents claimed that autism is a complex condition that requires the intervention of various kinds of professionals (such as behavioral therapists, speech therapists, occupational therapists, etc.), the common focus on the specificities of autism would amount to so-called "specialized treatment". Instead, autistic children currently have to share the Centers for Psychosocial Attention for Children and Youth (CAPSi)[2] with children with all kinds of problems—from alcohol and drug addiction and various kinds of mental disorders to domestic violence, social vulnerability, and homelessness. According to many parents, if their autistic children get grouped together with children with widely different problems and needs, and treated with non-specific therapeutic approaches, they would not acquire the necessary skills to get past their impairments.

I then became intrigued with the meaning of "specialized treatment". First because it implies that a person can be "only" autistic. The specialization imperative begs questions such as what to make of other possible comorbidities and, most of all, what to make of other problems not directly caused by or related to autism (but which might nonetheless be aggravated by it). Putting it simply—how is one to separate autism from the rest of the lives of autistic people and of those around them?

On the other hand, it seemed pretty intuitive that if autistics share some common traits they might benefit from similar interventions. The claim is certainly not that simple and obvious, since it requires a common agreement on what is "wrong" with autistic people and the best approach to deal with it. In spite of Brazilian parent activists' argument that evidence-based therapies equate to the best intervention, such proposition is far from obvious and uncontroversial. While a behavioral approach tends to be the favored approach in autism interventions nowadays, there are many different therapies that fall under this general category. The so-called Applied Behavioral Analysis (ABA) is the most famous treatment worldwide and the one most frequently quoted by Brazilian parent activists. Yet, what that actually means in terms of therapeutic practice has changed a great deal since it was first developed by Ivar Lovaas and his team, and also tends to vary from place to place (see Lima et al., this volume).

Given that parents' associations such as *Círculo da Esperança*, were created by parents to treat their autistic children, it made sense to pursue the question of specialization in such settings. I conducted participant observation there for a period of two years and talked to parents and professionals, both formally (in semi-structured interviews) and informally. I also participated in various kinds of activities developed by its professional and non-professional members: I have joined study groups with professionals, sat in on mutual help meetings with parents, and spent time with kids and their families in their day-to-day lives, ranging from routine activities to family gatherings and celebrations.

9.3 From "Specialized Treatment" to Autism Expertise

Associations such as *Círculo da Esperança* are a good place to investigate the cultivation of autism expertise not just because of the specialized services they provide, but also because the "new economy of exchanges" (Eyal and Hart 2010, 5) between parents and therapists, made possible by these associations, fosters a unique combination of credentialed and local experiential knowledge. Autism associations created and run by parents were the first type of specialized service providers in the country.

The first of them was founded in 1980s, by a group of parents in São Paulo. The founders of the association, known as *Associação de Amigos do Autista* (AMA),[3] visited important centers of autism treatment in the United States and Europe, importing to Brazil technical expertise in well-known models of intervention such as TEACCH and ABA. Over the years, AMA São Paulo has become a reference for other parent associations, providing a model of organization that was followed by associations throughout the country. AMA São Paulo also played a key role in promoting these foreign models of intervention through short-term courses and workshops to train professionals and parents not only from São Paulo but also from all over Brazil. Therefore, parent associations in Brazil stand at the intersection of globally circulating expert discourses and situated, context-particular knowledge.

When parent activists in Brazil demand "specialized treatment" for their children in the public health system they are not only making claims about what kinds of services best suit their children, but also making claims about who has authoritative knowledge about autism and who has not. Not surprisingly, given the history of parents' associations in Brazil, this authoritative knowledge often comes from sources well outside of their local worlds. Overall, Brazilian parents tend to attribute a lot of power to foreign diagnostic tools and interventions, positioning themselves mostly as consumers of knowledge produced abroad. For example, in 2013 the Brazilian Federal government, in partnership with AMA São Paulo and other parents' associations published a book called *Retratos do Autismo no Brasil* (Portraits of Autism in Brazil). The book's main goal was to provide a general account of the specialized services for autism throughout Brazil (mostly parents' associations like AMA), describing their history and their current work, that should help with the development of public policies for autistic people in Brazil. Two chapters of the book were written by a professional expert, the therapist Meca Andrade, who played a major role in the history of AMA São Paulo. She establishes her authority as an expert right at the title of one of the chapters—"Lessons learned - Working with autism in the USA: what this experience tells me about working with people with autism in Brasil" (Mello et al. 2013, 75). In a footnote, her credentials are listed as follows: she "is a psychologist who worked for 15 years at the New England Center for Children, in Boston, one of the largest institutions specialized in assisting people with autism in the USA" (Mello et al. 2013, 75).

Meca Andrade's status as an expert refers both to the highly socially valued international credentials granted by the Boston center, and to her ability to (re)act in situations where her ability as a therapist is required. Nevertheless, a growing focus on the performative nature of expertise has opened up the possibility of recognizing somebody as an expert in the absence of socially and institutionally recognized credentials.[4] The whole idea of parents acting as "cotherapists" of their autistic children is premised on this possibility. Eyal and Hart point out that the term "expertise" is defined by the Oxford Dictionary as "an authority by reason of special skill, training or knowledge" (quoted in Eyal and Hart 2010, 5). As such, they note, "it could derive from credentials or from experience, from professional status or personal involvement, it could be abstract or practical" (2010, 5). These authors also argue that there are good reasons to treat expertise as a network property, and not simply as a set of attributes that a select group of professional experts have. When professionals and lay people in a given network are no longer clearly set apart by professional credentials, the whole notion of expertise in a given field of knowledge and/or of professional practice changes. In fact, the very object of knowledge/practice in that field tends to change as well. The history of autism diagnosis is a great example of such shifts.

According to Eyal and Hart (2010), starting in the 1960s in the United States, parent activism has been responsible for a rearrangement in parents' relations to professionals, redefining not only flows of information and types of intervention but also the whole concept of relevant expertise in the field of autism. For these authors, autism expertise involved "blurring boundaries between expert and layman", more specifically between professionals and parents, who both engaged in the "co-production of common objects of inquiry and treatment" (Eyal and Hart 2010, 4. See also Jasanoff 2004).[5] In the case of autism, the new regime of relations between parents, activists, researchers, and therapists led to radical transformations in autism as an object of inquiry and treatment. It is not the case to review here the history of autism diagnosis and the institutional matrix that formed around it but, among other things, this rearrangement led to the shift from a psychogenic explanation to a neurobiological account of autism (see Eyal et al. 2010; Eyal and Hart 2010 for a detailed account).

Rabeharisoa (2003) identified a similar pattern in her research with the French Muscular Dystrophy Association (AFM), but she distinguishes various modes of knowledge production based on the models of collaboration established between patients and researchers. While the AFM managed to establish what she calls a "partnership model", where patients managed to take a leading role in the knowledge production process itself, the "experiential knowledge" (Borkman 1976; Rabeharisoa 2003) developed by patients does not always guarantee them an active role in this process. Patients' mutual help groups for example, have historically played an auxiliary role in their relationship with researchers and professionals, providing "emotional and social support in addition to medical treatment" (Rabeharisoa 2003, 2129), without really questioning medical knowledge and practices. Rabeharisoa (2003, 2127) also recognizes different elements affecting such relationships such as the "institutional characteristics of each country, the specific features of each pathology, and the history of each organization, along with the individuals comprising it."

Given the way *Círculo da Esperança* was structured and the history of parents' associations in Brazil more broadly, it could be argued that *Círculo da Esperança's* parents also play an auxiliary role in their relationship with professionals, fitting into what Rabeharisoa described as the "auxiliary model" (2003, 2128). In other words, as non-professional experts on the credentialed knowledge and therapeutic interventions mobilized by professionals at the association, their role (auxiliary) is defined by reference to this credentialed knowledge and professional techniques. However, since much of the discussion on the topic of expertise has focused on how epistemic authority is established and regulated in these situations, important but less obvious aspects of autism expertise are left out of such a classification scheme. For example, a good part of what autism experts do (and that includes both parents and professional therapists), is to help people with autism develop skills and acquire knowledge that are not really specialized.[6] Rather than specialized knowledge, what is at stake in this case are basic knowledge and skills that people acquire by virtue of being part of a given society and that help them navigate their way through life. Nevertheless, as we shall see, these parent experts also mobilize specialized knowledge about the typical cognitive styles of people with autism in translating their local worlds to their autistic children, and vice versa. For these parents, to *specialize* in autism is to develop a certain mode of attention to everyday *non-specialized* social competency.

9.4 Expertise in Context: Who Is an Expert After All?

I first got to *Círculo da Esperança* for a welcoming meeting, held every last Saturday of each month. It was very early in the morning and a number of anxious parents were already waiting for a presentation of the work done at this parents' association. Most of them got there through a doctor's referral, and simply wanted to schedule a professional evaluation of their child with Maria, the speech therapist. When it was founded, *Círculo da Esperança* was meant to be simply a support group for parents of autistic children, but mostly through the dedication and hard work of these two women, it became a well-known service provider for lower income families and their autistic children. Aside from the professional evaluation conducted by Maria, and used to assist medical doctors with the diagnostic process, *Círculo da Esperança* offers regular services focused on the development of communication and social skills of autistic children. It is also a place where parents can share their experiences with autism and help each other to cope with it.

During the introductory presentation on that Saturday, I was pleased to hear Maria talking about ideas that sounded very respectful of autistic differences and of parents' knowledge and experience in a parents' association situated in an area where many families sometimes know little to nothing about autism. According to Maria, the philosophy of *Círculo da Esperança* could be summarized in four principles, which she called the *Bem Viver com Autismo* (Living well with Autism). The principles, as listed in one of the slides of her PowerPoint presentation, were:

Four principles of *Bem Viver com Autismo* (Living well with Autism)

1. We are all different
   autism as an expression of human diversity
   neurodiversity
2. Parents are the experts
3. Building support networks
4. Life difficulties are opportunities.

According to Maria, the principles of *Bem Viver*[7] should not only help parents make sense of their experience with autism in a positive way, but also promote a less pathologized approach to autism and a less hierarchical relationship between parents and professionals. Commenting on the second principle of *Bem Viver*, Maria says that parents are experts on their own child because they spend more time with them than a single professional will ever do. Professional experts on the other hand, tend to have a very narrow approach to their object of expertise. To illustrate her point, Maria compares a professional expert to a doctor who specializes in fingers and does not know much about the rest of the body. As a speech therapist, Maria says she focuses only on language problems, but there is obviously a lot more to an autistic child than just language problems. Ultimately, only parents should know what is best for their child. Although at first sight that seemed a pretty self-evident assertion for me, throughout my fieldwork I noticed that, in spite of all the efforts of Maria and Inês, getting parents to embrace their own expertise and engage with the work developed at *Círculo da Esperança* was not always an easy task in this particular sociocultural context. Parents arrived at the association looking for the authority of professional experts, not the experience of other parents. They asked questions like "Is my child going to be able to speak?" and expected precise answers. Some left their children there for a short period of time, until they found a new promise of what they expected to be a miraculous cure. Others simply acted as if it was up to the professionals to "fix" their children and resisted taking responsibility for the whole process.

A little background on parent activism and autism in Brazil is necessary to understand the reasons for this. Historically autism was widely ignored as a diagnostic category until the 1980s. The creation of AMA São Paulo, set in motion the mobilization of a larger network of parents and professional experts on autism. As other associations like this proliferated across the country throughout the 1990s, other parental advocacy groups, more focused on awareness-raising and political lobbying, also emerged. Overall, parents' organizations have been playing a double role in the biosocial field of autism in Brazil: while many of them provide specialized services, they are also largely responsible for creating the very urge to adopt specialized treatments in dealing with autism. As already mentioned, the demand for specialized treatments has become a focal point for parent activism. Such demand also relates to the structure of the Brazilian mental health system and the kinds of services it provides. The country's mental health policy emphasizes deinstitutionalization and the creation of outpatient mental health facilities (the CAPS for adults, and CAPSi for children and youth). These facilities offer psychosocial services for people experiencing "mental suffering", regardless of their specific diagnosis. In other words, one of the defining characteristics of the mental health system in Brazil is that it is not structured around specific diagnoses or specialized treatments. That not only sharpened the antagonism between parent activists and mental health professionals, but also contributed to making professional specialization in autism a valuable asset, embodying additional material and emotional value for parents of autistic children in Brazil.[8] Thus, while an autism diagnosis is said to leave room for improvement, especially when it is identified and treated early, it also sets in motion a booming therapeutic market for autism.

While *Círculo da Esperança* is one among the many service providers that have benefited from this booming market, its history was also shaped by the unique conditions in which it was founded. A network of expertise on autism in Brazil was still in the process of consolidating itself, so what constituted relevant knowledge on autism and autism interventions, and the means to achieve that, was still a very open question. At the risk of simplifying, it is possible to say that the association was born out of the encounter between a desperate mother (Inês) and a socially engaged and spiritually inspired speech therapist (Maria). Maria's experience assisting the neurologist at the hospital where Inês' son (Ivan) finally got his autism diagnosis was also enhanced by Internet searches on the topic. Since she speaks English, she had access to a wide range of literature on the subject. The combination of Internet research, autism literature in English, her previous expertise as a speech therapist, and what she learned from talking to the neurologist or simply seeing a wide range of autistic children in the public hospital, turned Maria into a professional expert on autism. Today, after more than fifteen years of experience applying screening tools and making evaluations at *Círculo da Esperança*, Maria is a well-respected professional in the field of autism in Rio de Janeiro. Although she does not have all the academic credentials, such as a Ph.D., she has the symbolic capital to gather respect from the medical doctors that refer children to *Círculo da Esperança*.

Inês on the other hand, had not even completed high school when she migrated to Rio from a poorer part of the country. As already mentioned, her very ability to understand what autism is was questioned by one of the doctors she encountered in her search for a diagnosis. Such attitude towards patients is not unusual in the public health system in Brazil. On the one hand, doctors often underestimate their patients' abilities to understand and deal with their health conditions. On the other hand, many lower income patients actually have very limited understanding of medical and psychiatric jargon, and easily hand over the responsibility for diagnosis and treatment to professional experts.[9]

Inês still remembers the moment she got the diagnosis, along with an adequate explanation. Her enormous sense of relief for finally learning what her son had was an inspiration for Maria to carry on her old dream—forming a support group where Inês and other desperate parents like her, could share their experience and learn from each other. Although Maria insisted from the beginning that these group should be organized and run by parents, the group would not have continued without her participation and professional guidance. After the first few meetings, the group was reduced to Maria and Inês. During those weekly Saturday meetings, when the two of them sat there by themselves, they developed a strong friendship and set the basis for the association as it is structured today.

Inês recalls that she learned a great deal about autism with Maria. At first, she learned about autism by discussing the Internet material translated by Maria during those weekly meetings. Throughout the years Inês would also come to Maria for expert advice every once in a while, in moments where she simply did not know what else to do with her son. When I ask Inês how she learned about autism, though, she says she never read specialized books or first-person accounts, or watched films about autism. For Inês, in these books and films things are too organized and successful, unlike real life when she often has to improvise and deal with very stressful situations. She complains that parents arrive at *Círculo da Esperança* today too anxious with the diagnosis and the future of their child. They get overwhelmed with the amount of information (now in Portuguese) that they find on the Internet,[10] and do not really enjoy the network of support and experience that *Círculo da Esperança* has to offer. Inês says for example, that when they come to her asking if their two-year-old child will be able to marry and graduate from school, she laughs and says that she herself has still not graduated from school. For her, by obsessing about the future, these parents are missing valuable time with their child, enjoying their childhood years, getting to know them for whom they are and teaching them skills and limits, like any parent should do with their child.

Yet, this fascinating and wise woman gets awfully insecure when she has to act as a spokesperson for the association. Although she is good in talking about her son, calming anxious parents, and dealing with daily administrative and financial problems at the association, she is not fluent in the credentialed knowledge that secures the necessary funds to keep the association functioning. So, Maria is in charge of the presentation at the welcoming meeting, explaining the work done there, its principles and, most importantly, the "evidence-based" approach they use. Her presentation includes a description of their Living Well philosophy, as well as an explanation about the main methodology adopted there, the SCERTS Model. This model is basically a research-based educational approach developed in the US, which addresses common challenges faced by children with ASD and related disabilities. According to Maria, SCERTS summarizes and systematizes everything they already did. In other words, according to her, the SCERTS Model did not teach them any novel content. Instead, it gave Maria and other professionals working at *Círculo da Esperança* a structured approach and an extensive assessment tool to measure the children's progress. It also gave them a way to display credentialed knowledge to parents in search for "specialized treatment for autism".

Were I to focus solely on the services offered by *Círculo da Esperança* and the work performed by Maria, it would be easy to conclude that the assessment tools provided by the SCERTS model as well as other forms of credentialed knowledge were the most important elements in creating a network of expertise among parents and professionals in this association. Yet equating expertise to fluency in credentialed knowledge ends up challenging the very idea that any parent, or anyone for that matter, can be an expert on autism. In this specific setting for example, although anyone can, in theory, get trained in various specialized tools and techniques, access to knowledge is limited by other factors such as fluency in English or in professional language and jargon, and, ultimately, by the very ability to enact autism expertise in socially valued and authenticated ways (Carr 2010, 21).

But as I spent more time talking to Inês and other parents who were active at *Círculo da Esperança*, about random aspects of their routines, I started noticing that there was more to being "an expert on your own child" than I thought at first. There were parents who seemed better at being experts in their own child than others, and this was not necessarily related to fluency in credentialed and specialized knowledge about autism. These parents did not just hand their children to professional experts but were also concerned about educating their child to live in their local worlds. They created a number of strategies to deal with them based on their immediate socioeconomic realities, family and work arrangements, and the daily routines they manage to develop for their kids. For sure, being able to articulate general information about autism and its main characteristics is also a part of such expertise. Even though Inês criticizes parents' anxious search for information at the expense of spending time to get to know their children, she herself did not learn about Ivan's autism simply by spending time with him. Having Maria as someone she could consult with at times of doubt and despair, certainly helped a lot. As we shall see, she also learned from other professional sources. And yet, she is right in saying that things never happen exactly as the books and manuals describe.

9.5 Experts in What? Raising A(n Autistic) Child in Rio de Janeiro

I started my first interview with Inês by asking her to tell me her story. She launched into a detailed narrative of how she ended up in Rio, after migrating from one of the poorer states of Brazil. Although her son was and still is assisted at *Círculo da Esperança* a couple of days a week, the real breakthrough for Inês and for him came through another institution, the Ann Sullivan Center, which used a method called Functional Natural Curriculum (FNC).[11] Inês explains FNC as "the obvious thing that you need to do for your child. It's normal children education." Every two weeks, according to her, she had to attend a "school for parents", where they teach to you teach the child the "obvious". It is beyond the scope of this chapter to get into details about this methodology. Instead, it is interesting to examine what she understood to be the goal of this "training" and what happened after it.

A story she told me then, and that she had already told me before, illustrates her perspective. Ivan is hyperlexic, having learned to read by himself at age 2, and because of that is completely obsessed with newspapers, magazines, flyers, catalogues, etc. There was a newsstand right by the bus stop where they got off to go to the Center. In order to the get him to the FNC training, Inês agreed to give him rewards—such as magazines, old newspapers, or even snacks—every time they passed by the newsstand. Each trip to the Center involved negotiations and compromises on both parts. For example, once she managed to get him to switch the highly caloric and unhealthy snack he would usually get, for a box of his favorite fruit (Ivan was overweight at the time and she was concerned about it). Another time, he got the magazine he wanted and then wanted to go back home straight away. She reminded him of their deal and he agreed to go all the way to the Center. One day though, the salesperson at the newsstand changed, and the old man who was now in charge did not let Ivan handle the newspapers and magazines as freely as he was used to. Even as Ivan had a major meltdown, Inês remained firm in setting limits with him. As they walked to the Center, a considerable distance from the bus stop, she had to deal both with Ivan pulling her hair and cursing her out loud, and with the moral judgment of people who were passing by and did not understand what was going on. When they finally got to the Center, she was shaking and not feeling well[12] but, she says, his episode helped her realize she had to be in charge, otherwise both of their lives would be controlled by these meltdowns. That is actually one of the first things Inês and Maria tell parents arriving at *Círculo da Esperança*—"you have to learn how to teach them limits when they are kids, because they will grow bigger and you will grow older. So, it will only get harder with time." According to Inês, an autistic child needs to learn basic things that any child needs to learn; you just have to work harder to teach them.

The kind of negotiations involved in each trip to the Center, that eventually failed on that particular day, were also part of the routine of other parents I met at *Círculo da Esperança*. They were not simply about imposing their will as parents or some impossible goal for their kids, but most of all, about learning when to respect the child's limits and when to push the child a little further. I then started paying more attention to what exactly these parents needed to know to become "experts on their own kids."

First, I realized that such expertise is not just about the child, or just about autism for that matter. It is also about the sociocultural worlds they both inhabit. In that sense, it involves engaging with their immediate environment with a special kind of attention. Learning to identify obstacles and challenges to be faced in a regular trip to the doctor using public transportation, for example, and planning ahead how to deal with them. Or making sure people in the surrounding community know about the child's special needs and that they will keep an eye on the child in case s/he elopes. Since the community around *Círculo da Esperança* struggles with drug trafficking and police violence, autistic children's elopement can have a really tragic ending.

The area is also densely populated, especially around the subway station and where local commerce is concentrated. Thus, living in that area means having to deal with intense sensory stimulation and moving through crowded and narrow pathways. A mother of an autistic child of *Círculo da Esperança*, who is also a self-identified "Asperger", first called my attention to that as we walked through this area one day: "This is what me and my son have to deal with on a daily basis. It's so awful! I put on earphones and listen to music, to make it more bearable. But I'm still teaching my son to tolerate all this." I later mentioned that story to Inês, who said she did something similar with her son and then invited me to join her and Ivan in their Saturday outings in that same area. Ivan walked a couple of meters ahead of us, and as we followed him she talked about how much progress he'd made since they started these outings. In the beginning, she had to walk very close to him, sometimes holding his arm, so that he would not take magazines away from newsstands or simply act in ways that would create problems for them and those around them. He now follows a well-defined route, going from shop to shop to gather free promotional flyers to read later. I was particularly amazed when I saw him entering an overcrowded supermarket during its anniversary sale, getting the flyer and leaving, apparently undisturbed by the loud anxious crowd. Sometimes Ivan flirts with a girl he finds attractive. He approaches her, and with his sometimes-incomprehensible voice asks her name. Inês then gets between the two of them, smiling at the girl with reassurance, and explains he wants to know her name. For me, it all looks as a very graceful well-rehearsed ballet routine—she knows just when to intervene, and when to keep her distance; how to let him flirt, and how to keep the girl from getting scared.

João, father of one of the children at *Círculo da Esperança*, told me that he quitted his regular job to take care of his autistic son, because he knew his wife would not be able to put the necessary effort in providing the best for him. João managed to enroll his son in every available public service for autism in Rio, in addition to *Círculo da Esperança*. He uses public transportation (mostly subway) to take his son to these different services and to school. During these subway trips, he takes the opportunity to teach him different lessons: "I do not let him sit in the preferential seats for handicapped because I know that judging solely by the looks, you often cannot tell someone is autistic. One day when he grows up, he might take the subway alone, without me or someone who can tell others that he has a disability. So, he'd better not get used to the privilege, because if he does, then it will be really hard to teach him otherwise. He is also learning how to walk in the middle of the crowd without bumping into others. He has made tremendous progress, you should see." In that sense, a parent who is an expert on his own child does more than planning the immediate future; he also strategizes and thinks about the long-term consequences of what his child is learning now.

Parents like João and Inês engage in practices of radical translations (Hart 2014; Eyal et al. 2010; see also Chew 2013), constantly attempting to make their child's behavior intelligible to others. Yet, they also became experts in conveying knowledge about their sociocultural worlds to their autistic child. In the process, they learn about the particular cognitive styles of their children but try not to lose sight of what it means to educate any child in the sociocultural worlds they inhabit. This means making very subtle moral distinctions and on-the-spot decisions about how to react to certain situations. I noticed for example, that professionals at *Círculo da Esperança* would use a particular expression for autistic meltdowns, *dar comportamento* (which could be literally translated as "to manifest behavior"), and distinguish that from a regular *birra* (a child tantrum). For them, an autistic child can manifest both kinds of behavior, and making such distinction can help parents decide when to accommodate to the child's needs, and when to resist their *birra*, impose some limits and push them a little further when necessary. Inês' story about the trips to the Ann Sullivan's Center is actually a story of how she came to realize she needed to make such distinctions. During our Saturday outings, I noticed that this is an ongoing apprenticeship,[13] and that making such distinction does not necessarily make things easier. And although I am not entirely convinced that this distinction can always be made, the very attempt to make such distinction is a major part of what made her an expert in this context.

9.6 A Context Sensitive Model of Autism Expertise

In arguing that expertise should be taken as a network property, and not as a set of attributes that a select group of professional experts have, Eyal and Hart (2010, 7) start from the premise that "experts and expertise are not the same thing". Yet, as already discussed, experts are usually recognized as such by virtue of a socially recognized network of expertise. As such, the concept of expertise does not simply refer to skill and knowledge in themselves, but to the social practices that organize a set of skills and knowledge within an "epistemic jurisdiction" (Boyer 2008, 38). Nevertheless, while such network regulates a specific set of skills and knowledge, what makes a parent an expert is not simply knowledge about autism. That does not mean of course, that there is no specialized knowledge involved in autism expertise. My point is that part of what one needs to know to be an expert on autism is highly context specific. The object of autism expertise refers both to a certain way of being in the world currently described under the rubric of ASD, and to the sociocultural worlds in which people diagnosed with such condition and their families live. The ways in which parents model their parenting styles and engage with their sociocultural worlds is deeply informed, but not totally determined, by what they learn about ASD.[14] As I hope to have shown with the stories of parents at *Círculo da Esperança*, much of their lives might be permeated by specialized knowledge on autism, but at the end of the day they are still parents, not therapists (and autistic children are still children, not just autistic). A big part of their parenting style might orbit around therapies and specialists, but not all of it. Like any other parent, they do their best to educate their children to live in the world they were born into.

Distinguishing what is determined by autism and what is part of the child's unique personality and life history is crucial for these parents, because this will help them balance between attending to the child's special needs and treating them like any other child growing up in that specific environment. Such distinction is obviously informed by professional descriptions, experience shared by other parents and, more and more often these days, by first-person accounts of what autism is and what it feels like. But the very fact that these parents—and professionals at *Círculo da Esperança* as well—do not see only autism in the child, paradoxically makes such a diagnostic category both less stable and pervasive, and more well-defined and objectified. Autism signs become more readily recognized by these parents and professionals, but the autistic condition might or might not be actualized in a given context, making space for other interpretations of a given behavior or personality trait.

Another key aspect of the kind of autism expertise I observed in parents and professionals at this association, is that a good part of it involves turning tacit knowledge (i.e., what they learned intuitively, as a result of having been socialized to a given sociocultural world) into explicit knowledge that can be taught to the autistic child, or used to build short- or long-term strategies for both the child and the family.

The stories of Inês and João are good examples of that—they often mentally reenact ordinary situations of their local sociocultural worlds, and rehearse their possible responses and strategies based on what they tacitly know both about these situations and about their children. I also observed that professionals at *Círculo da Esperança* often taught social skills to children with Asperger's Syndrome[15] by accessing examples from their local moral worlds and making inferences about intentions and moods of the people involved in a given situation. Such therapeutic approach is obviously not unique to professionals at *Círculo da Esperança*. Many autism therapies are based in the same principle. But professionals tend to conceal the sociocultural assumptions and inferences embedded in their how-to handbooks and trainings.[16]

On the other hand, parents like Inês and João, whose expertise is not so deeply shaped by professional knowledge on autism, become experts mostly by virtue of learning to make their own tacit knowledge of the social world explicit. After all, turning tacit into explicit knowledge is a skill that also demands expertise. As Collins points out, while there has been a great deal of interest on tacit knowledge as "knowledge that *cannot* be made explicit" (Collins 2010, 4; see also Polanyi [1966] 2009), the really interesting question is that knowledge can be made explicit at all: "There is … nothing strange about things being done but not being told–it is normal life. What is strange is that anything *can* be told" (Collins 2010, 7). According to Garro's process-oriented anthropological perspective to cognition, knowledge is not just about *what* we learn but also about *how* we learn (2007). These parents develop certain "ways of knowing" (Garro 2007, 59) the world around them that are highly focused on turning tacit into explicit knowledge. Interestingly, in doing that, they become deeply attuned to their own child's "ways of knowing".

It was not my intention in this chapter to suggest that these parents are representative of all Brazilian parents, not even of all the parents at *Círculo da Esperança*. I also do not claim that these parents' way of raising their children is totally unique and singular. I am sure that other parents of children with autism around the world develop similar strategies. Instead, my main goal in this chapter was to call attention to a model of autism expertise that is not so dependent on credentialed scientific knowledge, although still informed by it. The parents at *Círculo da Esperança* are not exactly "co-producers" of scientific knowledge, but many of them develop strategies to raise their autistic children that take this knowledge into account as well as their own knowledge about their local realities. As I see it, their approach to autism expertise has the advantage of not abiding uncritically to imported credentialed knowledge and of expanding the existential horizons of their children beyond a diagnostic category alone. Such approach also helps us understand how this association, in spite of all the challenges and lack of resources, managed to be so successful for such a long time. It seems as if Inês finally understood what autism is, maybe better than that doctor would ever have imagined.

Notes

1. For the sake of brevity, I will simply use the term "autism" throughout this chapter.
2. CAPSis were created as part of the first governmental attempt to provide assistance for autistic people and their families in the public health system. See Cascio et al. and Lima et al. (this volume), Rios and Costa Andrada (2015) for more information on the topic.
3. In English, Association of Friends of Autistics.
4. Collins and Evans (2007) have frame this in terms of an opposition between a "sociology of the acquisition of the expert status" and a sociology that treats expertise as something "real and substantive". The anthropological literature on expertise does not make such a stark distinction between these two approaches. Carr (2010) for example, writes a review of the anthropology of expertise, highlighting right in the abstract that "the anthropology of expertise focuses on what people *do* rather than what people *possess*, even in the many circumstances where the former is naturalized as the latter" (my emphasis).
5. The growing involvement of lay people in scientific debates and activities they are concerned with became the subject of a new wave in Science Studies, what Collins and Evans refer to as the Studies of Expertise and Experience (2002). These studies also bring to the fore the figure of the "lay expert", as someone whose expertise is experience-based, rather than based on credentials and academic certification (Collins and Evans 2002; Epstein 1995).
6. I do not mean to argue that all therapeutic practices related to autism are focused on cognitive and behavioral goals, but here it is important to consider the major influence of the normalization principle in therapeutic practices for autism after the process of deinstitutionalization. For an excellent review of the history of autism therapies, see Eyal et al. (2010).
7. Although these principles were officially named *Bem Viver com Autismo*, people usually referred to it simply as *Bem Viver*.

8. As far as education is concerned, the country's educational policies have focused on promoting the inclusion of autistic children in regular classrooms. That has created major controversies not only between parents and schools, but also among parents themselves. Parents of autistic children with more severe impairments do not think that inclusion in a regular classroom is a viable option for their kids. Others, whose children are not so severely impaired, still complain about the lack of special support for their children at schools. I will not have the chance to discuss this topic in depth in this chapter, but suffice it to say that overall parents and teachers tend to think of autism mostly as a medical and psychiatric problem, over which health professionals have more expertise than education professionals. One extreme example should illustrate that—I once attended a day seminar for teachers of the public school system of a lower income municipality of Rio de Janeiro on school inclusion of autistic children. One of the presenters, a professional from the field of psychopedagogy and an expert on ASD, stressed the importance of the DSM-V by recommending that every teacher take with them to the classroom a translated copy of the ASD diagnostic description as presented in the DSM-V. Fortunately, that is not a common practice in Rio de Janeiro. But the assumption that you are preparing school teachers to receive autistic children in their regular school classrooms by handing them copies of the DSM-V shows how much power is still attributed to psychiatric knowledge in Brazil.
9. These comments are not based on direct observations of doctor's appointments, but on participant observation in the welcoming meeting at *Círculo da Esperança*, where an ongoing flux of all kinds of parents share their stories after they hear Maria's presentation. Even though these families do not come from highly literate backgrounds, the level of health literacy among these parents varies immensely.
10. Internet searches range from autism symptom checklists to available treatments and personal testimonies (the latter usually in blogs written by parents of autistic children and/or social networks). Stories of children who managed to "get out of the spectrum" are especially popular among these parents, and create high expectations towards the work developed by professionals at *Círculo da Esperança*.
11. This methodology was created by the Ann Sullivan Center in Peru. The Functional Natural Curriculum follows the general guidelines of Applied Behavioral Analysis (ABA), and focuses on teaching abilities that are useful for the student in the present and near future (functional), in real life situations or in very similar circumstances to their normal occurrence (natural).
12. According to Inês, her blood pressure went up with all the stress. Recently, she reported having problems keeping her blood pressure under control, and commented this is probably related to all the stress she faced raising her son.

13. At *Círculo da Esperança*, the moments when parents and/or professionals have the chance to share with each other stories and anecdotes of their daily lives living/working with an autistic child, are especially important to the development of the ability to make such distinctions. In the routine of the association these moments of sharing can happen during formal activities such as the group therapy offered to parents, or more informal conversations taking place before or after other activities.
14. The argument for a context sensitive model of expertise is also an attempt to move beyond the dichotomy that underlies the debate on the relationship between evidence-based practices and cultural competence in mental health services. As we shall see, a context sensitive model of autism expertise is not about turning evidence-based practices into culturally appropriate services, but most of all, about inquiring into what is the real object of expertise in the case of autism. The cultural competence discourse, on the other hand, focuses on offering culturally appropriate services in multicultural settings. Moreover, patients' perspectives are treated as "ethnocultural beliefs, values, attitudes, and conventions" (Whitley 2007, 1588) and not as legitimate forms of knowledge. For more on that subject see Gone (2015) and Whitley (2007).
15. Professionals at *Círculo da Esperança* are quite aware of the changes at DSM-V, but still use Asperger's Syndrome as a diagnostic category to refer to certain people in the spectrum.
16. Ochs et al. critique this tendency within psychological literature on autism. According to them, "although autism is characterized as a social disorder, social functioning tends to be arbitrarily configured and under-conceptualized in clinical diagnostic manuals and in many psychological studies of the disorder" (Ochs et al. 2004, 154).

References

Borkman, T. 1976. "Experiential Knowledge: A New Concept for the Analysis of Self-help Groups." *Social Science Review* 50: 445–455.

Boyer, Dominic. 2008. "Thinking Through the Anthropology of Experts." *Anthropology in Action* 15 (2): 38–46.

Carr, E. Summerson. 2010. "Enactments of Expertise." *Annual Review of Anthropology* 39: 17–32.

Chew, Kristina. 2013. "Autism and the Task of the Translator." In *Worlds of Autism*, edited by Joyce Davidson and Michael Orsini, 305–317. Minneapolis: University of Minnesota Press.

Collins, Harry. 2010. *Tacit & Explicit Knowledge*. Chicago: University of Chicago Press.

Collins, Harry, and Robert Evans. 2002. "Third Wave of Science Studies: Studies of Expertise and Experience." *Social Studies of Science* 32 (2): 235–296.

Collins, Harry, and Robert Evans. 2007. *Rethinking Expertise*. Chicago: University of Chicago Press.

Epstein, Steven. 1995. "The Construction of Lay Expertise: AIDS Activism and the Forging of Credibility in the Reform of Clinical Trials." *Science, Technology, & Human Values* 20 (4): 408–437.

Eyal, Gil, and Brendan Hart. 2010. "How Parents of Autistic Children Became Experts on their Own Children: Notes Towards a Sociology of Expertise." Paper Written for the Annual Conference of the Berkeley Journal of Sociology. https://works.bepress.com/gil_eyal/1/.

Eyal, Gil, Brendan Hart, Emine Onculer, Neta Oren, and Natasha Rossi. 2010. *The Autism Matrix: The Social Origins of the Autism Epidemic*. Cambridge: Polity Press.

Garro, Linda. 2007 [2005]. "'Effort After Meaning' in Everyday Life." In *A Companion to Psychological Anthropology*, edited by Conerly Casey and Robert B. Edgerton, 48–71. Malden, Oxford, and Victoria: Blackwell.

Gone, Joseph P. 2015. "Reconciling Evidence-Based Practice and Cultural Competence in Mental Health Services: Introduction to a Special Issue." *Transcultural Psychiatry* 52 (2): 139–149.

Hart, Brendan. 2014. "Autism Parents & Neurodiversity: Radical Translation, Joint Embodiment and the Prosthetic Environment." *BioSocieties* 9 (3): 284–303.

Jasanoff, Sheila. 2004. The Idiom of Co-production. In *States of Knowledge: The Co-production of Science and Social Order*, edited by Sheila Jasanoff, 1–12. New York: Routledge.

Mello, Ana Maria, Helena Ho, Inês Dias, and Meca Andrade. 2013. *Retratos do autismo Brasil*. Secretaria de Direitos Humanos da Presidência da República (SDH/PR). https://www.autismo.org.br/site/images/Downloads/Retrato-DoAutismo-20131001.pdf.

Ochs, Elinor, Tamar Kremer-Sadlik, Karen Gainer Sirota, and Olga Solomon. 2004. "Autism and the Social World: An Anthropological Perspective." *Discourse Studies* 6 (2): 147–183.

Polanyi, Michael (1966) 2009. *The Tacit Dimension*. Chicago and London: The University of Chicago Press.

Rabeharisoa, Vololona. 2003. "The Struggle Against Neuromuscular Diseases in France and the Emergence of the 'Partnership Model' of Patient Organisation." *Social Science & Medicine* 57: 2127–2136.

Rios, Clarice, and Barbara Costa Andrada. 2015. "The Changing Face of Autism in Brazil." *Culture, Medicine and Psychiatry* 39 (2): 213–234.

Whitley, Rob. 2007. "Cultural Competence, Evidence-Based Medicine, and Evidence-Based Practices." *Psychiatric Services* 58 (12): 1588–1590.

CHAPTER 10

A.S.: Classification, Interpellation

Enrico Valtellina

10.1 Introduction

What is autism/Asperger's Syndrome (AS)? It seems like a silly question, given the extraordinary proliferation of public discourse on the condition in the present time. It is exactly for this reason that I find it interesting to propose this question anew, in the simplest and most preliminary of ways. My analysis will start from the most immediate of the responses: Autism is a clinical diagnosis. But, in fact, what is a clinical diagnosis? At what levels does its performativity perform? What does it say about the life of those who receive it? How is AS, in particular, specific among other DSM diagnoses? And beyond that, how does the diagnosis enter into the lives of the people who receive it or identify with it? In what ways is it a call, a particular cultural interpellation, constituting a specific collective subjectivity? Things are already getting complicated, but let us proceed in an orderly way, as I said, beginning from the historical and cultural contextualization of clinical diagnosis.

Translated by M. Ariel Cascio

E. Valtellina (✉)
University of Bergamo, Bergamo, Italy

E. Fein and C. Rios (eds.), *Autism in Translation*, Culture, Mind, and Society, https://doi.org/10.1007/978-3-319-93293-4_10

10.2 The Diagnosis

The term "diagnosis" was coined by Thomas Willis in 1681 (Jutel 2011a, 6). The subsequent constitution of medical knowledge as clinic—through the fundamental reorganization of the medical gaze, described by Foucault in *Birth of the Clinic* (Foucault 1963)—gradually puts focus on the diagnostic moment and the taxonomies within which that moment is structured. This text aims as a preliminary task to map the diagnostic moment in its constitution and articulation, in order to frame AS as one of its specific forms. It puts into place an (unavoidably preliminary) attempt at analysis, aiming to investigate the epistemological foundations of clinical classification, particularly in mental health. Thereby it calls into question the realism with which such classification is treated—by whom is it requested? by whom is it dispensed?—and articulates the nominalism of a genealogical gaze, recounting that to which the diagnosis makes reference.

Despite the centrality and historical pervasiveness of medicalization, only in recent years have the human sciences focused their attention on the diagnostic moment.[1] The following argument is based upon the productive theorizing of these works.

"Diagnosis" is at the same time both the name of a naming procedure and the act of naming itself. A recent book characterizes it as follows:

Diagnosis:

- is a way of experiencing, doing, and thinking that is pervasive in western culture.
- is constructed by lay people as well as professional experts.
- is socially situated and culturally sensitive.
- is a process and product of social interaction and social discourse.
- can have a life altering impact on those diagnosed. (Duchan and Kovarsky 2005, 11)

Just as there is unmistakable evidence that the medical gaze is a pervasive epistemological framework in the present era, so the diagnosis—insofar as it is certified only on the order of professional medical discourse—has made its way into daily discourse.[2] To approach the object of our research—autism and, in particular, Asperger's Syndrome—we need to turn our gaze to two specific aspects of the diagnosis: the diagnosis as *classification*, or the cataloging of problematic conditions (that continuously growing table of names given to individual clinical entities by medical and psychiatric knowledge), and the diagnosis as *event*, the moment of identifying a person within a definite set of problems with a name given by medical science.

10.3 The Diagnosis as Classification

> (N) Questions
> THOUGHTS/SORTS
> What does the forward-slash mean?
> What exactly is the question? Whether I think before I sort? Whether I sort before I think? How do I sort out my thoughts? What thoughts do I have when I want to sort them out?
> (Perec 2009, 121)

Diagnosis is a complex cultural construct. It is the form through which medical knowledge differentiates its objects, classifies specific pathologies into a clinical semiotic, and proceeds to treatment through a process of nomination. Georges Perec's suggestion of *Penser/Classer* addresses an essential aspect: the link between thought and classification, and its intimately problematic nature. Ian Hacking (2001) also talks about classificatory thought, in his inaugural lecture at the Collège de France. He recalls how classification evokes the fundamental opposition between realism and nominalism in medieval philosophy, reproduced today in the epistemological debate between foundationalist and antifoundationalist factions. His argument then takes into account the famous 58th paragraph of *The Gay Science*:

> 58. Only as creators! *This has caused me the greatest trouble and still does always cause me the greatest trouble: to realize that what things are called is unspeakably more important than what they are. The reputation, name, and appearance, the worth, the usual measure and weight of a thing—originally almost always something mistaken and arbitrary, thrown over things like a dress and quite foreign to their nature and even to their skin—has, through the belief in it and its growth from generation to generation, slowly grown onto and into the thing and has become its very body: what started as appearance in the end nearly always becomes essence and effectively acts as its essence! What kind of a fool would believe that it is enough to point to this origin and this misty shroud of delusion in order to destroy the world that counts as 'real,' so-called 'reality'! Only as creators can we destroy!—But let us also not*

> *forget that in the long run it is enough to create new names and valuations and appearances of truth in order to create new 'things.'* (Nietzsche 2001, 69–70)

Hacking analyzes this quote to show how classifications are historically, socially, and mentally produced but are at the same time performative. You can deconstruct them in a convincing way, but we live in a world that relies on them in order to make sense, and the only way to overcome them is by way of constructing new objects, "by creation." And the creation happens with usage: not in immediate way, but in a stratification of sense that gives birth to new objects, "layer after layer," until the new thing is finally produced. The naming procedure is the starting point of a social ontogenetic process.

> Objects come into being. We have a technical word in philosophy for the study of being: 'ontology.' It was traditionally thought of as a timeless discipline. Nietzsche speaks of the appearance and disappearance of objects, not of being in general but of being in particular, being in time. He speaks, we might say, of a historical ontology. That is an expression that Michel Foucault was using in 1982. Perhaps the most succinct way to state my debt, in some of my work, to the ideas and practices of Michel Foucault is by mentioning the title of a book that I shall publish next year: *Historical Ontology*. (Hacking 2002b)
>
> Michel Foucault did far more than historical ontology. He helped bring things into being. His was a creative ontology as well as a historical one. *Nur als schaffende!* [only as creators!] (Hacking 2002a, 7–8)

The nomination process creates objects through a gradual and culturally overdetermined process of stratification. That which it constructs does not remain the same object in perpetuity, but constantly evolves. Hacking discusses this particularity, this constitutive *dynamic interaction*, as peculiar to the objects of the human sciences. The theme of the distinction between *Naturwissenschaften* and *Geisteswissenschaften* (natural sciences and human sciences), is not resolved through the contrast between objective and interpretative methods of inquiry. The human sciences:

> [...] differ because there is a dynamical interaction between the classifications developed in the social sciences, and the individuals or behaviour classified. When we characterise a type of person or behaviour, it can affect some people so classified in a direct way, and may even change them.

> Hence regularities about individuals of that kind may change. Our knowledge of those individuals must be revised as they change, and our classifications themselves may have to be modified. I have called that the looping effect of human kinds. (Hacking 2002a, 10)

In the human sciences, we are, therefore, dealing with interactive classifications; diagnostic classifications provide a key example. In the following years, Hacking's courses at the Collège de France elaborated upon the propositions of this inaugural lecture, substantiating them through argumentation and examples. For our purposes, we are particularly interested in the lectures of 2004–2005 relating to autism, in which the dynamic and interactive character of classification in the human sciences is reaffirmed. In those lessons, Hacking stresses the importance of the first-person accounts of autism, what Donna Williams, one of the most famous autistic advocates and authors, calls "aut*ie*biographies," for understanding the condition from the inside, and how these interpretations have changed the public perception of ASD over time, and in some ways the medical one too.

Medical diagnosis as taxonomy has also been analyzed from a sociological and social constructivist tradition. A good example is the first chapter of Annemarie Jutel's (2011a) *Putting a Name to it: Diagnosis in Contemporary Society*, dedicated to examining and retracing the discourses and history of medical classification. In the last two centuries, with the emergence of the medicalization phenomenon—the gradual extension of medical power/knowledge beyond the borders of its original precincts and for good reasons not bound to its technical competence (Conrad 2007; Conrad and Schneider 1985; Szasz 2007)—medical classifications proliferate. Both medical classifications and psychiatric classifications have grown with the gradual differentiation of diagnostic categories because of the development of diagnostic tools. Psychiatric classifications have passed from the four Pinelian nosographic categories of melancholy, mania, dementia, and idiocy (as they were called) to the 1092 pages of the Italian edition of the *Manuale diagnostico e statistico dei disturbi mentali* (*DSM-V*) (American Psychiatric Association 2013). Jutel's text traces the histories of diagnostic repertoires, from Bertillon and the statistical list of causes of mortality to the *ICD* as its diagnostic development,[3] to the vicissitudes of the *DSM*, created from the necessity of psychiatric evaluation in military contexts,[4] and through its stages of evolution (most importantly, the *biological turn* of the third edition, published in 1980).

Shifting to a sociological perspective, let us recall Pierre Bourdieu's (2010, 481) suggestion: classification is the outcome of a *classification struggle* in which the social dialectic of nomination comes into play. "What is at stake in the struggles about the meaning of the social word is power over the classificatory schemes and systems which are the basis of the representations of the groups and therefore of their mobilization and demobilization [...] a separative power, a distinction, *diacrisis, discretio*, drawing discrete unites out of indivisible continuity, difference out of the undifferentiated" (ibid., 481–482). Therefore, classification is not the practice of neutrally and passively cataloging, but on the contrary is a place where a power relation takes form. "Classificatory *discretio*, like law, freezes a certain state of the power relations which it aims to fix forever by enunciating and codifying it" (ibid., 482).

Giving a name to a class of objects/subjects determines the nature of the differential relationship to the order within which they are located, bringing into being their social existence. Classification triggers dynamics of recognition and subsequent constraints—the exclusion of other incompatible determinations.

10.4 Aspergers Syndrome/AS

The realist attitude toward diagnosis makes sense when we are dealing with clinical entities with an etiology, a prognosis, and possibly, a cure. We will see that this is not the case of AS/autism. However, it is too easy to go from there to endorsing a nominalistic attitude, saying that the classification of AS/autism is just *flatus vocis*—an empty set of words with no real referent. This article will take a different stance, positing instead that the term "Asperger's Syndrome," through all of its fluctuations, points to something concrete: the relational problems that the diagnosis certifies. Ian Hacking, in a famous talk (Hacking 2006), introduces the notion of "dynamic nominalism" to illustrate his position and finds an easy example in his work on what he calls "transient mental illnesses," the *multiple personality disorder* and the *mad travelers*. He states that it is a lot more difficult to propose a radical nominalistic approach in the case of autism. It is true that there were no people with multiple personality disorder in 1950, and there were plenty of them in the eighties, but it is wrong, Hacking argues, to say that there were no autistic people before Kanner and Asperger.

In this paper, I will make reference to AS and autism as the names that the medical gaze gave since 1943 to a particular set of problems that happen during face-to-face interactions: what I call *relational disabilities*. To talk about relational disabilities, it permits us to refer to these same problems both outside the medical model and before the historical denominations of ASDs. It also permits us (as I did in Valtellina 2016) to consider the specificity of autism/AS in relation to the theoretical tools elaborated in the field of Disability Studies, and particularly at the singular shape that the partition of impairment and disability, central in the elaboration of the English Social Model of Disability (whose leading authors were mainly physically disabled), takes in case of relational disabilities.

Let us take a look now at how Asperger's Syndrome becomes characterized from its outset. In reviewing its history, we find it useful to map out its evolution, to "catch in the act" the progressive resignification process that Hacking calls the "looping effect" (Hacking 1995, 351).

As a clinical classification, Asperger's Syndrome emerged nearly forty years after its discovery, with Lorna Wing's (1981) article "Asperger's Syndrome: A clinical account," in which she describes the work of Hans Asperger,[5] and proposes to dismiss Asperger's term "autistic psychopathy" in favor of adopting the term "Asperger's Syndrome." We can, therefore, establish 1981 as the birth of Asperger's Syndrome in the world of psychiatric nosography—after a gestation period starting in 1943. We can see briefly how Wing and Asperger characterized the objects of their dedication. The first piece of evidence is the gender balance of their populations. Asperger's autistic children were almost exclusively male. Later, AS changed its gendered character with the gradual emergence of *aspergirls*.[6] For now, we note that, in its origins, AS was fundamentally characterized as a masculine pathology.

> It is fascinating to note that the autistic children we have seen are almost exclusively boys. Sometimes girls had contact disturbances which were reminiscent of autism, and there were also girls in whom a preceding encephalitis had caused the state. [...] How can this be explained? There is certainly a strong hint at a sex-linked or at least sex-limited mode of inheritance. The autistic personality is an extreme variant of male intelligence. (Asperger 1944, quoted in Frith 1991)

Wing synthesized the characteristics of the syndrome, drawing from Asperger's text, following his very same list of key points (Wing 1981). Let us take a brief look at those problematic points that define AS. Language acquired in the expected times, tends to be pedantic in its use, with echolalia and a strange passion for word games; nonverbal communication is lacking in the domains of ability to express feelings and to understand nonverbal communications from other people. Another fundamental characteristic, the one that permits me to talk about "relational disabilities" with reference to AS, is being "out of phase" with other people, manifesting in a seeming inability to manage social customs, codes, and implicit norms. All of these things are difficult to handle, resulting in inappropriate and awkward behavior, leading to many interpretations that have reduced this complex, problematic orientation to formulas such as "lack of empathy"[7] or of a "theory of mind."[8] Another determining aspect is what Kanner called predilection for "sameness," discomfort with changes and attitude for *routines*. People with AS usually lack motor coordination, and tend to show inadequate posture and stereotypical movements. A positive trait is the attitude toward developing special skills and interests, although at times, they turn into obsessive dedications, like that of the trainspotter. Certainly the school is the first place in which such eccentricities find socially visible expression—the nonconformity that identifies people as having relational disabilities. "They give the impression of fragile vulnerability and a pathetic childishness, which some find infinitely touching and others merely exasperating" (Wing 1981).

These characteristics, these original coordinates, identify the object of our research. However, even from the outset of its assertion, the syndrome has changed its face. Lorna Wing finds it necessary to supplement Asperger's interpretation.

Wing notes, in fact, some additional characteristics not identified by Asperger, specifically the manifestation in the first years of life of recurrent traits: scarce attention to the surrounding world; absence of communication of one's own wants through gestures and movement; absence of laughter, smiling, and other typical expressions in early infancy such as showing one's toys and other objects to parents; absence of pretend play, or when present, play that takes rigid and stereotypical forms without involving peers.

Beyond these supplementary observations, Wing takes her distance from Asperger with respect to two issues. In the first place, Asperger sustains that people with Asperger's Syndrome develop language before learning to walk. He makes reference to an "especially intimate relationship with language" and to "highly sophisticated language skills." This development is usually considered fundamental for a differential diagnosis with Kanner's autism (Van Krevelen 1971), in which motor development is normal while language development is delayed or absent. From her observations, Wing notes that language development is not always early and brilliant, but for the most part, behind an adequate grammar and a refined vocabulary for age level, careful investigation reveals that "the content of speech is impoverished and much of it is copied inappropriately from other people or books" (Wing 1981, 116), sometimes displaying awareness of the meaning of archaic or technical terms, but often not showing understanding of commonly used terms.

The second point Wing raises regarding Asperger is that he gave attention to the creative capacities and originality of his patients in their areas of interest, however restricted. "It would be more true to say that their thought processes are confined to a narrow, pedantic, literal, but logical, chain of reasoning" (ibid., 118). Even with respect to the claim of the sometimes superior intelligence of his children, Wing objects that such an affirmation does not rely on any standardized measure of IQ. That which is certain is that the rote intelligence of children with Asperger leads for the most part to partial or grossly incorrect comprehension. "Those with the syndrome are conspicuously lacking in common sense" (ibid., 118). Hans Asperger's emphasis on the positive characteristics of the condition became tempered by Lorna Wing's attention to the moments of deficit. As soon as it was born, Asperger's Syndrome was no longer the same. Having been brought to light in the English-speaking world by Wing, Hans Asperger's research began to circulate and to spread around the world, catalyzing a growing attention to the nascent syndrome. That which could be resolved in a fleeting, retrospective glance—the attention to an unknown predecessor—little by little, layer by layer, from its incubation in the 1980s to its canonization in the *DSM-IV* in 1994 (American Psychiatric Association 1980, 1994), took the form of a defined object following Hacking's formula.

A text by Lorna Wing and Judith Gould (Wing and Gould 1979, see also Feinstein 2010), based on research conducted in the London quarter of Camberwell on 173 children with autism and high levels of support needs, introduces a highly successful supplementary interpretation of autism: the "triad of autism," now the three principal diagnostic criteria. The three problem areas, the ***triad of impairments***, are (1) qualitative impairment in social interaction, (2) qualitative impairment in communication, and (3) restricted, repetitive, and stereotypical behaviors, interests, and activities.[9]

The growth of attention to autism and Asperger's Syndrome is reflected in a diagnostic explosion. These conditions were rare in the 1980s, with a prevalence of 1 in 5000 (numbers vary, higher or lower according to the authors, but at the time were assessed at this level). A study conducted in Korea in 2011, "Prevalence of Autism Spectrum Disorder in a Total Population Sample,"[10] found 1 person in 38 on the autism spectrum. The increase of diagnoses of severe autism can be accounted for via a wide range of factors—among which the subsumption of the previously quite prevalent category of "mental retardation" into the autism spectrum (indexical of a fundamental change in the dominant interpretation from a "mental" capacity to a "relational" one[11]), and the greater acceptability to parents of a diagnosis considered less stigmatized and full of more hope for change. Overall, the explosion of the diagnosis of Asperger's Syndrome was a complex and culturally fascinating phenomenon. Over time, according to Hacking's *looping effect*, the form of Asperger's Syndrome has changed, has gradually meant more things, and has evolved to the point of disappearing from the *DSM-V* in May 2013.[12] I linger here to identify a characteristic absolutely particular to Asperger's Syndrome, that is, that we are speaking of the only psychiatric classification in the *DSM* not only not stigmatized, but full of positive connotations (as stated, starting from the pioneering research of Asperger himself). Certainly this fact has determined a good part of the extraordinary cultural attention to which it has been subjected.

The diagnostic classification, more than just a taxonomy, is also something that happens in people's lives. Let us try, therefore, to analyze it as an *event*, something traumatic that happens into the vital flow, reorganizing it in critical ways.

10.5 Diagnosis as Event

> There is a class of performatives which I call *verdictives*: for example, when we say 'I find the accused guilty' or merely 'guilty', or when the umpire says 'out'. When we say 'guilty', this is happy in a way if we sincerely think on the evidence that he did it. But, of course, the whole point of the procedure in a way is to be correct; it may even be scarcely a matter of

> opinion, as above. Thus when the umpire says 'over', this terminates the over. But again we may have a 'bad' verdict: it may either be unjustified (jury) or even incorrect (umpire). So here we have a very unhappy situation. (Austin 1962, 42)

Austin's theory of speech acts, which brought attention to the performative dimension of language, would situate diagnosis among the *verdictives*—sentences in which the performativity is displaced across many levels, depending on the type of diagnosis, up to the most severe cases in which the sentence is death. In each case, it is a judgment (*Ur-teil*, original partition) that creates a before and after, a schism that transforms one's existence that reformulates it with respect to expectations for the future.

Regarding the event of inscription in a psychiatric disorder, Asperger's Syndrome also presents absolutely peculiar, sometimes paradoxical, aspects. The human kinds who carry the individual characteristics of the diagnostic criteria of AS are deeply affected, at the affective, occupational, and social levels, by these particularities. The disinclination toward face-to-face social interaction can be extremely debilitating, to the point of bringing on a state of severe distress, depression, isolation, social deprivation, and substance addiction. It is, therefore, understandable the cathartic effect activated by the discovery of a reason for all of those things. Punshon et al. (2009) dedicate their text "The 'Not Guilty Verdict': Psychological reactions to a diagnosis of a diagnosis of Asperger syndrome in adulthood" to this theme. Based on focus groups with people diagnosed with AS, the authors identify six specific thematic moments: "(1) negative life experiences, (2) experiences of services (prediagnosis), (3) beliefs about symptoms of Asperger syndrome, (4) identity formation, (5) effects of diagnosis on beliefs, and (6) effect of societal views of Asperger syndrome" (ibid., 270–271). After a lifetime of being blamed for these disinclinations, people with relational problems find in the diagnosis a justification that absolves them. They find themselves to be this way and to not be able to be any other way, so they often welcome as an essential element of their personality the diagnosis of Asperger's Syndrome. Since the 1990s, this diagnosis has created a space for something like an affirmation of identity. On the social stage, the evocative and curious figure of the "Aspie" finally appeared. A highly unusual situation: a psychiatric category was reclaimed and rearranged with an endearing nickname.[13] Given that for the most part, people with

AS are able to manage their lives, and in unproblematic contexts (that is, familiar and without stressing factors, and in the ecological niche in which they structure their existence); in many cases, they do not present any particular problems, it happens often that their diagnosis is called into question. One odd consequence of this is the search for proof. An Aspie activist friend of mine who had helped bring renowned Aspie American author of an "auto-bio-patho-graphy," John Elder Robison, to Italy for a conference circuit told me how Robison boasted a good seven diagnoses of Asperger's Syndrome, made by the world's most esteemed experts on autism. Jealously, she added that she herself had only two such diagnoses.

In the 1990s, it even became sensible for AS to be at the center of a collective reclamation campaign based on the American minority model (the civil rights model of collective affirmation of "minority" subjectivities affirmed in the 1960s and 1970s by African-Americans, women, and LGBT groups).

In 1998, Judy Singer coined the term "neurodiversity" (Singer 1998), taken up, and disseminated by neurodiversity.org, a website full of information on the syndrome. This concept is extremely interesting because it brings together two emergent discursive plains (AS and *neuro-hype*[14]), and identifies a synergistic interaction. Afterward, this identitarian discourse manifested its macroscopic limits (starting from the choice of the name "neurodiversity"[15] that attached it to an extreme biological reductionism and that, ultimately, means nothing, given that no such thing as two structurally identical brains exist), and remained only a generic backdrop for the affirmation for the imploring of "Aspie" activists. The term "neurodiversity" is now being used even by parents who seek biological and curative interventions for their children, and the political tone of neurodiversity activism has shifted drastically, away from an Asperger-specific separatist discourse and toward a wider embrace of all forms of cognitive development.

In the real lives of people that I have had the chance to meet in the last ten years of my dedication to this topic, I have observed a process that recurs frequently enough to make note of here: a gradual development of the relationship of people on the spectrum with their diagnosis of AS, corresponding to that which you can find in the recent anthropological literature.[16] Nancy Bagatell's (2007) work "Orchestrating Voices: Autism, Identity and the Power of Discourse," is particularly illuminating; as is the research of Sara Ryan, published in 2013 in an excellent volume edited by Joyce Davidson and Michael Orsini, with the title "Capturing Diagnostic Journeys of Life on the Autistic Spectrum"[17]:

> Why Seek Diagnosis? Although participants had varied backgrounds, they all described experiencing difficulties in their lives. Some ostensibly led successful lives with families and long-term careers but talked about consistently struggling with social interaction, expectations, and social norms. Others struggled with education, employment, and relationships and had been involved with mental-health services over the years. Several participants had been misdiagnosed with conditions including personality disorder, schizoid personality, and social anxiety. Others had had more derogatory labels applied to them. (Ryan 2013, 197)

Bagatell's ethnographic approach focuses on the process of construction of identity, something that is particularly problematic and challenging for people living in a situation of disablement. For those manifesting relational disabilities, that happens in a peculiar, and little analyzed, way. Relying on the theory of *dialogue* elaborated by Michail Bakhtin as an interpretative framework, her ethnographic research shows, through a protracted interaction with a young autistic, how difficult and laborious it is to cope with the conflicting discourses that surrounds diagnosis, and to find a personal narrative, through the polyphony of different voices, in a singular and effective way. The approximate path is this: more or less macroscopic evidence of constraints on their existence linked to problems of interaction, to sensory particularities, to interests, to ways of relating to the world, therefore, lead to diagnosis or self-diagnosis.

> At the conference, Ben attended a session on Asperger's syndrome and came away with a new way of understanding himself. Hearing a doctor talk about the neurological aspects of autism helped Ben to construct a new life narrative, to reframe his experiences and behaviors. Ben became aware that his actions, given his neurological make-up, were 'a normal part of my experience' instead of shameful or deviant. (Bagatell 2007, 419)

Bagatell describes the turning point that brought forth a determination to know as much as possible (for many, researching AS took the form of a symptom: an obsessive, exclusive, and restricted interest), to meet other people recognized as having the very same condition, and to follow—on the stockpile of awareness cultivated by precisely their limits and resources—a reorganization of their very existence, through an *orchestration* (taking up the sense of the title of Nancy Bagatell's article) of often dissonant discourses that constitute the cultural object of AS/autism:

> Ben began to realize that while he could be himself and not have to monitor his actions in the Aspie world, being in this world was not enough. What Ben was realizing is that while autism was one identity, he needed to construct multiple identities through experiences in multiple communities or figured worlds. (Bagatell 2007, 423)

The diagnosis, therefore, sought as an event, resignifies one's life: on the one hand, it brings an awareness, on the other, a self-absolution. Awareness that the difficulties that one meets in the life of relationships are similar to those experienced by many other people, awareness of the futility of blaming oneself, and that despite everything, there exists the possibility to valorize oneself and one's own abilities, to create an ecological niche in which to construct a horizon of sense conforming to one's own specifications—a self absolution in the case in which there comes an opportunity to withdraw, avoiding any potentially anxiety-provoking or frustrating interaction, even when doing so precludes the possibility of satisfaction and a full and fulfilling life.

To conclude this brief argument, I will now focus on a specific moment of the diagnosis as an event, that is, the self-recognition on the horizon of relational problems, through a discussion of the Althusserian key concept of interpellation.

10.6 "Hey, You There!" Ideology Interpellates Individuals as Subjects

Diagnosis is a process of inscription, of recognition. Someone who is diagnosed places himself on the horizons of meaning constituted by the specificities of the endorsed situation. For the most part, diagnoses are made by medical professionals certified to provide them. Indeed, the phenomenon of self-recognition seems far more pronounced in the case of AS and High Functioning Autism (HFA), that is, relational disabilities without cognitive impairment, than is the case with other diagnoses. Given a spectrum of problems that dishearten one's life, many people welcome the inscription of HFA/AS, as previously stated, as an integral part of their very person. They are *interpellated* by medical codification. If in turn, I am compulsively engrossed in the topic of relational disabilities, it is because 15 years ago I noted in myself several crucial characteristics identified by Asperger and Wing, and I had accepted it on the order of *subjectivation*, as something that was part of my *self*. Many people who work on autism—such as Ian Hacking—link their dedication to the topic to similar forms of partial self-recognition. The theme of *interpellation*,[18] of a call and response, explicit or implicit, is at the center of the dynamic constituting the subject and his relationship to ideology discussed by Louis Althusser, as we will see in the following argumentation.

> As a first formulation, I would suggest: all ideology hails or interpellates concrete individuals as concrete subjects, through the functioning of the category of the subject. This proposition implies that we should distinguish, for the moment, between concrete individuals on the one hand and concrete subjects on the other, although, at this level, there is no concrete subject that does not have a concrete individual as its support. We shall go on to suggest that ideology 'acts' or 'functions' in such a way as to 'recruit' subjects among individuals (it recruits them all) or 'transforms' individuals into subjects (it transforms them all) through the very precise operation that we call interpellation or hailing. It can be imagined along the lines of the most commonplace, everyday hailing, by (or not by) the police: 'Hey, you there!'
>
> If, to offer readers the most concrete sort of concreteness, we suppose that the theoretical scene we are imagining happens in the street, the hailed individual turns around. With this simple 180-degree physical conversion, he becomes a subject. Why? Because he has recognized that the hail 'really' was addressed to him and that 'it really was he who was hailed' (not someone else). (Althusser 2014, 190–191)

In substance, we concrete *individuals*, biological unities, are constituted as concrete *subjects* by the interpellations toward which we dispose ourselves or that dispose us. Althusser maintains that for the most part, the "call" is implicit, and often the "response" precedes the question (as in our case, in which the recognition of one's own relational problems in the cases of HFA/AS precedes the medical diagnosis, sometimes sought afterward). More, we are subjects before we are born, we already have a nationality, a religion, a given name, an expected social status.

To clarify further the dynamic relationship between ideology and subjectivity, Althusser takes the example of religious ideology, in which a symmetrical form of double recognition exists between God and the faithful, between the granting Subject and the subjected individuals.

> Thus the duplicate mirror-structure of ideology simultaneously ensures: 1) the interpellation of individuals as subjects; 2) the mutual recognition between subjects and Subject and among the subjects themselves, as well as the recognition of the subject by himself; and 3) the absolute guarantee that everything really is so: God really is God, Peter really is Peter, and, if the subjection of the subjects to the Subject is well respected, everything will go well for the subjects: they will 'receive their reward.' (Althusser 2014, 197)

In this case, the Subject that guarantees is God, but the same atemporal dynamic (in this sense Althusser states that ideology[19] has no history) produces subjectivity with reference to other Subjects, as the Nation with reference to nationalism. Bringing the homology to our theme, the eventual cathartic effect of the diagnosis of AS, as stated, proceeds from this "call", which is substantiated in the self-recognition into an order of categorized difference, that effectively is based on an a priori faith in the principle of justification, in the Subject, the practice of sorting that lies at the core of current medical-psychiatric knowledge.

We must bear in mind that Althusser's arguing happens in a text dealing with the Marxian theme of the reproduction of the relations of production, so the suggestion of the homology of the dynamic of interpellation needs to be further clarified. One important point that Althusser neglects but has been raised by many critics[20] of his work is the question of subjective *agency*. In a brief remark, he affirms that a "bad subject" can ignore the call, but that acting this way opens to consequences from the Repressive State Apparatus, that, differently from the Ideological State Apparatuses, "functions by violence" (Althusser 2006, 92). Without getting into a deep examination of the question, it is obvious that, while there is a spectrum of possible consequences to you if you do not pick up your diagnosis of AS, those consequences do not generally include direct violence from a repressive state. Stuart Hall gets the point at the ending of his "Signification, Representation, Ideology: Althusser and the post-structuralist debates" affirming:

> Contrary to the emphasis of Althusser's argument, ideology does not therefore only have the function of "reproducing the social relations of production." Ideology also sets limits to the degree to which a society-in-dominance can easily, smoothly and functionally reproduce itself. The

> notion that the ideologies are always-already inscribed, does not allow us to think adequately about the shifts of accentuation in language and ideology, which is a constant, unending process—what Vološinov [Bakhtin] called the "multiaccentuality of the ideological sign" or the "class struggle in language." (Hall 1985, 113)[21]

The work of Louis Althusser was taken up again in critical terms by Judith Butler (Butler 1997; Macherey and Bundy 2013). Her analysis proceeds from the text according to the method of symptomatic reading elaborated by the same Althusser, highlighting in it a dimension of religious introjection of guilt, and elaborating upon the problematic nodes of identitarian interpellations:

> Consider the force of this dynamic of interpellation and misrecognition when the name is not a proper name but a social category, and hence a signifier capable of being interpreted in a number of divergent and conflictual ways. To be hailed as a "woman" or "Jew" or "queer" or "Black" or "Chicana" may be heard or interpreted as an affirmation or an insult, depending on the context in which the hailing occurs (where context is the effective historicity and spatiality of the sign). If that name is called, there is more often than not some hesitation about whether or how to respond, for what is at stake is whether the temporary totalization performed by the name is politically enabling or paralyzing, whether the foreclosure, indeed the violence, of the totalizing reduction of identity performed by that particular hailing is politically strategic or regressive or, if paralyzing and regressive, also enabling in some way. (Butler 1997, 96)

Over time, my relationship with interpellation changed. Years ago, when I recognized autistic traits in myself that corresponded with Asperger's Syndrome, I had given maximum credit to the diagnosis. I read and wrote on the topic. With time and with study, the subject of AS revealed itself to me in its substance as a cultural assortment of human kinds that are divergent—legitimately divergent—and that find themselves atoning in infinitely different ways for the extremely scarce social tolerance for involuntary transgressions of implicit codes of face-to-face interaction. I progressively unsubjected myself. Now if they call me, I do not turn, and this seems to me the most delicious of the autistic responses.

Notes

1. Ballerini (2007), Jutel (2010, 2011a, b), McGann and Hutson (2011), Brown (1990, 1995), Felson Duchan and Kovarsky (2005), Maj et al. (2002), Colucci (2013).
2. A good reference for the cultural implications of diagnosis remains the works of Susan Sontag (1988, 1989).
3. For the history of the *ICD*, the *International Classification of Diseases* of the World Health Organizations, see their website at http://www.who.int/classifications/icd/en/HistoryOfICD.pdf.
4. An interesting article by Roy Richard Grinker, an author we will discuss further below, reviews the origins of the APA's diagnostic manual and its origins as an instrument for psychiatric evolution in military contexts (Grinker 2010).
5. The original article by Hans Asperger was re-published by Uta Frith as "'Autistic psychopathy' in childhood" (1991, 37–92).
6. Regarding the reconfiguration of the gender of Asperger's Syndrome, see the book by Rudy Simone (2010): *Aspergirls: Empowering Females with Asperger Syndrome*.
7. Regarding autism as a "lack of empathy," a recurrent theme even if not identified by the founding fathers, refer to Baron-Cohen and Wheelwright (2004): "Thinking about autism spectrum conditions as empathy disorders may be a useful framework and may teach us something about the neuro-developmental and genetic basis of empathy". Such a deficit theory of autism has been brilliantly debunked, through a heated debate with the problematic notion of "empathy," by Patrick McDonagh (2013).
8. The theme of lack of theory of mind in autism is the primary interpretation in the cognitivist school, and is its definitive tool: the test of Sally and Anne. Once again see Baron-Cohen (1995), who lists lack of "theory of mind," or the ability to determine what happens in the minds of others, 'mindblindness.'
9. From the interview with Lorna Wing in Feinstein (2010): "They were the three aspects. We referred to imagination as a separate deficit. The Triad of Impairments we introduced was social, communication, and imagination. People misquote the triad as social communication and rigidity. We weren't saying anything new in that sense. But we were saying that you could have manifestations in different ways" (Feinstein 2010, 152).
10. Kim et al. (2011). Among the authors is Roy Richard Grinker, anthropologist and father of a young woman with ASD, who furthermore definitively deconstructs the language of an supposed "epidemic" of autism—promoted primarily by parents' associations—in his important cross-cultural and anthropological analysis of autism, *Unstrange Minds* (Grinker 2007).

11. Again, Roy Richard Grinker examines this process in depth in his *Unstrange Minds* (2007).
12. At the time of the removal of the specific category of Asperger's Syndrome from the *DSM* and its subsumption into the autism spectrum, I was asking myself what would become of the cultural construct that the diagnostic voice had generated. For now, people continue to talk about Asperger's, so it seems that it has survived as a cultural object despite its defenestration from the *DSM*.
13. Michele Capararo rightly notes, in an inaugural address, how improbable it would be to do something similar for each other psychiatric diagnosis. As someone with Asperger's Syndrome reclaims "Aspie," it is harder to imagine that someone with depression be identified as a "depre" or someone with bipolar disorder as "bipo". This fact is a direct consequence of the aforementioned "positive connotations" of AS's diagnosis (Capararo, unpublished personal communication).
14. Ortega (2009, 2011, 2014), Ortega and Vidal (2011), Ortega and Chodhury (2011). A recent book co-authored by one of the most famous testimonial writers on the Syndrome, Temple Grandin, remarks even from its title—*The Autistic Brain*—on the explanatory centrality reserved to the brain for these problems (Grandin and Panek 2013). Harvey Blume, journalist and co-creator of the term *neurodiversity* speaks of *different wiring* in the autistic brain (Blume 1997).
15. See moreover Jurecic (2007).
16. See in particular the special issue of *Ethos* edited by Olga Solomon and Nancy Bagatell (Solomon and Bagatell, eds. 2010), Bagatell (2007), and the work of Elinor Ochs. Elizabeth Fein's (2012) doctoral dissertation on the theme is also extraordinarily interesting.
17. While Nancy Bagatell's text retraces an individual history as it unwinds over several months after the diagnosis, Ryan's research results from interviews with several people diagnosed or self-diagnosed on the autism spectrum.
18. The philosophical work on the notion of interpellation undertaken by the authors of the school of Ljubljana is very interesting. See Mladen Dolar (1993).
19. Althusser's notion of "ideology" differs slightly from the usual Marxist one that sees it as "false consciousness," for him "Ideology represents individuals' imaginary relation to their real conditions of existence" (Althusser 2014, 226).
20. Althusser's "Ideology and the Ideological State Apparatuses (Notes Towards an Investigation)" (Althusser 2006) and *For Marx* (Althusser 1969) had a strong impact and gave rise to a wide theoretical debate since their appearance, particularly in the British Marxism of the seventies. Some fundamental references are Pêcheux (1982), Hall (1985, 1986), Laclau and Mouffe (2001), Therborn (1999), Žižek (2009), and Guilfoyle (2009).

21. This reference to Vološinov/Bakhtin is an important link to the aforementioned work on AS by Bagatell (2007): in some way interpellation, in this manifold view, ends up being something very similar to "orchestrating voices."

References

Althusser, Louis. 1969. *For Marx*. New York: Pantheon Books.

———. 2006. "Ideology and Ideological State Apparatuses (Notes Towards an Investigation)." In *The Anthropology of the State: A Reader*, edited by Aradhana Sharma and Akhil Gupta. Malden, MA: Blackwell.

———. 2014. *On the Reproduction of Capitalism: Ideology and Ideological State Apparatuses*. London: Verso.

American Psychiatric Association. 1980. *Diagnostic and Statistical Manual of Mental Disorders: DSM-III*. Washington, DC: American Psychiatric Association.

———. 1994. *Diagnostic and Statistical Manual of Mental Disorders: DSM-IV*. Washington, DC: American Psychiatric Association.

———. 2013. *Manuale diagnostico e statistico dei disturbi mentali: DSM-5*. Milan, IT: Cortina Raffaello.

Asperger, Hans. 1944. "Die 'Autistischen Psychopathen' im Kindesalter." *Archiv fur Psychiatrie und Nervenkrankheiten* 117: 76–136.

Austin, John Langshaw. 1962. *How to Do Things with Words*. Oxford: Oxford University Press.

Bagatell, Nancy. 2007. "Orchestrating Voices: Autism, Identity and the Power of Discourse." *Disability & Society* 22 (4): 413–426.

Ballerini, Arnaldo. 2007. *La diagnosi in psichiatria*. Roma: Carocci.

Baron-Cohen, Simon. 1995. *Mindblindness: An Essay on Autism and Theory of Mind*. Cambridge, MA: MIT Press.

Baron-Cohen, Simon, and Sally Wheelwright. 2004. "The Empathy Quotient: An Investigation of Adults with Asperger Syndrome or High Functioning Autism, and Normal Sex Differences." *Journal of Autism and Developmental Disorders* 34 (2): 163–175.

Blume, Harvey. 1997. "*'Autism & the Internet' or, 'It's the Wiring, Stupid'*." MIT Communications Forum. http://web.mit.edu/m-i-t/articles/index_blume.html.

Bourdieu, Pierre. 2010. *Distinction: A Social Critique of the Judgement of Taste*. Oxon: Routledge Classics.

Brown, Phil. 1990. "The Name Game: Toward a Sociology of Diagnosis." *The Journal of Mind and Behaviour* 11 (3 and 4): 385–406.

———. 1995. "Naming and Framing: The Social Construction of Diagnosis and Illness." *Journal of Health and Social Behavior* (Extra Issue): 34–52.

Butler, Judith. 1997. "Conscience Doth Make Subjects of Us All." In *The Psychic Life of Power: Theories in Subjection*. Stanford: Stanford University Press.

Colucci, Mario. 2013. *La diagnosi in psichiatria. Aut aut 357.* Milano, IT: Saggiatore.

Conrad, Peter. 2007. *The Medicalization of Society on the Transformation of Human Conditions into Treatable Disorders.* Baltimore: Johns Hopkins University Press.

Conrad, Peter, and Joseph W. Schneider. 1985. *Deviance and Medicalization: From Badness to Sickness.* Philadelphia: Temple University Press.

Dolar, Mladen. 1993. "Beyond Interpellation." *Qui Parle* 6 (2): 75–96.

Duchan, Judith Felson, and Dana Kovarsky. 2005. *Diagnosis as Cultural Practice.* New York: Mouton de Gruyter.

Fein, Elizabeth. 2012. "The Machine Within: An Ethnography of Asperger's Syndrome, Biomedicine, and the Paradoxes of Identity and Technology in the Late Modern United States." PhD dissertation, University of Chicago.

Feinstein, Adam. 2010. *A History of Autism: Conversations with the Pioneers.* Chichester: Wiley.

Foucault, Michel. 1963. *La naissance de la clinique.* Paris: PUF.

Frith, Uta. 1991. *Autism and Asperger Syndrome.* Cambridge: Cambridge University Press.

Grinker, Roy Richard. 2010. "The Five Lives of the Psychiatry Manual." *Nature* 468 (11): 168–170.

———. 2007. *Unstrange Minds: Remapping the World of Autism.* New York: Basic Books.

Guilfoyle, Michael. 2009. "Using Althusser's Notion of Interpellation to Study the Politics of Therapeutic Practice." *Psychotherapy and Politics International* 7 (3): 159–173.

Grandin, Temple, and Richard Panek. 2013. *The Autistic Brain.* Boston: Houghton Mifflin Harcourt.

Hacking, Ian. 1995. "The Looping Effect of Human Kinds." In *Causal Cognition: A Multidisciplinary Debate*, edited by Dan Sperber, David Premack, and Ann James Premack, 351–383, 384–394. Oxford: Clarendon.

———. 2001. "Leçon inaugurale." (Speech, Collège de France, Paris, FR, January 11, 2001). http://www.college-de-france.fr/media/ian-hacking/UPL7027195376715508431_Le__on_inaugurale_Hacking.pdf.

———. 2002a. "Inaugural Lecture: Chair of Philosophy and History of Scientific Concepts at the Collège de France, 16 January 2001." *Economy and Society* 31 (1): 1–14.

———. 2002b. *Historical Onthology.* London: Harper University Press.

———. 2006. "Kinds of People: Moving Targets." In *Proceedings of the British Academy* 151: 285–318. https://www.britac.ac.uk/sites/default/files/hacking-draft.pdf.

Hall, Stuart. 1985. "Signification, Representation, Ideology: Althusser and the Post-structuralist Debates." *Critical Studies in Mass Communication* 2 (2): 91–114.
———. 1986. "The Problem of Ideology: Marxism Without Guarantees." *Journal of Communication Inquiry* 10 (2): 28–44.
Jurecic, Ann. 2007. "Neurodiversity." *College English* (69) 5: 421–442.
Jutel, Annemarie. 2010. "Framing Disease: The Example of Female Hypoactive Sexual Desire Disorder." In *Social Science & Medicine* 70: 1084–1090.
———. 2011a. *Putting a Name to It: Diagnosis in Contemporary Society.* Baltimore: John Hopkins University Press.
———. 2011b. "Classification, Disease, and Diagnosis." *Perspectives in Biology and Medicine* 54 (2): 189–205.
Kim, Young Shin, Bennett L. Leventhal, Yun-Joo Koh, Eric Fombonne, Eugene Laska, Eun-Chung Lim, Keun-Ah Cheon, Soo-Jeong Kim, Young-Key Kim, HyunKyung Lee, Dong-Ho Song, and Roy Richard Grinker. 2011. "Prevalence of Autism Spectrum Disorders in a Total Population Sample." *American Journal of Psychiatry* 168 (9): 904–912.
Laclau, Ernesto, and Chantal Mouffe. 2001. *Hegemony and Socialist Strategy: Towards a Radical Democratic Politics.* London: Verso.
Macherey, Pierre, and Stephanie Bundy. 2013. "Judith Butler and the Althusserian Theory of Subjection." *Décalages* 1 (2): 13.
Maj, Mario, Wolfgang Gaebel, Juan José Lopez-Ibor, and Norman Sartorius. 2002. *Psychiatric Diagnosis and Classification.* Chichester: Wiley.
McDonagh, Patrick. 2013. "Autism in an Age of Empathy: A Cautionary Critique." In *Worlds of Autism: Across the Spectrum of Neurological Difference*, edited by Joyce Davidson and Michael Orsini. Minneapolis: University of Minnesota Press.
McGann, P.J., and David J. Hutson, David J., eds. 2011. *Sociology of Diagnosis.* Bingley, UK: Emerald Group.
Nietzsche, Friedrich Wilhelm. 2001. *The Gay Science.* Cambridge: Cambridge University Press.
Ortega, Francisco. 2009. "Deficiência, autismo e neurodiversidade." *Ciênc. saúde coletiva* 14 (1): 67–77.
———. 2011. "Il soggetto cerebrale e la sfida della neurodiversità." In *L'avventura delle differenze*, edited by Barbetta, Pietro. Napoli: Liguori.
———. 2014. "Cerebralizing Autism Within the Neurodiversity Movement." In *Worlds of Autism: Across the Spectrum of Neurological Difference*, edited by Joyce Davidson and Michael Orsini, 73–96. Minneapolis: University of Minnesota Press.
Ortega, Francisco, and Fernando Vidal. 2011. *Neurocultures: Glimpses into an Expanding Universe.* Frankfurt: Peter Lang.

Ortega, Francisco, and Suparna Chodhury. 2011. "'Wired Up Differently?' Autism, Adolescence and the Politics of Neurological Identities." *Subjectivity* 4 (3): 323–345.

Pêcheux, Michel. 1982. *Language, Semantics and Ideology: Stating the Obvious*. London: Palgrave.

Perec, Georges. 2009. *Thoughts of Sorts*. Boston: Godine-Verba Mundi.

Punshon, Clare, Paul Skirrow, and Glynis Murphy. 2009. "The 'Not Guilty Verdict': Psychological Reactions to a Diagnosis of Asperger Syndrome in Adulthood." *Autism* 13 (3): 265–283.

Ryan, Sara. 2013. "Capturing Diagnostic Journeys of Life on the Autistic Spectrum." In *Worlds of Autism: Across the Spectrum of Neurological Difference*, edited by Joyce Davidson and Michael Orsini. Minneapolis: University of Minnesota Press.

Simone, Rudy. 2010. *Aspergirls: Empowering Females with Asperger Syndrome*. London: Jessica Kingsley.

Singer, Judith. 1998. "Why Can't You Be Normal for Once in Your Life? From a 'Problem with No Name' to the Emergence of a New Category of Difference." In *Disability Discourse*, edited by Mairian Corker and Sally French, 59–67. Buckingham, UK: Open University Press.

Solomon, Olga, and Nancy Bagatell, eds. 2010. "Rethinking Autism, Rethinking Anthropology." Special issue, *Ethos* 38 (1). https://anthrosource.onlinelibrary.wiley.com/toc/15481352/38/1.

Sontag, Susan. 1988. *Illness as Metaphor*. New York: Farrar, Straus, Giroux.

———. 1989. *AIDS and Its Metaphors*. New York: Farrar, Straus, Giroux.

Szasz, Thomas. 2007. *The Medicalization of Everyday Life: Selected Essays*. New York: Syracuse University Press.

Therborn, Göran. 1999. *The Ideology of Power and the Power of Ideology*. London: Verso.

Valtellina, Enrico. 2016. *Tipi umani particolarmente strani: La sindrome di Asperger come oggetto culturale*. Milano: Mimesis.

Van Krevelen, D.A. 1971. "Early Infantile Autism and Autistic Psychopathy." *Journal of Autism and Childhood Schizophrenia* 1: 82–86.

Wing, Lorna. 1981. "Asperger's Syndrome: A Clinical Account." *Psychological Medicine* 11 (1): 115–129.

Wing, Lorna, and Judith Gould. 1979. "Severe Impairments of Social Interaction and Associated Abnormalities in Children: Epidemiology and Classification." *Journal of Autism and Developmental Disorders* 9: 11–29.

Žižek, Slavoj. 2009. *The Sublime Object of Ideology*. London: Verso.

CHAPTER 11

Who Owns Autism? Economics, Fetishism, and Stakeholders

Roy Richard Grinker

11.1 Introduction

What does it mean to talk about the economics of autism? The answer depends on one's definition of "economics." The economic literature on autism—and, for that matter, most health issues—not surprisingly focuses on medical costs (see, for example, Amendah et al. 2011) rather than the dynamic construction of value (whether monetized or not). In their review essay of the economic literature on autism, Amendah et al. found a small number of publications on nonmedical expenditures in any country. Much of the literature concerns estimates of loss of productivity of caregivers, costs of behavioral therapies, supported employment, and residential care in the context of the increase in autism prevalence throughout the world. The data gathered for these publications come from clinical, insurance (e.g., Medicaid claims), and educational records. Authors tend to provide estimates of lifetime costs per person with a developmental disability, or estimates of prevalence and cost of comorbid disabilities, such as calculating how much the treatment of cognitive disabilities associated with Fetal Alcohol Syndrome costs as a proportion

R. R. Grinker (✉)
George Washington University, Washington, DC, USA

E. Fein and C. Rios (eds.), *Autism in Translation*, Culture, Mind, and Society, https://doi.org/10.1007/978-3-319-93293-4_11

of the treatment of the total population of children with cognitive disabilities (Abel and Sokol 1983). Little has been written on how autism became such a valuable diagnosis.

There are several rather obvious absences in the literature on the economics of autism. First, missing from these assessments and estimates is an explicit concern with how these costs are related to the question of how the *concept* of autism has changed and gained traction in recent years. There is an implicit assumption that most of these costs are new because there are more people with a diagnosis of autism today than ever before, an assumption that begs the underlying question of whether the costs are new because the meanings of autism have changed so radically in recent years, leading to increased diagnosis, or if the costs are new because there is actually an increase in prevalence. Second, there is little information on the economics of the production of expertise related to the rise of autism as a diagnosis, and the rise of child development specializations more generally (i.e., special education training, child psychology and psychiatry fellowships, speech and language therapy). These areas of inquiry are important if we believe that the economics of autism goes beyond dollars and their flows to the analysis of how financial interests help constitute not only costs but also forms of knowledge.

To anticipate the sorts of ideas I will discuss below, I want to emphasize the power with which we have imbued this concept of autism. Autism, in many memoirs authored by autistic people and their relatives, completely defines a person, or even possesses a person (like a demon), so it can shape personhood and social identity. It is codified so it becomes standardized in our vocabulary about human behavior. It is the foundation of a wide range of institutions and can even constitute a kind of "culture" (as for some self-advocates, as a way of life mediated through distinctive skills, challenges, etc.). Once established, autism feeds an industry of therapists; complementary and alternative medicines; pharmaceuticals; special educators; group homes, and other facilities that are established and maintained by government or nonprofit organizations. This industry is necessitated by, requires, and produces new laws, high-cost diagnostic and screening tools, new forms of evidence and analysis, and even new forms of aesthetics. These new phenomena are supported by sources of capital. These include philanthropists, advocacy organizations, schools, governments, research foundations, researchers in need of funding. In other words, autism may be imagined as a singular phenomenon, but it does not exist in isolation from a web of relationships, almost all of which have easily identifiable economic causes and consequences.

11.2 Prevalence and the Growth of Expertise

In a recent paper, Polyak et al. (2015) found no statistically significant change in "the overall proportion of children in special education ascertained under the IDEA [Individuals with Disabilities Education Act]." This act, passed by the U.S. government in 1990, is a permutation of an earlier act, the Education for All Handicapped Children Act of 1975, which recognized the right of all children with disabilities to have a free and appropriate education, as well as due process before the law. Between 1990 and 2016, both the number and percentage of students served under IDEA have varied, between 11 and 14%. However, both the number and percentage declined from 2004–2005 through 2011–2012 (National Center for Education Statistics 2016). Indeed, the proportion of students served under the IDEA was lower in 2009–2010 (13.1%), 2010–2011 (13.0%), and 2011–2012 (12.9%) than in any previous year up until 2000 (13.3%). Yet between 2000–2001 and 2010–2011, the classification of autism as a proportion of students in special education under the IDEA increased by 331%. Much of the increase is attributable to the steady decline in the United States of Intellectual Disability and Specific Learning Disability as classifications (though SLD remains, by far, the most common IDEA diagnosis), as well as the rise of autism, traumatic brain injury (TBI), and Other Health Impaired (OHI) as desirable categories in the U.S. What makes these categories desirable is partly what they are not. A parent of a child with TBI or autism does not want to suffer what many believe is the indignity of a label of intellectual disability. The parent of a child with a rare, complex genetic disorder prefers "autism" because, through that parsimonious category, the child joins an ever-widening group of peers and their families, and perhaps fits more neatly in pre-established or new programs. As has been well documented in the U.S. state of Minnesota, administrative prevalence rates rise substantially over time within single-age groups, with students receiving first-time autism classifications, even in late adolescence, when by definition autism would have already been present (Gurney et al. 2003). It is not that people with absent, delayed, or otherwise impaired language, with challenges in social communication, and with repetitive and stereotyped behaviors did not exist before.

But only a narrow group of people warranted the autism diagnosis, given how autism was defined. The phenomena that constitute what we call autism today may be universal, but autism is not necessarily a valid comparative category, either across time or space. Polyak et al.'s study shows that the category of autism now comprises a host of conditions of which symptoms of autism are comorbid. Despite the fact that the DSM still considers autism idiopathic (as did Kanner), in actual practice autism has become a main diagnosis for many people whose symptoms have an identifiable etiology. Research conducted over the past two decades has demonstrated overlap between genetic syndromes and ASD in Down's, Angelman, Cohen, Williams, Fragile X, Rett, Cornelia de Lange, 22q11 deletion, and Prader Willi syndromes (see Gillberg and Coleman 2000 for a review of this literature).

The increase in autism diagnosis is reflected in changes in clinical practices. As of this writing, for example, the American Speech, Language and Hearing Association (ASHA) has 182,000 members and affiliates, up from 25 members in 1925. Much of the growth is due to an increase in longevity, as much of speech language pathology (SLP) is devoted to the elderly, but an ASHA report on private practitioners also notes that 59% of SLP clinical time of ASHA members was spent with infants and toddlers, preschoolers, and school-age children (ASHA 2012). In 2013, 20% of the pediatric caseload of private practitioners was with patients with a diagnosis of autism (Brook 2013). Apart from private practice, in school settings, more SLPs served students with articulation/phonological disorders (93% of SLPs) and autism spectrum disorders (90% of SLPs) than any other disorder. The majority of public school children with autism (60%) were identified using both school and nonschool (typically private) resources (Yeargin-Allsopp 2003). At the same time, private therapy is not universally used since the far more flexible state and federal education codes and regulations used by the schools, and not the DSM, drive eligibility decisions. In one study in Atlanta, only 3% of children with autism were identified using solely nonschool resources (Yeargin-Allsopp 2003). The larger principle at work here is that where the availability of school resources increases, so too will special education classifications. Hence, in the U.S. approximately 13% of students in public schools receive some sort of special education service, while in a country like South Korea, with a robust and internationally respected medical system, but a weak special education infrastructure, only 2% of students in government schools receive special education services (Kim et al. 2011).

An epidemiological study of children with ASD in Venezuela, based solely on medical and school records, found a prevalence of only 0.17%. In this case, the likely underestimated rate of ASD is due to a combination of limited governmental resources, lack of awareness among professionals, and parents that do not recognize that the behavior of their children is different (Montiel-Nava and Peña 2008). Similar results have been found in other Latin American countries like Ecuador with a prevalence of 0.11% (Dekkers et al. 2015) and Brazil with a prevalence of 0.27% (Paula et al. 2011). The fact that three different Latin American countries with varying levels of economic development have such low prevalence rates of ASD compels us to recognize that the need for special education, and the delivery of services, can be determined by a multitude of factors that have little to do with any scientifically validated disease.

The specialization of child psychiatry also increased rapidly in recent decades. By the early 1970s in the U.S., there were only a few hundred child psychiatrists; it was a low prestige medical specialty because psychoanalysis was still the dominant paradigm, and largely an area of adult psychiatry. Today, there is a serious shortage of child specialists, as documented both anecdotally by parents waiting months for appointments, and by the U.S. Bureau of Health Professions, which in 2003 projected that, based on diagnostic practices, by 2020, the number of child psychiatrists needed to address the pediatric population with the same level of service would be double the number that existed in 1995 (Kim 2003; Thomas and Holzer 2006). If 2003 recruitment levels remained constant, there would only be a projected supply of 8312 clinicians in 2020, though more than 12,000 would be needed. The problem was most acute for poor and rural populations. Alaska, Alabama, Oklahoma, and Wyoming had less than 4 child and adolescent psychiatrists per 100,000 youth. For example, in 2001, there were 6 child and adolescent psychiatrists in Alaska, and 5 in Wyoming. Given the cost of psychiatric care, the highest rates of child specialization were in the wealthiest states, and within those states, clinicians were concentrated in wealthier areas. The prevalence of autism is significantly higher in wealthier states than in poorer ones, as evidenced by the CDC estimates, in which the proportion of children with autism in New Jersey is five times that of Alabama. This is likely due to the fact that wealthier states are capable of providing more services, and the CDC can only count those cases that appear in service records. A more nuanced analysis within any state would also find prevalence rates lower in poorer districts, as has been shown by Bearman and colleagues in California (King and Bearman 2011).

Today, universities offer Master's degrees in autism (Florida State University, for example); concentrations within psychology PhD programs on autism; programs focusing on autism and play therapy, and social skills; and Master's degrees in Applied Behavior Analysis (ABA), which training institutions justify in terms of increased prevalence. Drexel's MS program in ABA, for example, notes on its Homepage: "Within the past decade, the number of children diagnosed with autism or Asperger syndrome has increased drastically, resulting in the need for educated behavior science professionals. Drexel University's accredited online Master's in ABA prepares clinical, behavioral health, and educational leaders to use analytic theory and tools to care for and educate this growing population" (https://online.drexel.edu/online-degrees/education-degrees/ms-aba/index.aspx. Accessed October 30, 2017).

Many other factors need to be considered in any analysis of prevalence trends. For example, advocacy organizations, such as Autism Speaks Foundation and the Autism Society of America, have increased awareness of autism dramatically (though there is no way to quantify awareness) and likely, therefore, also diagnoses of autism at earlier ages. Autism also increases as a primary diagnosis for children who reside in states in which fiscal incentives promote a greater number of school diagnoses of autism. Cullen (2003), for example, demonstrated a link between fiscal incentives and a 40% growth in student disability rates in Texas. As she notes, the 1975 Education for All Handicapped Children Act provided greater financial support to schools if they identified and provided services to children with disabilities, especially those conditions (such as mild learning disabilities) that had been under-identified. And, importantly, state and school criteria for autism diagnoses are generally significantly broader than DSM criteria. Kwak (2010) describes how in 1996, when California began to determine levels of special education funding based on total enrollment rather than the enrollment of disabled students, special education classifications fell or remained flat. Diagnoses or diagnostic adjustments are possible given the great variability in diagnostic practices across the country, although there were clearly financial limits on how many children could be considered disabled: despite the desire to diagnose for financial reasons, diagnosis itself, let alone the special education services, can be costly. Scholars tracking funding streams for special education in a range of different countries often estimate that special education of a student incurs double the cost of regular (mainstream) education (Sigafoos et al. 2010).

Furthermore, the increased attention to evaluate schools on the basis of educational testing measures may have promoted greater numbers of school-based diagnoses of autism to exclude low-performing students from standardized tests, if it was believed that those test results might reflect poorly on the school. Another important economic factor contributing to rising diagnostic rates is the rise of special education litigation, and litigation specifically for autism-related services, the costs of which have yet to be clearly studied; however, we do know from one study of a comprehensive sample of published court decisions that children with autism accounted for about one third of published court decisions concerning appropriate education and the least restrictive environment, under the Individuals With Disabilities Education Act (Zirkel 2011). Zirkel notes that this rate is disproportional to enrollment of students with autism in special education programs in the U.S. under the IDEA, and that this disproportionality has spanned the period of analysis, from 1993 to 2006, and occurred across states with both high and low prevalence estimates. The reasons for the disproportionality are unclear, but it is certainly conceivable that because autism-related services tend to be more expensive than those for other disabilities, schools may be more likely to withhold services, and parents, thus, more likely to feel the need to litigate.

Boyle et al. (2011) suggest that reported prevalence of a developmental disability increases with poverty. They note that, compared with families with private insurance, there was a nearly two-fold higher prevalence of developmental disability among children receiving Medicaid. Within schools, there has been a consistent rise in special education funding, but less in real terms than in proportion, as funding has shifted toward special education. Between 1967 and 1991, regular education expenditures dropped nationally from 80% of total education expenditures to 59%, and the share devoted to special education rose from 4 to 17% (Rothstein and Miles 1995). Autism accounts for much of the upward trend in relative terms, although high prevalence conditions such as Attention Deficit Hyperactive Disorder (ADHD) far exceeded autism in terms of increased numbers of cases.

Anne McGuire was one of the early writers to formally publish the phrase "autism industrial complex" in reference to this emerging infrastructure for autism awareness, philanthropy, research, training, and treatment. The phrase comes from former U.S. president Dwight Eisenhower who, after leaving office in 1961, expressed concern about the "military industrial complex," by which he meant the symbiotic relationship between American industry and the U.S. military. The intimate relationship between industry (and capitalism in general) and military was certainly not new. What was new was the explicit recognition that the symbiosis might insulate the military and its corporate partners from the normal operations of the competitive market, since that relationship is to a great extent shielded *by* the government, and shielded *from* the actions and interests of the wider American public. While some economists have attributed the complex to the inevitable effects of technological progress, others have hypothesized a more Schumpeterian view of "creative destruction" in which new forms of economic power emerge only by replacing (i.e., destroying) existing economic power (Adams 1968, 653). Phrased differently, there was no accretion of new forms but an emerging web of interconnected, bounded interests.

The literature on autism similarly suggests that the costs, prevalence rates, numbers of programs and experts, etc. reflect a new reality in which there is, in fact, an increase in the incidence of autism, and new scientific knowledge. But it seems just as likely that there is a mutual feedback between autism and society, such that even small increases in rates of autism diagnosis (for whatever reason) lead to new realities (such as educational programs and clinical services) that validate the increases in diagnosis as a true increase in incidence. Why would there be more autism programs if there were not more autistic people? Why would there be so many more people with expertise in autism if autism was not a legitimate object of study? Ian Hacking's looping mechanism suggests something similar: that we interact with our classifications.

Timothy Mitchell (2007, 244) asks, what if we think of economics as "a set of instruments of calculation and other technical devices, whose strength lies not in their representation of an external reality but in their usefulness for organizing sociotechnical practices, such as markets?" Similarly, psychiatry is a set of representations that organize difference, and forms of suffering, into specific practices, such as the naming, definition, classification, and treatment of mental illnesses. But the most crucial point is that these organizing devices take on an often-unanticipated economic power. Each new revision of the DSM, for example, may be motivated less by radical changes in psychiatric knowledge, than by the need for the American Psychiatric Association to develop what is widely known to be its greatest source of ongoing revenue.

Commenting on the "autism industrial complex," Anne McGuire (2013) notes that even the body of the autistic person is measurable in capitalist terms. She writes of "the untimely body" of the autistic person, whose delays on so-called milestones (relationships between specific ages and specific tasks, and pegged to a definition of normality), generate a multibillion dollar industry of advocacy, pharmaceutical, and service interests. She writes:

> The Starbucks cup, World Autism Awareness Day and the sheer breadth of the 'autism industrial complex' all gesture towards the cultural fact that, under neoliberal rule, social and/or economic investment in the untimely autistic child is not just an investment in the realization of the 'future-citizen-worker' but in the potential for its realization. In one unbroken—and clearly very lucrative—move, our market-driven times, at once, produce and regulate, create and constrain conducts that are beyond the norm. (124)

She notes that politicians and clinicians often lament the high cost of autism. But costs did not suddenly arrive full blown. The costs of caring for people with autism could not increase unless it was believed that the costs provided benefits—moral and practical goods. The economics of autism had to await the high awareness (if not prevalence) of autism, which replaced the cases that used to be called something else, or nothing at all. And awareness is certainly more lucrative than research in terms of producing expenditures and donations. The Autism Speaks Foundation has grown rapidly since its founding in 2005 due to philanthropy, and thus, it seems rational (in an economic sense) that it would focus its efforts on fundraising. In 2009, awareness campaigns comprised 19% of its annual budget. That figure rose to 31% in 2011 and 64% in 2013. Research funding and science grants declined as a percentage of overall expenditures (see publicly available tax returns).

11.3 Fetishism

This constructivist approach often provokes criticism, as if one is denying the reality of suffering. If I say, for example, that autism is a mid to late twentieth century construction that is a historically contingent assemblage of specific and observable behaviors, I do not mean that the phenomena that we today call autism do not exist. My daughter will have problems with social communication and repetitive behaviors no matter what diagnosis she has. A constructivist approach does not deny that there is an underlying biological condition that can produce suffering. Rather it acknowledges first that our models of those conditions are historically contingent and second, that, in the words of the anthropologist Paul Brodwin (2013, 59–60), our models typically “race ahead of what is actually known, reclassify knowledge through educated guesses and grand syntheses,” and justify practices that surround identification and treatment.

Because when we speak about autism (or when, as in the foundation name, autism speaks), we often think we are—to paraphrase the philosopher Jacques Derrida—talking about *that of which we speak*, as opposed to that *out of which* we speak. Given that I am an anthropologist, one might expect I would talk about how autism is similar or different across cultures. But I think the value of an *anthropologically* informed approach to autism is not just its contribution to particularism (in which we describe cultural differences) or relativism (in which we appreciate autism for its differences from an assumed norm). Rather, I think an important contribution anthropology can make at this time is to help unmask the cultural foundations of the various representations of autism (especially in science and in advocacy), including the “high cost” of autism.

Derrida writes that nothing exists outside of context (1988), and Foucault has persuasively argued that we live within epistemes (1994)—the totality of the discursive practices that gives rise to forms of knowledge, such as medicine, economics, history. In the history of psychiatry, in particular, the doctor or expert first emerges not as a person who possesses knowledge but as a person who could establish order. Foucault, in fact, likens early psychiatrists before and up through Freud to *magicians*, because their authority and also their effectiveness came not from science and knowledge but from a moral, humanistic strategy to provide care and to do so in a way that was systematic, ordered, and institutionalized. Why? Because the history of psychiatry did not really proceed on the accumulation of knowledge but on the coattails of modernity, we now know that the rise of institutions in Europe—schools, prisons, hospitals, etc.—accompanied the rise of capitalism, and along with capitalism came a new way of thinking about and ordering the world. New modes of production do not just change how we behave. They also change the way we think and the way we organize our ideas and classify behaviors. In other words, capitalism is a pervasive condition.

What changed from, say, Pinel (who is credited with the first humane care of the mentally ill) to Freud was less about generating new knowledge than about a new system of ordering knowledge, of which psychiatry was just one small part. With the rise of psychiatric disorder, constructs, and the various practices surrounding those constructs, become organized and coherent—and therefore intelligible as a distinct body of knowledge. We need only think about the DSM to understand this point. The DSM is a system of classification, presumably based on a system of knowledge, but it is also a form of governance or psychiatric governmentality (not to mention a commodity). I think it is difficult to be in the fields of psychology, psychiatry or social work, and not own the DSM because the DSM owns the classification of mental illness.

Our academic disciplines emerge in particular contexts for particular reasons. And they emerge, as the word discipline suggests, as *forms of discipline*—in the sense that they control, correct, and train human beings. They are organized hierarchically and inflict micropenalties on us for our transgressions (lateness and absences at schools or jobs; talking out of turn; not citing the appropriate references or writing outside the conventions of scholarship). For many, it is unimaginable to conceive of hospitals, schools, prisons, or militaries, organized in any way other than to be divided up and ordered into small units with highly formalized, controlled, and orderly operations. Abstract oppositions like right and wrong, good and bad, normal and abnormal, rational and irrational, derive from this order and are the poles within which we conceive of ourselves.

Knowledge becomes a form of power and governance, exercised by those who claim to possess it or those who societies endow with the authority to possess it. Science becomes a form of political power, then, not through coercion or imposition, but "by aligning diverse agents through shared vocabularies" (Thornton 2010, 315). The power is not out there in the open, obvious to us, because it is enclosed within the ideology that simultaneously legitimates and masks it. So any particular psychiatric disorder becomes conceived not as a form of governance that guides human action but as a medical or scientific problem to be solved through medicine or science.

It is important to challenge autism as a singular or exceptional category because, otherwise, we risk naturalizing it. The sense we often have that autism is something new, special exceptional—a thing in and of itself—is a product of what philosopher Hannah Arendt (1958) considered the *appearance of freedom* in the universe. "It is in the nature of beginning," she wrote, "that something new is started which cannot be expected from whatever happened before" (177–178). Antecedents fade into the distance. Autism was childhood schizophrenia; then it was not. It was considered to be unrelated to seizures and intellectual disability, and then, it was related. Autism was a mental illness; then it was a developmental disability. Asperger's Disorder existed; then it did not. Autism is a concept discussed by DeSanctis in Italy in 1906, Heller in Austria in 1908, Bleuler in Switzerland in 1911, Sukhareva in Kiev in 1926, and Freud in Austria in 1921 (DeSanctis 1906; Heller 1908; Bleuler 1911; Sukhareva 1926; Freud 1921). Yet there is, for all intents and purposes, a belief in a single origin—Leo Kanner, the person who prefaces every historical account of autism as if autism was born in 1943 (note: Steve Silberman's, *Neurotribes* (2015), changes this origin story to privilege Hans Asperger, and consider Kanner derivative). In situating autism in society and history, my goal is to complicate the idea that autism is unique or—another way of saying unique—exceptional. Many researchers working in the field of autism treat it as an island, to be explained in terms of itself, though the histories of many conditions across medicine share themes and patterns.

Consider all the new kinds of people—what Ian Hacking calls "Making Up People" (2006)—that exist today that did not, in a classificatory sense, exist before. PTSD, Multiple Personality Disorder, Fetal Alcohol Syndrome. Yet people have always had trauma; there have always been people who have had severe dissociation; there have always been women who drank large amounts of alcohol during pregnancy. What we have not always had is a certain group of experts who created these classifications, justified them as valid, integrated them into a range of institutions, and then diagnosed them in individuals who came to see themselves in terms of the diagnosis—all of which made the classification feel legitimate and authentic. This process—what Ian Hacking (2000) calls the "looping effect"—can lead to stigma when individuals adopt this new category of person. Given how total this looping effect can be, it is hard to resist it.

New models are often validated not just in spite of their occasional failures but because of them. In the context of autism prevalence, it may be useful to look at Mackenzie et al.'s critique of the Fama's well-known efficient-market hypothesis (2007, 4). Simply put, the hypothesis states that prices within a market will always reflect the information available within the market. The idea behind this proposition is that one can never "beat" the market (because prices already reflect information before anyone can buy or sell based on that information). In response to the increased popularity of the hypothesis during the 1980s and 1990s, economists developed a large number of financial tests that failed to support it. When tests failed, instead of questioning the hypothesis, economists developed strategies that would profit from the failures. Index funds, in which people invest in the market as a whole, were one result. Strategies to profit from failed tests or anomalies then validated the very hypothesis of which failures created the strategies in the first place. Some economic models take on an almost sacred quality, such that they must always be protected. And when a particular perspective does not show what we expect from the model, we can simply change the perspective until we do show it.

One could make the argument that autism and other kinds of diagnoses have become such sacred objects, that they have been fetishized in the interests of the industrial complex. I do not mean fetish in a sinister or sexual sense, or even in the religious sense, though there are some illness categories that have been defended as almost sacred objects. Rather, I mean fetish in the sense of something singular, set apart, and whose conditions of being do not depend on its similarities with other phenomena. It is set apart in a system of classification as something real.

Marx, of course, described the commodity as fetishized. Marx argued that money is fetishized as having real and objective value—and even a life of its own, as when we talk about the stock market liking or disliking an event, or animate it as a bull or bear. We come to believe that it has a real and objective existence, with real value, when in fact, a piece of paper money has value only because that value has been produced by a complex set of social relations of production. Just as the value of money is self-evident in an economy based on markets and commodities, so too is autism made real by all the activity that takes place around it—from the basic sciences to epidemiology, treatment, and intervention. In the midst of so much science, it becomes difficult to see that we may have taken the medicalized, neuroscientific, and genetic approaches to the point at which a disease construct is so profoundly fetishized that we fail to see its cultural constitution. There is now simply too much at stake to threaten the integrity of autism.

Consider, for example, the stubborn persistence of another fetishized psychiatric representation, schizophrenia as a "split mind," an idea defined in large part by the oppositions between dark and light, good and evil in eighteenth and nineteenth century European arts and literature (Barrett 1998). Remarkably, more than 140 years after Dostoevsky wrote about the "second self" as the sign of the disintegration of the mind, even a cursory examination of advertisements for antipsychotic pharmaceuticals in 2015 will yield representations of psychosis as a divided mind. Images of young men break into pieces, or the floor cracks beneath their legs. These representations, which owe their existence largely to European Romanticism, and certainly not to any scientific discoveries, are circulated through an economy in which just one antipsychotic medication, Risperdal, earned Johnson and Johnson several billion dollars per year (more than $4 billion in 2007, and still, in 2012, after generic competition emerged, $1.4 billion).

The definition of autism and other conditions in terms of a group of deficits or impairments—a deficit model of autism—may be another legacy of the tradition of explaining difference as diversion from a norm and motivating the call for costly services. Consider New York University's Child Study Center's 2007–2008 advertisements for their diagnostic and treatment business, called "Ransom Notes" (Kras 2010). The ads, posted on bus stop shelters and in other print media, were letters from kidnappers. One letter to a parent, and signed "Autism," read, "We have your son. We will make sure he will not be able to care for himself or interact socially as long as he lives. This is only the beginning." This view of the autistic person as lost, abducted, kidnapped, is not the result of scientific research, but of a particular objectification of the human mind, and the idea that the person with autism has been damaged. The autistic person, from this perspective, is deficient and dysfunctional and the responsible parent must, in this view, purchase services from the New York University. In many memoirs of autism written by parents, diagnosis becomes both a proxy for the onset of autism and the sudden disappearance of the child. In her book, *The Accidental Teacher*, Annie Lehman calls autism "a greedy disability," because it takes so much away (2009). And each article on the costs of autism details its drain on society, from families to the economy as a whole. Paradoxically, autism is at once a threat to economic growth and (at least for many parts of American society) an engine of economic growth. It is not surprising that drug companies sponsor research not only into treatment but into *prevention* (where everyone is a possible candidate for medication), and into disease awareness campaigns.

11.4 Conclusion

To conclude, it is worth continuing this line of thinking about autism as fetish. First, autism experts and other "stakeholders" have endowed the diagnostic category with the central features of a fetish: It is an exceptional category—a thing, *sui generis*—the power of which is consolidated as it subsumes an increasingly broad array or *spectrum* of heterogeneous elements, and its reification masks the relations of its production. Despite the fact that autism may contain within it a wide range of variation, we have accepted autism as an objective, discursive object. If autism as a totality feels surprisingly new, well, it is. But so are many other seemingly autonomous areas of knowledge. The idea of the economy as a "self-evident totality" (Mitchell 2007, 88) emerges between 1930 and 1950 in the U.S. and Britain. Before that time, people who called themselves economists did not say they studied "the economy" but rather economic topics. Autism, of course, used to exist just in its adjectival form too—autistic—and is first nominalized in the DSM in 1980 with the publication of the DSM-III.

Second, to continue with the metaphor of the fetish, autism is a representation that has the power to order our ideas and experiences, and even mask its economic underpinnings. (For example, it does not sound right to refer to an organization like NYU's Child Study Center as a "business," and so, it is referred to as a "service provider.") How can something that exists at the level of representation also exert so much power? The answer may be that there is something more fundamental beneath the representation that reinforces its singularity and reproduction over time. And perhaps that "something" is not just discursive but is actually something material and objective. Perhaps that something is the system of ordering to which I referred before—the system of ordering that is an integral part of the larger systems in which we live.

Imagine how hard it is, then, to resist any of these forces. Even if new and innovative "stakeholders" want to lead the fight for some aspect of autism advocacy, they have no way of matching the networks and finances of this matrix, let alone of just one of the large corporate or philanthropic entities. It might be useful to reflect on the word "stakeholder" itself (commonly used by autism advocacy organizations to mean anyone with any involvement with autism—although, in its texts, Autism Speaks has generally separated scientists and stakeholders, despite the fact that scientists are among the biggest stakeholders in autism). A "stakeholder" is typically defined as a person or institution with a concern or interest, especially financial, in ensuring the success of an organization. When an organization calls me a "stakeholder" because I have a child with autism or because I do research on autism, there is an implicit assumption that everyone who has an autistic child or is an autism researcher has an interest in either helping support the organization or at least the object of that organization's work. Advocacy is fundamentally about absorbing as many people as possible into a community organized around a particular object, an object that is defined by the advocates. Just as citizens have an obligation to the interests of their nation or state, so too do stakeholders have an obligation to support and sustain the interests in which they are told they have a stake, and which may define them personally or professionally. Of course, in practice, advocates also delimit stakeholder communities, sometimes—as in early AIDS advocacy and in some autism self-advocacy efforts—by distinguishing between authentic or inauthentic stakeholders (i.e., people who are HIV positive or have AIDS, and people who are autistic) and shaping relationships between interest groups. Indeed, management scholarship treats the stakeholder as a form of social organization that structures relations between suppliers, customers, owners, employees, governments, advocates, and so on (Freeman 1984). Through the concept of the stakeholder, advocacy efforts sustain autism as both economic object and activity. And when advocates do delimit communities they may do so in order to influence the distribution or concentration of money and power (especially decision making and policy making).

There is an answer to the question "Who owns autism?" We all own autism, because it is now so integrated into our society and economy. But this answer presumes a "buy in" to the concept of the autism as a real and stable phenomenon rather than something we create—and that is exactly what this chapter has argued against. Marx's idea of the fetish was that humans create an economy that then appears to be natural, and to have an (independent) existence of its own, to which we are then subordinated. My argument about autism is that we have created a concept that then appears to us to be natural, and to have an (independent) existence independent of our scientific ideologies, and around which we organize a multitude of activities and shape identities.

Thus, to illustrate my argument, it might be better to turn the question of ownership on its head and ask "Who does autism own?"—thus giving us an answer that may be most accurate, and most faithful to the concept of the fetish. Autism owns us.

References

Abel, Ernest L., and Robert J. Sokol. 1983. "Incidence of Fetal Alcohol Syndrome and Economic Impact of FAS-Related Anomalies." *Drug and Alcohol Dependence* 19 (1): 51–70.

Adams, Walter. 1968. "The Military-Industrial Complex and the New Industrial State." *American Economic Review* 58 (2): 652–665.

Amendah, Djesika, Scott D. Grosse, Georgina Peacock, and David S. Mandell. 2011. "The Economic Costs of Autism: A Review." In *Autism Spectrum Disorders*, edited by David Amaral, David Geschwind, and Geraldine Dawson, 1347–1360. Oxford: Oxford University Press.

American Speech and Hearing Association (ASHA). 2012. *School Survey: SLP Caseload Characteristics*. Rockville, MD: ASHA. http://www.asha.org/uploadedFiles/Schools-2012-Caseload.pdf.

Arendt, Hannah. 1958. *The Human Condition*. Chicago: University of Chicago Press.

Barrett, Robert. 1998. "Conceptual Foundations of Schizophrenia I: Degeneration." *Australian and New Zealand Journal of Psychiatry* 32 (5): 617–626.

Bleuler, E. 1950 [1911]. *Dementia Praecox oder Gruppe der Schizophrenien*. Translated by J. Zinkin. New York, NY: International Universities Press.

Boyle, C.A., S. Boulet, L.A. Schieve, R.A. Cohen, S.J. Blumberg, M. Yeargin-Allsopp, S. Visser, and M.D. Kogan. 2011. "Trends in the Prevalence of Developmental Disabilities in US Children, 1997–2008." *Pediatrics* 6 (1): 1034–1042.

Brodwin, Paul. 2013. *Everyday Ethics: Voices from the Front Line of Community Psychiatry*. Berkeley: University of California Press.

Brook, Gail. 2013. "SLP Health Care Survey Report: Private Practice Trends 2007–2013." *ASHA*. December 2013. http://www.asha.org/uploadedFiles/2013-SLP-Health-Care-Survey-2007-2013-Private-Practice-Trends.pdf.

Cullen, Julie. 2003. "The Impact of Fiscal Incentives on Student Disability Rates." *Journal of Public Economics* 87: 1557–1589.

Dekkers, L.M., N.A. Groot, E.N. Díaz Mosquera, I.P. Andrade Zúñiga, and M.F. Delfos. 2015. "Prevalence of Autism Spectrum Disorders in Ecuador: A Pilot Study in Quito." *Journal of Autism and Developmental Disorders* 45 (12): 4165–4173.

Derrida, Jacques. 1988. *Limited, Inc*. Evanston: Northwestern University Press.

DeSanctis, S. 1906. "Sopra alcune varieta della demenza precoce." *Rivista Sperimentale de Feniantria E. di Medicinea Legale* 32: 141–165.

Foucault, Michel. 1994. *The Order of Things: An Archaeology of the Human Sciences*. New York: Vintage.

Freeman, R. Edward. 1984. *Strategic Management: A Stakeholder Approach*. Boston: Pitman.

Freud, Sigmund. 1921. "Introduction to J. Varendonck's *The Psychology of Daydreams.*" Standard Edition. 18: 271. Edited by James Strachey. London: Hogarth.

Gillberg, Christopher, and Mary Coleman. 2000. *The Biology of the Autistic Syndromes.* 3rd ed. London: High Holborn House.

Gurney, James, Melissa S. Fritz, and Kirsten K. Ness. 2003. "Analysis of Prevalence Trends of Autism Spectrum Disorder in Minnesota." *Archives Pediatrics & Adolescent Medicine* 157 (7): 622–627.

Hacking, Ian. 2000. *The Social Construction of What?* Cambridge, MA: Harvard University Press.

Hacking, Ian. 2006. "Making Up People." *London Review of Books* 28 (16): 23–26.

Heller, T. 1908. "Dementia Infatilis." *Zeitchrift fur die Erforschung und Behandlung des Jungenlichen Schwashsinns* 2: 141–165.

Kim, W.J. 2003. "Child and Adolescent Psychiatry Workforce: A Critical Shortage and National Challenge." *Academic Psychiatry* 27: 277–282.

Kim, Young Shin, Bennet Leventhal, Yun-Joo Koh, Eric Fombonne, Eugene Laska, Eun-Chung Lim, Keun-Ah Cheon, Soo-Jeong Kim, Young-Key Kim, Hyun Kyung Lee, Dong-Ho Song, and Roy Richard Grinker. 2011. "Prevalence of Autism Spectrum Disorders in a Total Population Sample." *American Journal of Psychiatry* 168 (9): 904–912.

King, Marissa D., and Peter S. Bearman. 2011. "Socioeconomic Status and the Increased Prevalence of Autism Spectrum Disorder in California." *American Sociological Review* 76 (2): 320–346.

Kras, Joseph F. 2010. The "Ransom Notes" Affair: When the Neurodiversity Movement Came of Age. *Disability Studies Quarterly* [serial online]. Winter 30 (1): 23. Available from: Education Source, Ipswich, MA. Accessed June 28, 2018.

Kwak, Sally. 2010. "The Impact of Intergovernmental Incentives on Student Disability Rates." *Public Finance Review* 38 (1): 41–73.

Lehman, Annie Lubliner. 2009. *The Accidental Teacher.* Ann Arbor: University of Michigan Press.

Mackenzie, Donald, Fabian Muniesa, and Lucia Siu. 2007. "Introduction." In *Do Economists Make Markets? On the Performativity of Economic*, edited by Donald Mackenzie, Fabian Muniesa, and Lucia Siu, 1–19. Princeton: Princeton University Press.

McGuire, Anne. 2013. "Buying Time: The S/pace of Advocacy and the Cultural Production of Autism." *Canadian Journal of Disability Studies* 2 (3): 98–124.

Mitchell, Timothy. 2007. "The Properties of Markets." In *Do Economists Make Markets? On the Performativity of Economic*, edited by Donald Mackenzie, Fabian Muniesa, and Lucia Siu, 244–275. Princeton: Princeton University Press.

Montiel-Nava, C., and J.A. Peña. 2008. "Epidemiological Findings of Pervasive Developmental Disorders in a Venezuelan Study." *Autism* 12 (2): 191–202.

National Center for Education Statistics. 2016. "Children and Youth with Disabilities." Accessed October 5, 2016. http://nces.ed.gov/programs/coe/indicator_cgg.asp.

Paula, C.S., S.H. Ribeiro, E. Fombonne, and M.T. Marcadante. 2011. "Brief Report: Prevalence of Pervasive Developmental Disorder in Brazil: A Pilot Study." *Journal of Autism and Developmental Disorders* 41 (12): 1738–1742.

Polyak, Andrew, Richard M. Kubina, and Santhosh Girirajan. 2015. "Comorbidity of Intellectual Disability Confounds Ascertainment of Autism: Implications for Genetic Diagnosis." *American Journal of Medical Genetics* 168 (7): 600–608.

Rothstein, Richard, and Karen Hawley Miles. 1995. *Where's the Money Gone: Changes in the Level and Composition of Education Spending*. Washington, DC: Economic Policy Institute.

Sigafoos, Jeff, Dennis Moore, Don Brown, Vanessa A. Green, Mark F.O. Reilly, and Giulio E. Lancioni. 2010. "Special Education Funding Reform: A Review of Impact Studies." *Australasian Journal of Special Education* 34 (1): 17–35.

Silberman, Steve. 2015. *NeuroTribes: The Legacy of Autism and the Future of Neurodiversity*. New York: Avery.

Sukhareva, G.E. 1926. "Die schizoiden Psychopathien im Kindesalter." *Monatschrift für Psychiatrie und Neurologie* 60: 235–261.

Thomas, Christoper, and Charles Holzer. 2006. "The Continuing Shortage of Child and Adolescent Psychiatrists." *Journal of the American Academy of Child and Adolescent Psychiatry* 45 (9): 1–9.

Thornton, Davi. 2010. "Race, Risk, and Pathology in Psychiatric Culture: Disease Awareness Campaigns as Governmental Rhetoric." *Critical Studies in Media Communication* 27 (4): 311–355.

Yeargin-Allsopp, Marshalyn, Catherine Rice, Tanya Karapurkar, Nancy Doernberg, Coleen Boyle, and Catherine Murphy. 2003. "Prevalence of Autism in a US Metropolitan Area." *Journal of the American Medical Association (JAMA)* 289 (1): 49–55.

Zirkel, P. 2011. "Autism Litigation Under the IDEA: A New Meaning of 'Disproportionality?'" *Journal of Special Education Leadership* 24 (2): 1–12.

CHAPTER 12

Commentary: What Are We Talking About When We Talk About Autism?

M. Ariel Cascio

12.1 A Cultural Constructivist View of Autism

What are we talking about when we talk about autism? I pose this question from a cultural constructivist perspective, one which does not take the word autism for granted. It is worth stating now some basic premises of my constructivist approach. I describe autism—or more specifically "the autism concept"—as a social construct. This does not mean autism is not "real," in any meaningful sense of the word. Autism is a concept (a category, a label, a topic, an idea) which both describes and constructs real people's real experiences, be they of suffering, joy, creativity, diversity, pride, etc. A social constructivist approach does not deny lived experience or the consequences of social constructs. Indeed, constructivist approaches often highlight lived experience to demonstrate that all concepts are socially mediated.

M. A. Cascio—The work described in this commentary was carried out at the Department of Anthropology, Case Western Reserve University.

M. A. Cascio (✉)
Institut de recherches cliniques de Montréal, Montréal, Canada

M. A. Cascio
McGill University, Montréal, Canada

E. Fein and C. Rios (eds.), *Autism in Translation*, Culture, Mind, and Society, https://doi.org/10.1007/978-3-319-93293-4_12

Returning to our question then, what about autism? What are we talking about when we talk about autism? It is not always easy to talk about autism, particularly because of all the different meanings the term holds. This difficulty is especially clear when engaging in interdisciplinary or multidisciplinary conversations, or when navigating between different roles—both of which we do in this volume by including research from US, Brazilian, and Italian authors; scholars and physicians; anthropologists, musicologists, linguists, philosophers, psychoanalysts, and more. All of these writers might provide very different answers if asked to define autism.

Valtellina opens his piece by asking "What is autism/Asperger's Syndrome (AS)?" (p. 207) In response to this deceptively simple question, he discusses autism as a diagnosis—both in the sense of classification and in the sense of event. He describes the term "Asperger's Syndrome" as a diagnosis which impacts the subjectivity of people who experience it through the process of interpellation (though it is not all-powerful), and also as a term which "through all its fluctuations, points to something concrete: the relational problems that the diagnosis certifies" (p. 212).

Rios writes (p. 186) that she uses the term autism for the sake of brevity, to refer to autism spectrum disorder. She talks about autism as the object of expertise, the focal point for contests over what counts as expertise anyway, and as tangential to the notion of being an expert on one's child regardless of autism. Expertise, Rios explains, "is not just about the child, or just about autism for that matter. It is also about the socio-cultural worlds they both inhabit" (p. 198). While autism, in the sense of "a certain way of being in the world currently described under the rubric of Autism Spectrum Disorders (ASD)" is a part of the object of autism expertise, the other part is "the socio-cultural worlds in which people diagnosed with such condition and their families live" (p. 201). Rios also talks about autism as a way of being different from others, which necessitates translation, even "radical translation" (drawing on Hart 2014; Eyal et al. 2010; see also Chew 2013). Parents not only translated their autistic children's communications to others, but also translated the workings of their local worlds to their children (much, indeed, as any parents do).

Grinker talks about autism as a "valuable diagnosis" in the context of an "economics of autism." He challenges the current literature on autism economics for ignoring "how these costs are related to the question of how the *concept* of autism has changed and gained traction in recent years" (p. 232). Indeed, it is this very *concept* that concerns this commentary. Taking a Derridean constructivist approach, Grinker consider autism as that *out of which* we speak (p. 240), exploring the historically and culturally specific foundations through which autism (and autism economics) is represented.

12.2 The Autism Concept

Like Rios, I also tend to use the term autism in my work, and often when referring to Autism Spectrum Disorder as it is termed in the DSM, but less for the sake of brevity and more for the sake of being intentionally and—from some positivist perspectives—overly inclusive. When I write about autism, I write about "the autism concept" (Cascio 2015). I describe autism as a "concept" because the term is used to mean many different things. Kleinman and Good (1985, 2) once wrote that depression is "considered mood, symptom, and illness," and similarly Chloe Silverman (2012, 2) writes that "autism refers to a symptom, a disorder, and a syndrome" (see Cascio 2014). Autism may refer to diagnosis of something conceived of in a variety of ways: as a disease to be cured, a disability to be managed, or a neurological condition to be embraced as a part of human diversity (Cascio 2012; Eyal et al. 2014). The term autism may stand for "autism spectrum disorder," a DSM-5 diagnostic category. It may stand for "classic autism" in contrast to the "other" autism spectrum disorders of the DSM-IV, for example, or the current ICD. It may refer to a diagnosis made on the basis of a validated instrument such as the ADOS. It may be a historically particular term for "relational disability" (Valtellina) or for "problems with social communication and repetitive behaviors" (Grinker) that would exist regardless of time period or specific terminology. It may refer to a symptom the way that Eugen Bleuler (1950) used the term to describe a characteristic of schizophrenia (Hacking 2010). It may refer to a way of being, an integral part of an autistic person's experience and not, in the words of Jim Sinclair, "an appendage" (1993). Autism is both a medical or psychiatric diagnosis (and which of the two, if either, is often a point of contention) and also a locus of increasing popular culture fascination. In this volume, autism may also refer to an economic fetish (Grinker), an object of expertise (Rios), an interpellation (Valtellina), an identity, an online social space, and so much more. Due to the multiple meanings of autism, I have introduced the idea of "the autism concept," paralleling Margaret Lock's (2013) discussion of "the Alzheimer phenomenon," to encompass the range of ways that autism is or might be conceptualized and to avoid limiting myself to a particular understanding of autism (see Cascio 2015). This strategy allows me to explore a variety of meanings, to encompass the wide range of ways that the term autism is invoked, deployed, mobilized, rejected, negotiated, defied, defined, and discussed.

This constructivist perspective of the autism concept involves understanding how this idea of "autism" as a diagnosis and cultural phenomenon has emerged at a specific time and place (see Nadesan 2005). This constructivist perspective is not concerned with identifying an objective reality of autism that is outside of the social world—indeed, nothing is outside of the social world. The autism concept refers not to some sort of objective reality itself, but to a way of making meaning, such as the many meanings discussed in the above paragraph. But understanding the autism concept involves not only exploring what's "new" about autism—what specific features of time and place make autism a meaningful way to describe certain people. It also involves looking at what is "old" about autism. In other words, what sorts of continuity can we find between current studies of the autism concept, and previous studies of other concepts and phenomena? To answer this question, I now turn to the chapters in this section to highlight their continuities with classic questions in the field of anthropology (from which I, as an anthropologist, am inclined to speak and within which I am moreover biased by my North American anthropological training—any other commentator would surely raise other perspectives).

12.3 Exploring Classic Anthropological Questions

The chapters in this section address many big questions. They address questions of the classification of boundaries between normal and other; the formation of self, identity, and subjectivity; processes of socialization and enculturation; political economy; and social organization. In a way, autism is a lens researchers like those in this volume use to understand these big questions. Perhaps because autism means so many things to so many people, it is a rich concept through which to explore big debates across a range of topics. This range also highlights the importance of a social studies perspective to understanding autism by looking at the experiences around autism holistically, not just from a medical or psychiatric perspective. In order to understand autism—both the autism concept and the experiences of people living under the label of autism—scholars delve into these broader literatures. As the following paragraphs will show, these literatures inform and are informed by the social study of autism.

The study of autism as a classification addresses classic anthropological questions about the border between normal and abnormal (Canguilheim 1978; Benedict 1934; Devereux 1980). Who decides where the border lies? What are the consequences of that decision? What is the role of beliefs, norms, and values? Autism is a contested category (Silverman 2012). Grinker outlines several ways in which this category has changed over time, and that people currently diagnosed with autism might previously have been given another diagnoses, or no diagnosis at all. The relationship between Kanner's autism and Asperger's syndrome is also highly contested, as Valtellina discusses. Notions of normality and abnormality are also gendered in autism, as autism is often associated with masculinity and diagnosed more often in boys and men (see Valtellina). Although diagnosis as classification is one way of marking something (or someone) as "abnormal," the valence of this abnormality varies. Valtellina (p. 216) argues that Asperger's Syndrome is "the only psychiatric classification in the *DSM* not only not stigmatized, but full of positive connotations (as stated, starting from the pioneering research of Asperger himself)." Although we might argue that Asperger's is still stigmatized in some contexts, and certain other *DSM* labels are sometimes valorized, nonetheless Asperger and Autism Pride movements exist in local and global contexts to a scope not seen for other current *DSM* classifications. Indeed, as Valtellina points out, the neurodiversity movement that began in autistic communities has broadened such that some proponents argue it covers a wide range of human diversity conceptualized through the lens of the brain as neurological, psychiatric, psychological, and so on.

Not only has the concept of autism changed over time, as has its origin story (Grinker, this volume), but it has been and remains difficult to place autism within predefined categories. Grinker alludes to this when he notes "autism was a mental illness; then it was a developmental disability." Autism has fit differently across time and place with the category of mental health or psychiatry. While the history of psychiatry is important to the history of autism (see, for example, Nadesan 2005), attempts to place autism within or outside of the domain of psychiatry invokes the US obsession with mind/body dualism: is autism part of "medicine" or the "psy professions" (Rose 1998)? Is it of the body or is it of the mind? Autism studies further contribute to the deconstruction of that divide, long a central theme of US medical anthropology (e.g., Kirmayer 1988).

Similarly, the study of interpellation in autism develops theory about the formation of self, identity, and subjectivity and social context. What is the impact of institutions (in the broad sense of the word)—especially sociomedical institutions—on individual sense of self, identity, and subjectivity? What is the relationship between names and the named (Hacking 2006)? Autism is one name, but theories derived from the study of autism relate closely to many other names, for example those that Estroff (1993) calls "I am" illnesses. Valtellina explores in depth the way that diagnosis forms individuals into subjects, and also the way that he "unsubjected" himself from the Subject of Asperger's Syndrome. Upon hearing a diagnosis of Asperger's, people might welcome this diagnosis as an affirmation, "an essential element of their personality," or even a relief from a lifetime of being blamed for relational problems (Valtellina, p. 217). The diagnostic event allows people to "re-signify" their lives, re-interpreting their personal and interpersonal histories. Grinker also notes how autism is described in memoirs as completely defining and shaping the diagnosed individual's personhood and social identity. We might also note that it goes further to define the social identity of a family, "the family with autism" (Murray 2008). Grinker and Valtellina both draw on Hacking's philosophies of classification to explore these questions. Valtellina finds useful Hacking's observations that classifications are performative, and act on the world to create sense and structure. Grinker draws on Hacking's notion of the "looping effect," specifically as it appears in the creation of more and more autistic people and autism experts, groups which mutually reinforce each other as more diagnoses means greater need for experts, and more experts means greater reinforcement that autism is "a legitimate object of study." Autism studies therefore contribute to longstanding questions on the relationship between groups, individuals, and categories by exploring what the concept—the label, the word—of autism does to self-understanding and relationships with others, organizations, and categories themselves.

Autism studies also explore classic anthropological questions of socialization and enculturation: how do people learn to become members of societies? How does autism change this process, if at all? As Rios repeatedly points out, much of what she observed in her fieldwork with respect to autism parenting is really common to all parenting, and all boils down to "do[ing] their best to educate their children to live in the world they were born into" (p. 201), i.e., socialization and enculturation. The parents she describes were informed in their parenting strategies by credentialed autism experts and specialized autism expertise, but this type of knowledge was not the only source of their parenting styles and strategies. As Rios explains, a lot of the specific parenting work done by her participants involved turning tacit knowledge into explicit knowledge. This process makes explicit a lot of not only what is implicit about learning how to be a member of a particular society, but it also meant that parents became attuned to their children's different way of knowing and being in the world. This discussion expands theory about socialization, enculturation, and different (tacit and explicit) ways of learning.

The study of the economics of autism delves into important questions about political economy. Whose interests are being served? How is power operating in this situation? How is it negotiated? What is the language of power? What antecedents impact the current political-economic arrangements? Grinker dedicates his chapter to many of these questions, particularly through the metaphor of autism as a fetishized diagnosis. Rios and Grinker both describe the rise of specialized autism services, which can be understood in this political-economic framework. Specialized services depend of course on discrete diagnoses and involve not only a specialized market of consumers, but also attention to "the economics of the production of expertise related to the rise of autism as a diagnosis" (Grinker, p. 232) by means of professional specializations. Rios highlights also the international flows of power in the emergence of autism expertise, reporting that Brazilians consider North American and European sources—both traditional experts and lay experts—to be more authoritative than Brazilian. Although political-economic approaches are not often favored by constructivists, who sometimes see themselves as outright opposites (Gaines 1991), the two approaches have been successfully combined by some (Estroff 1993; Jorelamon 2015; McDougall 2015) and attention to key questions of the flow of money and power can be informative within any framework. The notion of the "autism industrial complex" raised by Grinker highlights the relationships between this network of autism actors and services and economic and financial interests. Autism has become "a valuable diagnosis" (Grinker, p. 232), a word and concept that wields economic power, shaping not only financial expenditures but also forms of knowledge. In these ways, autism studies contribute to understanding how diagnosis interacts with money and power, by exploring the flows of each within the broad networks that address autism.

Finally, the study of autism activism and advocacy addresses classic anthropological questions of social organization. What brings people together? In what communities do people imagine themselves, and on what bases? How does knowledge operate in these organizations? What types of knowledge are authoritative, and how are they deployed by whom and for what purposes? Grinker includes activism and advocacy organizations in the web that makes up the economics of autism, an economics that implicates social organization and social relationships. Indeed, one of the reasons an autism label might be more desirable than others, writes Grinker, is that it opens up opportunities for relationships with others living under the same label. Valtellina also addresses social organization, specifically through the neurodiversity movement, at first as a movement of activists with Asperger's and later as a broader political discourse used even by cure-oriented parents of people with autism (and also by Rios's participants as part of the philosophy of *Bem Viver*, living well), and stretching beyond the autism spectrum to include any cognitive difference. This movement, Valtellina notes, draws on a particular type of knowledge: the "neuro hype" of the brain sciences. Rios explores questions of social organization most directly of these authors, in her study of Brazilian autism services and expertise—both autism-specific and not, but always context-specific, demonstrating that expertise about autism is dependent on interactional and sociocultural contexts. As Rios points out, not all of this expertise is necessarily specific to autism. Rather, autism studies further theorization on expertise through the lens of a particularly discussed object of expertise.

We walk a fine line in taking these critical perspectives on autism and yet at the same time participating in the autism industrial complex, as Grinker describes it. On the one hand, we network with other autism researchers (and write books with them, and contract with publishers who sell said books), we seek autism-specific funding, and we are and/or care about people living under the label of autism. On the other hand, it is important to avoid reifying autism. The "autism concept" attempts to do so, by asserting that autism is a concept like any other. To describe autism as a concept is more than to describe it as a category, although that is certainly an important part of it. Autism-as-a-concept is a lens through which researchers, scholars, professionals, parents, and people with autism address important questions in their fields or in their lives. The chapters in this section have used autism as a lens to explore classic questions, but have also used these classic questions to understand how autism has become such a popular lens for such exploration.

References

Benedict, Ruth. 1934. *Patterns of Culture*. Boston, MA: Houghton Mifflin Harcourt.

Bleuler, Eugen. 1950. *Dementia Praecox or the Group of Schizophrenias*. Oxford, UK: International Universities Press.

Canguilhem, Georges. 1978. *On the Normal and the Pathological. Studies in the History of Modern Science*, vol. 3. Dordrecht, Holland and Boston: D. Reidel.

Cascio, M. Ariel. 2012. "Neurodiversity: Autism Pride Among Mothers of Children with Autism Spectrum Disorders." *Intellectual and Developmental Disabilities* 50 (3): 273–283.

Cascio, M. Ariel. 2014. "New Directions in the Social Study of the Autism Spectrum: A Review Essay." *Culture, Medicine, and Psychiatry* 38 (2): 306–311.

Cascio, M. Ariel. 2015. "Biopolitics and Subjectivity: The Case of Autism Spectrum Conditions in Italy." Ph.D. dissertation, Case Western Reserve University.

Chew, Kristina. 2013. "Autism and the Task of the Translator." In *Worlds of Autism*, edited by Joyce Davidson and Michael Orsini, 305–318. Minneapolis and London: University of Minnesota Press.

Devereux, George. 1980. *Basic Problems of Ethnopsychiatry*. Chicago: University of Chicago Press.

Estroff, Sue. 1993. "Identity, Disability, and Schizophrenia: The Problem of Chronicity." In *Knowledge, Power, and Practice: The Anthropology of Medicine and Everyday Life*, edited by Shirley Lindenbaum and Margaret M. Lock, 247–286. Berkeley: University of California Press.

Eyal, Gil, Brendan Hart, Emine Onculer, Beta Oren, and Natasha Rossi. 2010. *The Autism Matrix: The Social Origins of the Autism Epidemic*. Cambridge, UK: Polity Press.

Eyal, Gil, Des Fitzgerald, Eva Gillis-Buck, Brendan Hart, Martine D. Lappé, Daniel Navon, and Sarah S. Richardson. 2014. "New Modes of Understanding and Acting on Human Difference in Autism Research, Advocacy and Care: Introduction to a Special Issue of BioSocieties." *BioSocieties* 9 (3): 233–240.

Gaines, Atwood D. 1991. "Cultural Constructivism: Sickness Histories and the Understanding of Ethnomedicines Beyond Critical Medical Anthropologies." In *Anthropologies of Medicine: A Colloquium on West European and North American Perspectives*, edited by Beatrix Pleiderer and Gilles Bibeau, 221–258. Wiesbaden, Germany: Vieweg Und Sohn Verlag.

Hacking, Ian. 2006. "Making Up People." *London Review of Books*. August 17: 23–26.

Hacking, Ian. 2010. "Autism Fiction: A Mirror of an Internet Decade?" *University of Toronto Quarterly* 79 (2): 632–655.
Hart, Brendan. 2014. "Autism Parents & Neurodiversity: Radical Translation, Joint Embodiment and the Prosthetic Environment." *BioSocieties* 9 (3): 284–303.
Joralemon, Donald. 2015. *Exploring Medical Anthropology*. 3rd ed. Milton Park, Abingdon and Oxon: Routledge.
Kirmayer, Laurence J. 1988. "Mind and Body as Metaphors: Hidden Values in Biomedicine." In *Biomedicine Examined*, edited by Margaret Lock and Deborah Gordon, 57–93. Dordrecht, the Netherlands: Kluwer Academic.
Kleinman, Arthur, and Byron J. Good, eds. 1985. "Introduction: Culture and Depression." In *Culture and Depression: Studies in the Anthropology and Cross-Cultural Psychiatry of Affect and Disorder*, edited by Arthur Kleinman and Byron J. Good, 1–33. Berkeley: University of California Press.
Lock, Margaret. 2013. *The Alzheimer Conundrum: Entanglements of Dementia and Aging*. Princeton, NJ: Princeton University Press.
McDougall, Rosalind. 2015. "Reviewing Literature in Bioethics Research: Increasing Rigour in Non-Systematic Reviews." *Bioethics* 29 (7): 523–528.
Murray, Stuart. 2008. *Representing Autism: Culture, Narrative, Fascination*. Liverpool: Liverpool University Press.
Nadesan, Majia Holmer. 2005. *Constructing Autism: Unravelling the "Truth" and Understanding the Social*. New York, NY: Routledge.
Rose, Nikolas. 1998. *Inventing Our Selves: Psychology, Power, and Personhood*. Cambridge, UK: Cambridge University Press.
Silverman, Chloe. 2012. *Understanding Autism: Parents, Doctors, and the History of a Disorder*. Princeton, NJ: Princeton University Press.
Sinclair, Jim. 1993. "Don't Mourn for Us." Electronic Document, http://www.autreat.com/dont_mourn.html.

PART IV

Closing Commentaries

CHAPTER 13

Psychological Anthropology and the Study of Disability

Thomas S. Weisner

13.1 Introduction

Psychological Anthropology has studied disability and mental illness since the inception of the discipline, and many chapters in our volume bring Psychological Anthropology (PA) research and theory to bear on the study of autism. PA of course includes a much wider range of topics than mental illness, Autism Spectrum Disorder (ASD), and disability. Psychological Anthropology starts with some fundamental problems in the social and psychological sciences. PA includes the comparative, contextual, and cultural study of culture and the mind—culture and our mental life. In addition to disability, mental illness, and physical illness, Psychological Anthropology includes research on cognition, perception, memory, emotions and affect, child development generally, socialization and learning specifically, self and identity, the individual and culture, experience and consciousness, and others. A conceptual framework and empirical agenda like this surely are ambitious and aspirational, but nonetheless PA strives for valuable goals: holistic, open to plural methods, comparative, collaborative with other disciplines, and moving across levels of analysis. These are worthwhile goals for the understanding of ASD as well.

T. S. Weisner (✉)
Departments of Psychiatry and Anthropology, UCLA, Los Angeles, CA, USA

E. Fein and C. Rios (eds.), *Autism in Translation*, Culture, Mind, and Society, https://doi.org/10.1007/978-3-319-93293-4_13

Elinor Ochs et al. (2004) recently showed the importance of this PA tradition to the study of ASD specifically. ASD is "at once neurological and social" (171) in their view. They extend the conceptual frame of how to understand ASD to incorporate the sociocultural context. Solomon and Bagatell (2010) similarly suggest that ASD "is particularly well suited for psychological anthropology's concerns with the psychological and the social in an individual's experience and place in society" (3). They critique narrow biomedical and genetic studies of ASD, as well as emphasize "a multilogue of theories and voices, of scholarly research and personal experience, that intertwine perspectives intended to advance understanding of autism" (ibid., 2). Ochs and Solomon (2010, 5) see PA and other branches of anthropology as relevant to ASD due to sharing "a vision of autism as socially constructed across institutional, ideological, sociohistorical and social-interactional contexts." Many of the papers in our volume share this framework and further build on these insights.

From among the many connections between PA and the study of ASD and disability, there are six themes that seem particularly relevant, and that are reflected in the chapters in our volume: difference is both biological and social; experiences of disability are central; cultural beliefs regarding disability vary widely around the world; other inequalities in society influence disability, including structural and institutional constraints; social and sociolinguistic mechanisms important for understanding disability also are important for studying many other topics in psychological anthropology generally; and diverse family and parenting practices and daily routine activities are important in the field of PA, perhaps especially so for ASD, as are institutional and structural conditions in society.

13.2 Difference Due to Disability Is Biological and Social

Difference is constructed by culture and society, and is also a real fact of our biology (Stiker 1997). All of the chapters in our volume emphasize the fundamental power of diagnostic categories and their social–historical construction, the history of clinical services, and the organization and funding of social services in various national contexts. Yet none propose that there is no underlying neurological/physical condition. Roy Richard Grinker specifically raises this with regard to the argument that because a diagnosis arises for historical and medical-diagnostic reasons, those with the condition prior to the diagnosis did not suffer or that those with it now suffer "only" due to the diagnosis.

> This constructivist approach often provokes criticism, as if one is denying the reality of suffering. If I say, for example, that autism is a mid to late 20th century construction, that it is a historically contingent assemblage of specific and observable behaviors, I don't mean that the phenomena that we today call autism do not exist. My daughter will have problems with social communication and repetitive behaviors no matter what diagnosis she has. A constructivist approach does not deny that there is an underlying biological condition that can produce suffering. (this volume, p. 239)

Michael B. Bakan, citing Nick Walker, favors changing the conceptual frame for the study of ASD from disability and pathology to neurodiversity, including critiquing the ASD and disability labels themselves. Yet Bakan also recognizes at the same time the disabling (or disenabling) neurological condition itself.

> Walker calls for a comprehensive epistemological shift from what he terms the pathology paradigm of autism (essentially a subset of the medical model of disability critiqued in disability studies) to the neurodiversity paradigm of autism. It is noteworthy, however, that in doing so, neither he nor other Autistic self-advocates who have addressed such issues deny or underplay the significant and often profoundly disabling impact of ASCs on the lives of people who live with them, as well on the lives of those with whom they live, work, and play. That autism can be disabling, or as I prefer to phrase it, disenabling, is not in question. (3)

Elizabeth Fein also points to the ways that diagnostic labels (ASD, Asperger's Syndrome) can stigmatize and discount other ways of relating to the world, while also recognizing that the cognitive differences of Autism are innate—they are conditions that predate cultural input, even as they powerfully shape and are shaped by the nature of that input (5). Grinker also recognizes the power of the definition of ASD itself to come to "own us," to become a classification that is reified, which requires organization, control, and money for very expensive interventions and programs (which in turn defend their funding by justifying the labels). "The definition of autism and other conditions in terms of a group of deficits or impairments—a deficit model of autism—may be another legacy of the tradition of explaining difference as diversion from a norm and motivating the call for costly services" (Grinker, this volume, p. 244).

Finally, Enrico Valtellina provides a deep philosophical and social critique of social categories and clinical diagnoses such as ASD and Asperger's, yet also recognizes the autistic traits that he has. He explores the connections between autistic traits, a diagnosis, and the person experiencing ASD.

> Over time, my relationship with interpellation changed. Years ago, when I recognized autistic traits in myself that corresponded with Asperger's Syndrome, I had given maximum credit to the diagnosis. I read and wrote on the topic. With time and with study, the subject of AS revealed itself to me in its substance as a cultural assortment of human kinds that are divergent, legitimately divergent, and that find themselves atoning in infinitely different ways for the extremely scarce social tolerance for involuntary transgressions of implicit codes of face to face interaction. I progressively unsubjected myself. Now if they call me I do not turn, and this seems to me the most delicious of the autistic responses. (this volume, p. 223)

If the impacts of ASD can be profoundly disabling (and this deeply troubling impact appears to be the case for ASD symptoms across cultures, especially at more severe ends of the spectrum), these impacts and their many consequences clearly are empirical generalizable facts. Psychological Anthropology contributes to understanding the power of labeling and cultural categorization and the meanings of disability, while also recognizing, in a social and cultural context, the underlying disenabling condition.

13.3 The Experiences of Disability Matter

These comments regarding labels and disabling conditions speak to another central contribution of PA: disability deeply affects thought and consciousness, and the experiences of a disability are central to understanding the meaning of disability and its impacts on every person. As a matter of theory and methodological emphasis, PA nearly always includes the voices, the goals, and the points of view of those with ASD and other disabilities, often along with their families, using ethnography, fieldwork, and qualitative narratives as methods to explore these experiences.

Jurandir Costa and Roy Richard Grinker analyze texts from first person accounts from individuals with ASD, which they argue represent autistic experience and expressions. These accounts represent "the extreme diversity" of thought and experience of people with ASD. They ask, from the point of view of the person with ASD, what is the intention, meaning, purpose, and goal of the (repetitive, atypical, destructive, etc.) behavior that we hope to understand and treat? By this, Costa and Grinker mean that these difficult behaviors are presumptive "intentional states" having communicative goals, not exclusively behavioral symptoms to be eliminated.

> Understanding the meaning of the autistic experience depends largely on understanding the unusual way in which subjects communicate lived experiences to one another within their shared environment. These experiences are, in short, intentional states, processes or occurrences; that is, they represent needs, desires, thoughts, sensations, feelings, beliefs, judgments, actions, etc.
>
> The meaning of autistic expressions may, for the purposes of argumentative clarity, be divided into four major dimensions: *cognitive*; *sensory-motor*; *affective* and *communicational*. (this volume, p. 157)

First person accounts of disability written by anthropologists have explored the many pathways through which disability shapes experience. For example, Robert F. Murphy (1987), an anthropologist at the height of his career, a professor at Columbia University who worked for years in the Amazon with the Mundurucu, was struck by an inoperable spinal tumor in 1974, which gradually affected all of his physical abilities and ultimately killed him in 1990. Murphy describes the effects of this on his thought, consciousness, and the experience of gradually becoming disabled. His experience-based account is written with the autobiographical and scholarly clarity of a professional researcher and fieldworker. His colleagues gradually change in how they work with him, his eventual life in a wheelchair means that he is increasingly "looked over," and he comes to have "a damaged self."

Michael B. Bakan's essay concludes with a strong call for ethnographic and qualitative methods for understanding autistic experience.

> Understanding autism ought rightly to begin with listening to, communicating with, and learning from Autistic people—through their words and utterances, their actions and performances, not ours; on their terms and

> according to their values, not ours—to the greatest extent possible. This demands creativity, resourcefulness, flexibility, and patience on the part of all parties involved: it may require the recognition or establishment of completely novel modes of communication and interaction. (this volume, p. 124)

Ariel Cascio describes discourses and beliefs of psychiatrists and other care providers' interpretations and experiences. These can also differ widely and matter for treatment and public interpretations of ASD.

> Discourses of autism as a disability (in Brazil) and autism as a "way of being" (in Italy) articulate dissatisfactions with post-reform mental health services within these autism advocacy communities, through marshaling a biologically-based and diagnosis-specific rhetoric. (this volume, p. 55)

How to discover and represent these experiences is an important topic in Psychological Anthropology, and is a theme of many essays in our volume—expanding the methods for attempts to do this, as well as the importance of doing so. Although expanding methods and paradigms further certainly can lead to new discoveries, PA already is open to a wide range of methods, including physiological, behavioral, psychological, sociocultural, structural/institutional, and historical approaches. The use of plural, mixed methods has a long and important history in PA (Hay 2016).

13.4 Cultural Beliefs and Practices Regarding Disability Vary Widely Around the World

Disability is recognized in all known communities, although the forms and responses to it vary widely. Social practices for recognizing and responding to disability also vary widely, as we know from the ethnographic record around the world. PA and Medical Anthropology have made major contributions to the comparative empirical documentation and theoretical understanding of disability. There is quite wide variation in what counts as sufficiently troubling to lead to stigmatization or social exclusion due to disability. Difficulties with face-to-face interaction, for instance, might not be nearly as troubling in smaller scale communities where a person is known and accepted for other reasons—her family, work, and other areas of competence, physical abilities, or reliability, and predictability, for example—and where most are familiar with persons with ASD or other disabilities. Marshall (1996), for example, describes a small-scale Pacific Island culture that accepts physical disability and other problems as long as there is some level of community participation. Elizabeth Fein's chapter explores the similarly important question of why particular autistic modes of engagement become troubling in particular social and historical moments, similar to the cross-cultural question of why and how communities differ in the recognition and responses to troubling aspects of disability.

A more general claim from mental illness research is that prognosis and acceptance of those with schizophrenia and psychosis often are better (considering clinical outcomes and patterns of course, disability and social outcomes, and marital and occupational status) in many non-Western communities. However, there also is a counter argument questioning this generalization, arguing that treatments, well-being, and outcomes are not necessarily more positive in non-Western settings at least regarding more severe mental illness (Cohen et al. 2008; Edgerton and Cohen 1994). Arthur Kleinman (2008) also questions the view that mental illness outcomes were generally better in lower resource, more sociocentric societies. This is an important research question that will benefit from further study for a variety of disability conditions, including ASD. Unpacking the very unsatisfactory binary Western/non-Western category is essential as a start.

More generally, this connection between disability and broader societal inequalities and beliefs, reflects the long-standing theme in PA, Medical Anthropology, and many other fields recognizing that there is a close connection between disability and social context that extends to the many other differences in society that increase stigma and reduce opportunity. With regard to ASD more specifically, it is highly likely that it is more difficult to have ASD and to assist those with ASD in poor communities with few or unpredictable resources available for families and neighborhoods. Poverty, gender, kinship and family systems, class, caste and religion, ethnicity, race—all of these are intertwined with the expression of, and treatments for, disability. Those who are deprived, excluded, and vulnerable for reasons other than mental illness or ASD, are differently and more deeply affected by disability, and disability itself in turn can lead to deprivation, exclusion, and vulnerability (Ingstad and Whyte 1995). Lima et al. (this volume, pp. 33–37) point out in their chapter, for example, that fighting for services in Brazil for those with disabilities had to include fighting for the resources to "honor" the demands—that is to provide what is necessary in order to actually obtain those basic human rights to services.

> In Brazil social movements came together ... to fight both for individual liberties and for the public services that are essential to freedom and agency, such as the right to health care, education, food, and employment, among other things. However, in both settings (Brazil and the USA), scarcity of funding and limitations on resources have led to difficulties in honoring these rights in practice; many of the controversies around autism treatment arise out of these gaps between assumed human rights and the social resources necessary to honor them.

Another important debate in PA is whether or not there are certain seriously troubling domains of behavior among those with mental illness and disability that will be recognized and sanctioned everywhere. In addition to understanding the variations across cultures in patterns of support and outcomes, there clearly are circumstances in which all or virtually all societies find some of the behaviors and family and community consequences of mental illness and disability very troubling, and there is evidence that certain kinds of behaviors are more likely to be troubling nearly everywhere. These could include behaviors that are dangerous and threatening to others such as physical aggression or threat thereof; the disruption of essential community or family routines deemed essential for survival; the inability to communicate; and others. Furthermore, more severe, chronic, disruptive manifestations of mental illness and disability are more universally recognized and labeled as troubling in much of the world, whereas milder symptom patterns that do not even necessarily include all symptoms, and are not severe and chronic, have a much greater cultural and contextual variability in recognition, tolerance, and outcomes. The hypothesis is that in cases where ASD and mental illness more generally takes the form of milder symptoms, as well as with not all symptoms perhaps even present, early support and accommodations to the person will make their path easier. In such cases, there is a greater role for, and more influences of, social/community negotiations regarding what to do, degree of stigma, how to label and define a condition, and the extent of and nature of social tolerance (Edgerton 1969, 1992).

The more general hypothesis, with a considerable amount of cross-cultural evidence to support it, suggests that there are troubling behaviors that will be troubling everywhere. For these to be improved, families and individuals will require social support, benefactors, and an improvement not only in tolerant cultural beliefs and scientific evidence about the disorders and improved treatments but also a more general improvement in the societal circumstances of other unequal and disadvantaged groups, and the amelioration of broader inequality in society.

13.5 Social and Sociolinguistic Mechanisms Important for Understanding ASD and Other Disability also Are Important for Studying Many Other Topics in Psychological Anthropology

Sociality is a fluid, domain-specific, context-influenced process, which includes far more than dyadic interaction during sociolinguistic communication.

> Human sociality consists of a range of possibilities for social coordination with others, and autistic sociality is one of these possible coordinations. This perspective does not impose a dichotomous distinction between autistic and normative sociality but, rather, highlights the gray areas of sociality shared by those diagnosed with autism and neurologically unaffected persons. (Ochs and Solomon 2010, 2)

The socio-linguistic domains of communicative competence Ochs and Solomon describe include language, conversational turns/sequences, topics of discourse, body alignment, mediation, the communicative medium, emotional intensity/affect, and tempo of communication. Several chapters (Fein; Costa and Grinker; Bakan) describe how people experiencing ASD struggle within these domains of communicative competence. Social coordination for these domains among persons with ASD can be at least somewhat enhanced by recognizing and perhaps manipulating these domains. Those with ASD favor structure and routine in connections with the world, rather than disruption, sudden change, and shifting contexts, for example.

Psychological Anthropology also studies the social mechanisms that are involved in dealing with disability and mental illness, mechanisms common to everyone. These include universal social behavioral domains such as social responsibility, nurturance, emotion recognition and regulation, play and games, peer relationships, gender relations, and others. Passing, or the avoidance of stigma, is another important example of a universal social concern that of course is highly salient to those with ASD and their families. *The Cloak of Competence: Stigma in the Lives of the Mentally Retarded* (Edgerton 1967) describes this fundamental aspect of cultural learning and social engagement, which involves being able to "pass" as competent, to be "normal," accepted, or included. Furthermore, if we falter in our attempts to pass, as everyone does, it is important that we have a reason, narrative, or an account of our behavior that is believable in our community and that provides an acceptable explanation, a reasonable account, of why we cannot pass or do something normally expected (Goodley and Tregaskis 2006; Orbuch 1997). Those with ASD and other disabilities are like us in many ways, including in these respects—needing to pass, to feel competent enough, to act normal enough, and to be able to provide an account when we are socially incompetent—and we can see in their development and lives many of the same social processes, concerns, and fears about not meeting expectations, that to some extent we all have. The argument is that everyone requires a degree of social tolerance—that this is a universal condition, not only one facing those with ASD. As Edgerton (1967) describes this common experience (and fear), "perhaps normal persons see too clearly [in those with mental retardation] what they fear for themselves or for their children" (218).

Edgerton's (1967) classic study that led to the *Cloak of Competence* focused on 110 patients with mild to moderate retardation who had been released from Pacific State Hospital in California in the late 1950s. Edgerton and his team found 98 of these former patients. Fifty-three lived in the Los Angeles area and were contacted and followed with extensive ethnography and other assessments. Many had been able to pass, often with the help of benefactors. Edgerton called this the "benevolent conspiracy": benefactors who supported the tasks and functions that those with intellectual disabilities could not do, or scaffolded the ones they could do in part but needed help with. But successful benefactors then mostly let them do the things they could do (even if perhaps not in the optimal ways), and minimized and protected them from stigma as much as possible (Zetlin et al. 1985). Collective, community practices to increase social inclusion and reduce stigma, as well as individual benefactors, of course also can be beneficial (Skinner and Weisner 2007; Groce 1985, 1999). Clarice Rios's (this volume) studies in Brazil provide a contemporary illustration of how parents have to work with their children to inculcate culturally specific forms of social expertise in order to avoid stigma. Those with ASD and their benefactors continue to be crucial to inclusion and increase in well-being today.

Edgerton's (1967) studies suggested that these adults now living in the community could not always sustain their attempt to have a cloak of competence with all others. The adults "have been given a niche … in which they are permitted to live incompetently as long as in the course of this living they do not cause the wrong persons too much trouble."

> In the efforts of the former patients in the present study to evade the stigma that they feel and fear, we see an eloquent testament to man's determination to maintain his self-esteem in the face of overwhelming cultural rejection and deprecation. If we accept the unanimous findings of the behavioral and psychological sciences concerning the fundamental importance of self-esteem for any human being, then we can understand the dilemma in which these former patients find themselves, and we can appreciate their achievement in finding what is for them a cloak of competence. (218–219)

13.6 Family and Parenting in Response to Disability and Mental Illness Matter for Development: The Daily Routine and the Power of Activities and Institutional and Structural Conditions

Psychological Anthropology has a long-standing interest in parenting, culture and family life, and child development. One recurring theme includes the ways in which parenting and family life reproduce cultural goals and practices deemed desirable by their cultural community, ethnic group, class, and religious and other groups. Development and socialization are much more than stimulation seen in the context of back-and-forth dyadic interactions between autonomous individuals. Development has cultural goals and a moral direction: What kind of person do parents in their community want to create? What goals, with what moral meanings, do parents and others responsible for children and adults with ASD have for their children, for their families more broadly, and for themselves as caregivers or parents? Families that have children with ASD or other disabilities are fully a part of this much broader and deeper developmental agenda.

Several essays in our volume contrast the circumstances of parents, clinicians, community workers, and both children and adults with ASD in the US, Brazil (including different historical periods and institutional differences within Brazil), and Italy. Others describe the intentions, beliefs, and behaviors of those with ASD in the contexts of their particular circumstances within their familial and cultural ecology. Ecocultural theory and methods have been used to conceptualize, measure, and compare families with children with disabilities (Bernheimer and Weisner 2007; Weisner 2002, 2017). This theory begins with the daily routine of activities. People with ASD experience desired cultural goals in their life as practiced within their family's (or school's, or church's, or other context's) daily routine of cultural life. Cultural routines consist of activities children engage in (mealtimes, bedtimes, family visits, homework, reading together, chores, going to church or prayer, school, going for clinical treatments, play, "play dates," etc.). Activities are the primary mechanisms bringing culture to and into the mind of the child, since cultural activities are what a child directly experiences day in and day out, repeated thousands of times. Activities consist of at least these six core elements: goals and values for that activity and routine, including the kind of child or family that is desired; the tasks the activity is accomplishing; the scripts and norms for how to engage in that activity; the people present in the activity and their relationships with the child and with one another; the motives and feelings, affective and emotional experiences of those engaged in the activity; and the stability, routinization, and persistence of the activity in the lives of the child and family (Weisner 1996, 2002, 2015).

A *sustainable* routine involves fitting the routine to the family resources available, balancing the inherently diverse family interests and obligations and conflicts, making the routine and its activities meaningful with respect to goals and values, and providing reasonable stability and predictability of routines and activities. *Better resource fit, less conflict, more balance, more sense of meaning and purpose, and sufficient predictability in routines and activities for a child in any culture should enhance well-being.* Well-being arises out of engaged participation in the activities deemed desirable by one's cultural communities, and the psychological experiences that are due to this engagement. A child or adult with ASD would likely benefit not only from effective treatment, benefactors, and social tolerance but also from being a part of more sustainable routines and the activities that make up routines. The family and benefactors should also benefit. Routines gain some of their force to increase well-being through being frequent, sustainable, and part of a recurring pattern of activity that is culturally meaningful and hopefully also relatively predictable—which, of course, can be particularly comforting for an adult with ASD.

Parents have to *accommodate* to their child with disabilities, of course, and then attempt to maintain a sustainable routine for that child, as well as for others in the family, and for themselves, and this can be a very difficult process. Accommodations are changes made to the daily routine and family activities due to the child's ASD, including things not done that otherwise would have been (e.g., a father not changing jobs due to needs for health insurance; a mom not going to work; siblings assisting in care that otherwise would not have been needed; closer religious involvement due to support from the church, or leaving a church due to lack of support; a family deciding not to eat together because their child is too disruptive; etc.). The Project CHILD longitudinal study of 100 families with children with disabilities in Los Angeles, California mapped and reported some 800 distinct accommodations parents described during that study, across every domain of family life (Gallimore et al. 1996). The expectation from ecocultural theory is that maintaining a daily routine through continuing accommodations that attempt to be sustainable is an enduring family project that can support both the child and the family, not a transient stage in response to early disability identification of the child, or only an initial stage in family life (Weisner 2008).

A recent study of daily routines of 54 adults with ASD age 18–44, 82% male, in the middle and upper class in the New Delhi region in India also documented the life-long importance of routines to the adults and to their families (Brezis et al. 2015; Daley et al. 2014). In this study, all adult subjects lived with their parents; only one adult was married. This family residential pattern reflects the situation throughout India: the overwhelming majority of children and adults with developmental disorders, including ASD, live with their natal families. Contrary to expectations, most adults were not fully hidden from outside view, were out in public at least on some occasions, and 59% participated in some structured situations outside the home. However, adults located in smaller cities, villages, and towns may be less likely to have a diagnosis of ASD, would likely have fewer intervention and placement options than did these families, less contact with other families and adults in similar circumstances, and might be more hidden. At the same time, parents and most adults themselves favored careful scheduling and sequencing events in the same order each day; parents also had the challenge of matching very specific interests and activities the adults with ASD focused on, to the abilities of the individual adult.

Some 20 common daily routine activities of this diverse adult sample were identified. The provision of accommodations and sustainable routines included the challenge of finding the right fit for not only the adult but also the whole family. Both parents and adults told stories of remarkable resilience, creativity, acceptance, and perseverance embedded within the descriptions of the daily routines. But parents had a level of acceptance of what had to be let go in order even to have the routine they had crafted. Parents who focused on what made the adult with ASD happy, rather than on continuing to cultivate the adult's experiences or develop new and improved skills, had chosen a goal that may best fit and accommodate their family circumstances, and match with what the adult with ASD wanted. Parents described their awareness of the losses required to establish these routines: less time for extended family visits, mothers who are home more than they would have been otherwise, couples visiting families and doing activities separately so that someone is there at home with the adult with ASD, limited participation in other activities so that they will not be disrupted, and so forth (Daley et al. 2014).

Accommodations like these are beneficial, accepted and necessary in many cases, but they come at a cost. Summarizing what many parents said, "just because [we] have adapted doesn't mean that [we] would not welcome the opportunity to do things differently if we could" (ibid., 148). An intervention or support for a family with a disabled member will be most effective when it fits into the already-accommodated daily routine. By taking apart and highlighting the ordinary activities of adults and their families, we can better see where there are gaps and cracks where the routines are not satisfactory and identify what would make life easier for families in India or anywhere else (ibid.,148).

Through daily routines, we can identify potential levers of change, and a family routine can be adjusted in ways that may improve the well-being of adults and family members alike, even when institutional change is difficult, and individual change is slow. Adding new daily routines and alternative activities for adults and their parents alike in the New Delhi group, for example, led to new initiatives by NGOs in India by the study's research partner, Action for Autism, as well as a focus on changing regional and national institutional policies in New Delhi and elsewhere in India (ibid., 143).

Michael B. Bakan's chapter on the activity of music making and in particular his inclusion of Gordon Peterson's account of what Peterson needs in order to compose music and teach music illustrates the need for routine and the power of activity (and what happens when it is disrupted). These accounts from adults with ASD extend the general ecocultural theory of the importance of routines for children and families by describing the importance of routines for maintaining adults' own lives and goals. This broadens the discussion beyond the family or parenting context and incorporates the attempts by those with ASD to maintain a daily routine that supports activities that in turn can support them.

One of the parents in the Los Angeles CHILD study was asked about the stresses she faced in raising a child with disabilities and responded by commenting, "Just let me tell you what I do all day … ." in order for her to accommodate to the child and to all the family and personal and service-provider and other issues she has to manage (Bernheimer and Weisner 2007). This mother has deep local expertise that certainly is not sufficiently captured by asking her about "stress" using a standardized stress assessment scale. Clarice Rios's chapter focuses on the cultural, institutional, and local aspects of "expertise" about autism. Rios focuses on parent and community local knowledge by describing the role of expertise in pushing back against labeling based on the use of diagnostic categories. Her model of expertise also depends on local knowledge of "what is needed and what works" in everyday family life. This involves calling attention,

> to a model of autism expertise that is less dependent on credentialed scientific knowledge, although still informed by it. The parents at *Círculo da Esperança* [a community program and service provider in Rio de Janeiro, Brazil for parents and professionals] are not exactly "co-producers" of scientific knowledge, but many of them develop strategies to raise their autistic children that take this knowledge into account as well as their own knowledge about their local realities. As I see it, their approach to autism expertise has the advantage of not abiding uncritically to imported credentialed knowledge and of expanding the existential horizons of their children beyond a diagnostic category alone. Such [an] approach also helps us understand how this association, in spite of all the challenges and lack of resources, managed to be so successful for such a long time. It seems as if Inês [parent of an autistic son and worker in the association] finally understood what autism is, maybe better than that doctor would ever have imagined. (Rios, this volume, p. 202)

Finally, PA has turned increasing attention to institutional and structural conditions that shape emotion, belief, and practices regarding disability, including ASD. These conditions shape the daily routine and family responses, and the services and supports available. Elizabeth Fein (2015, 82), for example, links contemporary neoliberalism and individualism to a "market" orientation for selecting and maintaining friends and peers (she describes this as "the vicious cycle of social disorder in late modern identity markets"), which in turn affects youth with ASD. This shapes how "we become the people we are." In her chapter, Fein views autism as "a mode of engagement with the stuff of the world … a form of permeability, of deep existential vulnerability, to the order of things around us" (this volume, p. 130). She describes autism as deeply and fundamentally constituted by institutional and structural conditions.

There are several other examples in our volume of the different historical and clinical pathways ASD treatments, institutional ownership, and clinical labels took in Brazil, Italy, the US, and elsewhere, which influence everything from diagnostic systems, to choices available for treatment, to political and funding stream decisions. This is described in Clarice Rios' and Cascio et al.'s chapters. Cascio et al. contrast psychiatric reform policies with how they are instantiated in local practice in Italy and Brazil, beginning with deinstitutionalization movements in the 1960s and afterward. It is hard to overstate the complexity of the historical, clinical, political, institutional/service system, diagnostic, theory of ASD, emic and cultural belief systems, and many other complexities regarding autism in these two countries! A recently converging trend though, is that

> In both contexts, the discourses of parents and professionals reveal the flexibility of different concepts to be deployed for different political and clinical agendas. In Brazil and Italy, parents strongly advocate for a view of autism that is organicist—biologically based and diagnostically specific—in contrast to the anti-organicist, anti-positivist, and even anti-diagnostic perspectives of psychiatric reform. (Cascio et al., this volume, p. 77)

The emphasis in many papers in this volume is on the impact of differences in psychiatric reforms and institutional worlds, not the similarities. The structural split within Brazilian clinical and professional associations between "mental health" and "disability" advocates, for example, provides another case study of the importance of historical, political, and clinical context differences within Brazil regarding understanding who "owns" autism, as Roy Richard Grinker would put it. As Lima et al. state in their chapter,

> The conception of autism as disability [rather than a mental health issue seen in a community health and public health context] is historically tainted by negative connotations: it is associated with a history of excluding children considered retarded, who were predominantly poor and black, in public or philanthropic shelters, or even psychiatric hospitals, throughout the twentieth century. (this volume, p. 36)

13.7 Final Comments

Psychological Anthropology and Medical Anthropology have contributed in important ways to theory, methods, and empirical outcomes regarding mental health, disability, and ASD. The chapters in this volume contribute to the six themes I have covered, and no doubt suggest other themes as well. PA of course covers a wide range of topics relevant to the connection between culture and mind, and it recognizes that these connections have both a neurological and sociocultural basis. PA incorporates the experiences, consciousness, and emotions of those with disabilities into its theories, methods, evidence, and assessing outcomes. PA has documented the wide differences in beliefs and practices regarding disability found around the world, and how consequential these are for defining what is troubling about disability. PA and Medical Anthropology show how embedded disability and mental illness are in other differences and inequality found in a society, including structural, institutional, and historical influences. The many sociolinguistic and social–relational mechanisms that affect those with disabilities are at the same time general processes that affect everyone. Finally, PA examines the mechanisms, such as the daily routine and cultural practices, that drive socialization of children as well as adults. Raising a child with a disability also requires accommodation and changes to parenting, family routines, and socialization goals; more sustainable developmental and family routines likely benefit children with ASD as well as their families, and adults. This volume contributes to these wider theoretical conversations and also opens up possibilities for new approaches to ASD.

References

Bernheimer, Lucinda, and Thomas Weisner. 2007. "'Let Me Just Tell You What I Do All Day …': The Family Story at the Center of Intervention Research and Practice." *Infants and Young Children* 20 (3): 192–201.

Brezis, Rachel, Thomas Weisner, Tamara Daley, Nidhi Singhal, Merry Barua, and Shreya Chollera. 2015. "Parenting a Child with Autism in India: Narratives Before and After a Parent–Child Intervention Program." *Culture, Medicine and Psychiatry* 39 (2): 277–298.

Cohen, Alex, Vikram Patel, R. Thara, and Oye Gureje. 2008. "Questioning an Axiom: Better Prognosis for Schizophrenia in the Developing World?" *Schizophrenia Bulletin* 34 (2): 229–244.

Daley, Tamara, Thomas Weisner, and Nidhi Singhal. 2014. "Adults with Autism in India: A Mixed-Method Approach to Make Meaning of Daily Routines." *Social Science and Medicine* 116: 142–149.

Edgerton, Robert. 1967. *The Cloak of Competence: Stigma in the Lives of the Mentally Retarded*. Berkeley: University of California Press.

———. 1969. "On the 'Recognition' of Mental Illness." In *Changing Perspectives in Mental Illness*, edited by Stanley C. Plog and Robert B. Edgerton, 49–72. New York: Rinehart and Winston.

———. 1992. *Sick Societies: Challenging the Myth of Primitive Harmony*. New York: The Free Press.

Edgerton, Robert, and Alex Cohen. 1994. "Culture and Schizophrenia: The DOSMD Challenge." *The British Journal of Psychiatry* 164 (2): 222–231.

Fein, Elizabeth. 2015. "No One Has to Be Your Friend: Asperger's Syndrome and the Vicious Cycle of Social Disorder in Late Modern Identity Markets." *Ethos* 43 (1): 82–107.

Gallimore, Ronald, Jennifer Coots, Thomas Weisner, Helen Garnier, and Donald Guthrie. 1996. "Family Responses to Children with Early Developmental Delays II: Accommodation Intensity and Activity in Early and Middle Childhood." *American Journal on Mental Retardation* 101: 215–232.

Goodley, Dan, and Claire Tregaskis. 2006. "Storying Disability and Impairment: Retrospective Accounts of Disabled Family Life." *Qualitative Health Research* 16 (5): 630–646.

Groce, Nora. 1985. *Everybody Here Spoke Sign Language: Hereditary Deafness on Martha's Vineyard*. Cambridge: Harvard University Press.

———. 1999. "Disability in Cross-Cultural Perspective: Rethinking Disability." *The Lancet* 354 (9180): 756–757.

Hay, Cameron, ed. 2016. *Methods that Matter: Integrating Mixed Methods for More Effective Social Science Research*. Chicago: University of Chicago Press.

Ingstad, Benedicte, and Susan Whyte, eds. 1995. *Disability and Culture*. Berkeley: University of California Press.

Kleinman, Arthur. 2008. "Commentary on Alex Cohen et al: 'Questioning an Axiom: Better Prognosis for Schizophrenia in the Developing World.'" *Schizophrenia Bulletin* 34 (2): 249–250.

Marshall, M. (1996). "Problematizing Impairment: Cultural Competence in the Carolines." *Ethnology* 35 (94): 249–263.

Murphy, Robert. 1987. *The Body Silent: A Journey into Paralysis*. New York: Henry Holt.

Ochs, Elinor, and Olga Solomon. 2010. "Autistic Sociality." *Ethos* 38 (1): 69–92.

Ochs, Elinor, Tamar Kremer-Sadlik, Karen Sirota, and Olga Soloman. 2004. "Autism and the Social World: An Anthropological Perspective." *Discourse Studies* 6 (2): 147–183.

Orbuch, Terri. 1997. "People's Accounts Count: The Sociology of Accounts." *Annual Review of Sociology* 23: 455–478.

Skinner, Debra, and Thomas S. Weisner. 2007. "Sociocultural Studies of Families of Children with Intellectual Disabilities." *Mental Retardation and Developmental Disabilities Research Reviews* 13: 302–312.

Solomon, Olga, and Nancy Bagatell. 2010. "Introduction: Autism: Rethinking the Possibilities." *Ethos* 38 (1): 1–7.

Stiker, Henri-Jacques. 1997. *A History of Disability*. Ann Arbor: University of Michigan Press.

Weisner, Thomas. 1996. "The 5 to 7 Transition as an Ecocultural Project." In *The Five to Seven Year Shift: The Age of Reason and Responsibility*, edited by A.J. Sameroff and M.M. Haith, 295–326. Chicago: University of Chicago Press.

———. 2002. "Ecocultural Understanding of Children's Developmental Pathways." *Human Development* 45 (4): 275–281.

———. 2008. "Well Being and Sustainability of the Daily Routine of Life." In *The Good Life: Well-Being in Anthropological Perspective*, edited by G. Mathews and C. Izquerdo, 349–380. New York: Berghahn Press.

———. 2015. "Childhood: Anthropological Aspects." In *International Encyclopedia of the Social & Behavioral Sciences*, 2nd ed., vol. 3, edited by James D. Wright, 451–458. Oxford: Elsevier.

———. 2017. "Culture, Context, and the Integration of Qualitative and Quantitative Methods in the Study of Human Development." In *Advances in Culture and Psychology*, edited by M. Gelfand, C.Y. Chiu, and Y.Y. Hong, chapter 4, 153–215. New York: Oxford University Press.

Zetlin, Andrea, Thomas Weisner, and Ronald Gallimore. 1985. "Diversity, Shared Functioning, and the Role of Benefactors: A Study of Parenting by Retarded Persons." In *Children of Handicapped Parents: Research and Clinical Perspectives*, edited by S.K. Thurman, 69–95. New York: Academic Press.

CHAPTER 14

Joy

Dawn Prince-Hughes

There is an old saw of a question that people often ask when they gather in social situations. It is supposed to tell you something about the person who answers, though often the answer is just light language that fills an auditory space we think of as empty. There are a few permutations of the question, but it basically asks, "Who would you want to be stranded on a deserted island with?" Almost invariably, people choose celebrities or great thinkers from history. "Einstein," people say. Or "Mozart." Maybe they offer someone who has been in movies that they think would be interesting to talk to because they are brilliant, or because of the things they have done.

As a person who has been said to be on the spectrum, it has struck me more than once that people choose those with the very kinds of minds that they cannot stand to be with at the same social gatherings in which this island game is often played, let alone to be alone with on a deserted island. The people they choose, more times than not, are eccentric, focused on the immense immediacy of their sphere of interest, uncomfortably vibrating with a current of awareness and creative connection.

People are drawn to the products—but not usually the people—of such intense immediacy, who vibrate with the joy of their creative labor

D. Prince-Hughes (✉)
Carbondale, IL, USA

E. Fein and C. Rios (eds.), *Autism in Translation*, Culture, Mind, and Society, https://doi.org/10.1007/978-3-319-93293-4_14

pains, the joy of their immense vision. But just as people muse about feeding from it at the safe distance of social fantasy, so they also build culture on the back of the mental and emotional products of such people, at the safe academic distance of time, through the removed sources of what has already been written, or composed, or thought, or sung. But in so doing, they miss out on the joy.

The people who attended the conference in Rio are not typical. They invited several people on the spectrum to offer their views about what it means to experience a different way of living—in essence they invited us as people they would be trapped on an island with, as the conference itself was a kind of island—an intense "think tank" or better yet "gestalt tank" that contemplated the reality that spectrum people are not divided from non-spectrum people; that people from different countries are not separate; and in the end, that there is no divide between autism, the planet, ordinary life, intellectual inquiry, and the bonding ties of emotion. That is rare in our Western culture, and rarer still in academia.

Our culture—and academia as both parent and child of that culture—does not like its heroes too closely connected to immediate reality; we are not comfortable with the sweat, the agony, the tears, the craziness of direct interpretation and discovery—the barbaric cry of raw emotional, intellectual, and spiritual nakedness that is the stuff of real union with each other and the greater world.

As a person on the spectrum who chooses such blood and sweat, such immediacy, over the translated and removed, my answer to whom I would want to be stranded with is quite different from the normal one. For example, I would want to be on the island with an ancient ancestor or a contemporary person who understands survival on an island. Where most people think of some disconnected paradise, sipping drinks on the beach as Einstein regales them with supreme discourse as the sun sets, I think of the need for fire, for water, for the knowledge of sweet and bitter plants, someone who feels an abiding joy in finding just the right growing thing hidden near the earth or a tiny trickle of clean that can be drunk, who finds joy in the ability to make a simple place to sleep with the forest.

People have said I would make these kinds of choices in answer to the island question because I am "too literal." But there is nothing more literal than this life, this day, this survival, this opportunity for an old and profound connection with this island earth that we live on, right now. As our friend Roy Richard Grinker talks about in this volume, and I think he gets it right, autism is an archaic way of being. My own career started when I learned, somewhat by accident, to be social and how to find joy by becoming part of a clan of gorillas, and has grown as I have shared my belief that humans are not so different from gorillas, or all other living things.

When I talk to my adult friends they smile when I ask them a question in return. "Do you remember what it was like when you were a child and every tree, every stone, every stream, had its own personality?" I ask. Everyone remembers this, and almost everyone has forgotten what it feels like, as culture, painful experience, greed, pride, and lack of cultivation tears this joy away from them. This joy is the very thing I usually see lacking in my academic colleagues—in fact in the whole population of humans around me—because we have elevated the pursuit of happiness (with the attendant greed and pride that Western culture values) above the experience of joy.

I will clarify that the joy I am talking about, as I said above, is not the same as happiness. "Happiness," I believe, is something individual and therefore as much an illusion as separate personhood. Joy, on the other hand, is collective and recognizes that there is no one, separate entity that stands alone: we are every breath, every sip, every bite, and every moving, soulful atom of each other.

Those breaths, sips, bites, and moving, soulful atoms were alive and palpable at the conference that gave birth to this book. Those who contributed to this volume and participated in the conference have shared with a great openness; they are exceptional people in that they have approached the phenomena of autism, multi-level sensitivities, the current environmental challenge, and questions about human values and action with sincere equanimity.

Like so many previous endeavors, this volume and the conference that birthed it could have offered prim treatments about the isolation, the perseveration, the crippled communication of people on the spectrum, and nothing about the same elements in the lives of the people writing about "the other." Those contributing to both could have hidden their own passion and spiritual involvement in their work, could have dimmed the lighted threads that they saw firmly binding small ideas to infinite ideas.

What makes me proud to be a part of this present endeavor, to have been witness to this unfolding project, is that people were brave enough to talk about and experience these connections and the joy they ultimately bring. Sometimes each having to embrace the kind of potential social, physical, and emotional discomfort that people on the spectrum also face (and for similar reasons). We all endeavored, in the wise words our friend Enrico Valtellina shared at the workshop, to "strip bare what we think we know—inviting us … to re-view and reconsider what we take for granted about seeing, interpreting, and problematizing"—not only in regard to the phenomenon of autism, but every component of living.

Several examples stand out to me as examples of the connection between the self, the environment, and the great family of all sentient beings.

Elizabeth Fein shares that to her, autism is "a mode of engagement with the stuff of the world." She talks about "permeability" as an essential quality of autism. But further, she talks about the permeability of herself, as well as other people around her. With a rare frankness she shared some of her own traits that might be considered "spectrum" in a certain context and is not afraid to say that her sense of self, her physical body, and her body of work are all inseparable from those phenomena she studies. She discusses the idea of spectrum phenomena as a kind of disease of modernity—not that the individual him or herself is flawed—but that the context of modern life, as well as a polluted and toxic environment skew otherwise gifted ways of being sensitive in a living world.

And while she is beautifully articulate—allowing her inner poet to bring new dimensions to the scientific findings she describes—in the end she humbly acknowledges that words will never substitute for lived experience.

Many others, while also acknowledging the limitations of the spoken and written word, brought dynamic new ways of seeing spectrum phenomena and the global context it manifests in. Lima, Cascio, Andrada, Bezarra, and friends talked about the alleviation of suffering and the instilment of a life of meaning with the de-institutionalization of people on the spectrum—while underscoring the reality that the academe is also an institution. Lima et al. shares with us the history of the "warehousing" of people on the spectrum and how advances in evaluation, treatment, and mode of living have led to unfolding approaches that "encourage the respectful consideration of differences" and respect "multiple forms of being human." Social integration and collaboration blur the hard edges between individuals and urge a society that thrives like a living organism. Cascio et al. shared the Italian concepts of *relazionale*, *evolutivo*, and *umanista*, as a platform for considering the relational and evolutionary aspects of difference, and what it means to be human. They assert the importance of "profoundly questioning power relations within and outside" (this volume, p. 56) the monolithic cultural and academic structures we have constructed.

In her work that also advances the same awareness of power imbalance, Clarice Rios talked about the importance of reinventing autism expertise(s) by embracing and enfolding lived experiences, the importance of keeping lived experience alive in its local context while extrapolating its value to the wider world. She reminds us that autism expertise is a "network property" that is inclusive, multi-layered, and facilitates flow (this volume). There is danger in handing our power over to those who are designated as experts by a closed system that arguably has its own agenda. In order to move away from being consumers of products, we can blur the boundaries between us to manifest a co-production of shared knowledge, insight, and wisdom in vibrant sociocultural matrices. She reminds us that in a world of specialization, compartmentalization, and expertise—what we might call enforced disconnection—we are all experts on being ourselves. On being living beings. From the microcosm of spectrum people to the larger world, it is a natural step to uncover our expertise in the connections that sustain us and the ways we impact everything around us. In this way, what is asked of people on the spectrum is expected from everyone.

Other contributors to this project are keenly aware that the power vested in "experts" or in the hierarchies that create them are at best outmoded and at worst destructive. Like Rios, they offer the observation that those not in power are forced to meet the minds of those in control far more than half way to be considered worthwhile. In varying ways, they have all made it clear that we can replace the word "autism" with "being a living being." When Roy Richard Grinker asks, "who owns autism?" we are asking "Who owns human experience?" Those who have contributed here would say that we all own it collectively. We can all identify with archaic nature, its simple joys and visceral pain, its howling loneliness against the paradox of its absolute connection. We all embrace a deeper economy of natural connection. In this work is the implicit understanding that there are no lines to draw as we face and solve all the challenges inherent in human exchange, in human impact on everything around us.

Promoting this idea, Michael B. Bakan puts forth that we need to "look at old challenges in new ways" that utilize and inform society, culture, medicine, and politics. In this way, he says, we enable the living web to maximize its potential. His modes for this engagement are perhaps the most primal, as he provides opportunities for people—spectrum and otherwise—to literally make music together. He offers his gifts—his drums, his heart, his safe places, and vision—and steps back to allow the living web to grow organically. The results are genius. The films he showed us at the conference were deeply moving as we watched people who feel isolation as a daily weight break free to find their own rhythms become vital in a harmonious whole without losing their distinctness. I watched him do this same thing with a large group of people who showed up to the public event portion of our conference. Many people from the community showed up, looking to find experts on a stage, only to be gathered into a group experience of sound and connection while Michael led them in a primal beatbox style. These experiences moved our common academic assertions from the realm of the cerebral into that of the lived. All the Big Ideas we have shared here can be moved from the philosophical to the practical in such ways, and countless others.

I have (half) joked in the past that people invite me to conferences because I can get away with saying things that people restrained by academic convention cannot say themselves. Privately, they agree with me that we are all connected—people, other animals, the planet, and even the universe itself. They agree that only from a holistic standpoint can any of our current challenges be solved, whether we are contemplating autism or any other ground of being human that demands reflection and action. Prior to my experience of the conference, I had always found that my colleagues felt too constrained by social norms, personal fear, or academic convention to approach their areas of interest with a real sense of child-like wonder or even true open-mindedness. Research that seeks to involve itself with the real sensations of connection is *verboten*. We have been taught that it is not professional to feel.

I am so proud to say that my colleagues here know, and have proclaimed both academically and publicly, that we fool ourselves when we pretend not to let our emotions—our connections—get in the way of our "work." We are being less than alive when we try not to let our passion, our excitement—our joy—influence the experience of being one with what we study and find its way into our work. Time after time my heart has broken for the academic representative (or cultural participant in general) that is grim, disconnected, and suffers at the hacking edges of facts. Devoid of joy we say they are "serious" about their profession. In fact they are depressed, isolated … disabled. That is an important realization to face, especially as we define what disability is in the first place. I reflect on the reality that as academics we write reams of dead papers, made from dead trees, about disability, depression, or disconnection (the present example being autism) and how to treat it, but avoid talking about the crippling effects of the standard academic approach. Certainly we write and speak nothing about joy and how to find it, how to share it.

This reality does not just lead to the suffering of the individual. Our academic disconnection has set the stage for precedents that are not just ironic, but also cruel. I once heard a researcher many years ago speaking at a conference who was detailing his manipulation of empathetic responses in non-human primates in his lab—those showing the most empathy were then killed and their brains dissected so that he might look for the roots of that empathy. (See Roy Richard Grinker and Jurandir Freire Costa's comments on "weak central coherence theory").

When we talked about themes for this volume, based on what we learned at the conference, the word "psychic" came up for the first time in my experience as an academic. We let it hover at arm's length for awhile, and then moved in favor of "synergistic." We grappled with the fact that there is scant academic language to frame the transforming and revolutionary components of our ideas, exchanges, and shared vision. "Synergistic" was a good choice of words, but I think we should also have mentioned joy as an explicit product of that synergy. The conference—and this resulting volume—is an exercise in synergistic joy.

In the world of autism experts, it is often claimed that autistic people "can't see the forest for the trees." Once again replacing "autistic people" with "living beings," I would point out that in being the kinds of people we are we have ignored the trees and destroyed the forest both figuratively and literally. But there is hope.

One of the mothers in Ariel Cascio's study summed up her own hopeful belief in connection, saying, "don't take away the respect that each of us on this earth deserves" (this volume, p. 75). Her words extend to all on this island—humans, other animals, trees, water, rocks, the earth itself. Can we commit to the discomfort of immediate awareness? Can we willingly engage in the sacred compromise that enables all to survive and flourish? I thank those who contributed to this volume for saying yes to that question. I hope the reader also replies in the affirmative. In the end, we can all become the people we would choose to be on this joyful island with.

Index

E. Fein and C. Rios (eds.), *Autism in Translation*, Culture, Mind, and Society, https://doi.org/10.1007/978-3-319-93293-4

T

The manufacturer's authorised representative in the EU is Springer Nature Customer Service Centre GmbH, Europaplatz 3, 69115 Heidelberg, Germany. If you have any concerns regarding our products, please contact ProductSafety@springernature.com

Printed and bound by CPI Group (UK) Ltd, Croydon, CR0 4YY

30/09/2026

02225195-0007